Bob Beckman

Bob Beckman's reputation places him among the most successful and least conventional forecasters in London. He has an uncanny propensity for accuracy well proven on a wide range of topics, from the price of gold to the boom and subsequent decline of oil. He accurately predicted the start of the British recession and was alone in foretelling a fall in house prices, a subject he explores comprehensively in *The Downwave*. He has negotiated deals for billions of dollars between European and American institutions, and has been responsible for many transactions at government level.

An effusive New Yorker, Bob Beckman is an experienced economist who settled in London in 1963. Since then his writing and broadcasting have had an important impact on personal and business planning. He is the proprietor and editor of the weekly *Investors Bulletin*, and his daily radio programme 'The Beckman Report' on LBC has won him millions of followers. A frequent guest on radio and television, he lectures often throughout the country, and is a regular contributor to most major investment publications. His specialist books include *Share Price Analysis, The Elliott Wave Principle* and *Supertiming*.

WE ARE MOVING INTO A PERIOD WHERE THE WORLD AS WE KNOW IT WILL BE TURNED UPSIDE DOWN.

ALL THE THINGS WE ASSOCIATE WITH THE RIGHT COURSE OF ACTION DURING THE PAST 30 YEARS WILL SUDDENLY BECOME THE WRONG COURSE OF ACTION.

ALL OF THE THINGS WE WERE TOLD WERE THE WRONG THINGS TO DO WILL BECOME THE RIGHT THINGS TO DO.

WE ARE NOW MOVING INTO THE DOWNWAVE.

Robert C. Beckman

The Downwave
Surviving the Second Great Depression

Pan Books
London and Sydney

First published 1983 by Milestone Publications
This edition published 1983 by Pan Books Ltd,
Cavaye Place, London SW10 9PG
© Robert C. Beckman 1983
ISBN 0 330 28178 X
Printed in Great Britain by
Cox & Wyman Ltd, Reading

Design   Brian Iles
Jacket design   Satori
Index   Anne Coles
Illustrations   Gary O'Callaghan

Typeset by Inforum Ltd, Portsmouth

This book is dedicated to those persons whose actions are
deflected by thought along with the few remaining people
of intelligence who are still able to read and who do
sometimes purchase books. From this nucleus will come
the harbingers of the glorious twenty first century.

CONTENTS

ILLUSTRATIONS

ACKNOWLEDGEMENTS

Although my name appears as the author, a work of this nature could never be undertaken by one individual. There are many sources of toil and inspiration. In the area of toil my thanks go to Anthea Clift, Nils Taube, Michael Walters, Betty Stabler, Anne Dewe, Peter Carvel, Maggie Drummond, Colleen Toomey and Gary O'Callaghan who provided the illustrations. The sources of inspiration are many. To name a few, I must cite Dr. Edmund Goldberger, Dr. R. Opie, Professor Hayek, Ludwig von Mises, Herman Khan, James Bellini, and the great Jimmy Dines.

R.C. Beckman

INTRODUCTION

Most of our life is spent in a futile effort to halt the passage of time. We are told that history repeats itself. Georges Santayana tells us that if we cannot learn from history, we are condemned to repeat it. The only thing we can really learn from history is that nobody ever really learns anything from history.

We plan our lives as if the future is nothing more than a projection of the past into infinity. We demand higher wages because we believe prices will continue to go up. We have been brainwashed into believing that a steadily increasing standard of living is our inalienable right. So we continue to seek higher wages to pay for higher prices which we think will go on rising forever, because they have gone up for as long as we can remember.

Along with this inalienable right to a steady increase in living standards, we also believe that we are entitled to our own homes. It is part of the system. Over the past couple of years the rise in house prices has slowed. We assume this is temporary, because we believe house prices will always rise. It might be a tighter pinch nowadays to meet high mortgage repayments, but buying a house has always been a good investment. There is really no reason to doubt it. We are undeterred by recent sluggish prices. We will buy a house as soon as we can, or move into a bigger and better one.

As businessmen we have learned to live with inflation. By and large, inflation has been our friend. Interest rates may be high, but as long as we have inflation, we will be able to pass those borrowing costs on to our customers in next year's price increase. If we borrow now to expand, the money we pay back will be worth less than the money we are borrowing. Inflation is not really such a bad deal. The last thing a businessman wants is empty shelves when his customers come into the shop to buy. He will keep those shelves full, no matter the cost of borrowing. Inflation will always be around to bail him out. After all, it always has been.

As consumers, we are determined to live within our means even if we have to borrow to do it. The last thing we want to do is save. We see how inflation has ravaged our insurance policies. Twenty years ago when we took out a £5,000 endowment policy, we thought that £5,000 would see us clear through our retirement. Now we see that £5,000 barely provides the down-payment on a holiday home. No, we are certainly not going to get caught in that trap again.

Live today, pay tomorrow. Why not? The government will see to it that we do not starve. The unions will protect our jobs. Inflation will protect our businesses. Over the past few years we have learned how to keep up with inflation. Some of us have even learned how to beat inflation by buying gold, property and other things that have risen in value faster than the rate of inflation. Now that we have learned how to handle the problem, the rest of our lives should be fairly serene.

It is inconceivable that life as we perceive it would be subject to dramatic change. We have learned about the Great Depression and falling prices. We feel the government has learned a great deal since those days. It could never happen again. Most people are aware that over the past few years inflation has been accelerating at an alarming rate. But they think this is only temporary. Most assume that once the economy returns to normal, this persistent inflation will disappear, and life will return to the way it has always been. There may be temporary dislocations, but we are confident that government will be able to solve our problems . . . if not this government . . . another government.

If I were to describe public attitude during the early 1980s as one of self-satisfied complacency, I would not be too far off the mark. Anyone who challenges this complacency is coded, at best as a radical, at worst a lunatic.

Yet this complacency must be challenged. We are entering a social/political environment of dynamic change. For most of us, the vast changes that are taking place are totally unrecognised. To some they are unprecedented. To those whose perspective goes beyond recent history, they have happened before. Changes which lie beyond the experience of four or five decades are now taking place. What we are about to experience happens in only one decade in six. Personal experiences will be reversed, and the precedents of the previous few decades will no longer serve us. As I will demonstrate, we are now entering a period where the political, social and economic structure we know will be turned upside down, and our personal well-being will rely upon adapting to this much-changed environment. The savers, who have been penalised for the past four decades, will suddenly be rewarded. The spenders and borrowers, who have been rewarded over the past four decades, will suddenly be penalised.

Very few people will be prepared for the changes which lie ahead. In the following pages, I will try to broaden the horizons of the reader by showing the what and the why of the likely changes in everyone's lifestyle. And I will try to help my readers to cope with the changes ahead in our social and financial structure.

I do not forecast apocalypse and disaster ahead. I am doing nothing more than anticipating change. Those who are unable to adapt to it may suffer. Those who can make the adjustment may find they are about to enter the most rewarding period of their lives.

R.C. Beckman.

APRIL 1983

Chapter One

THE LEMMINGS WITHIN

The more extensive a man's knowledge of what has been done, the greater will be his power of knowing what to do.

Benjamin Disraeli

On they rush, headlong toward the sea. They scramble over one another. They bite and tear, shriek and squeal. Gripped by a seemingly mad compulsion, thousands of lemmings sweep down the countryside, destroying everything in their path, in a wild and frenzied stampede toward the Arctic Ocean in search of food. They cross tundra, rivers, even lakes, at an ever-quickening tempo. Finally they reach the water's edge. Then, something strange happens. The quest for sustenance is abandoned. Their mass migration continues, straight into the sea. Through some mysterious process of natural selection, a few remain on shore. They form the nucleus of the lemming population. And 3.86 years later, they are off again on a ritual of mass suicide.

Theories abound to explain their suicidal behaviour. Some say that when food supplies in their natural habitat are exhausted, the lemmings move on, en masse, to new vegetation near the sea. But this does not explain why these furry little creatures self-destruct on arrival. A more definitive theory points to radical hormonal changes. Intense stress induces shifts in their hormone balances. During the cold winter months the circulation system of the lemmings becomes saturated with steroid hormones which act like anti-freeze. This allows them to remain active in a climate where most other small animals would hibernate. Overcrowding is believed to be the trigger which releases these steroid hormones into the central nervous system, it soars to thirty times normal when the lemmings are most numerous. But even this scientifically-based theory has flaws. The life cycle of the lemming remains one of the many mysteries of the natural law governing this planet.

Repetitive patterns of plant and animal behaviour are all around us. There is a peak in the population of Canadian snowshoe rabbits averaging about 9.6 years. The life cycle of the lynx, marten, fishers, owls and hawk populations also averages 9.6 years. Each has its own self-correcting, self-destructing life sequence. Thousands of catalogued phenomena in our world occur over and over again with rhythmic regularity for which there is no logical explanation, no known cause. Yet, the knowledge of their existence can be of inestimable value in planning our future.

Knowing what the lemming does and when he's going to do it, is quite important . . . especially if you are a farmer tending land in the path of lemming mass migration every 3.86 years.

We humans suffer a major drawback because we have convinced ourselves we are not subject to the same behaviour patterns which exist elsewhere in the animal kingdom. Somehow, it seems demeaning that our lives may in some way be preordained by a force or forces still unknown and possibly uncontrollable by human effort. It is anathema to scientists, economists and forecasters to suggest that human life cannot be planned and regulated.

We choose to believe we are the masters of our destiny, and choose leaders who will master this destiny for us. Yet, our chosen leaders, regardless of political persuasion, continue to lead us into war, depression, recession, inflation, conflict and all sorts of economic and social mayhem with unfailing regularity. Inevitably we trail lemming-like behind, albeit unwillingly at times.

Are we so inept at choosing our leaders? The political party which is out of office claims it has the solutions to the problems created by the ruling party. Yet, as soon as it wins power, it too is landed with the same dilemmas, the same lack of solutions as the political party it ousted. Naturally, the dethroned party suddenly acquires the solutions whilst in opposition.

A gentle flirtation with logic and reason should tell you that if our leaders could prevent high unemployment they would. If they could prevent prices spiralling ever upwards or could keep us out of a recession, they would. If they could stamp out social disorder, they would. The idea that government can play a meaningful role in controlling these factors is a politically induced self-delusion.

For centuries, governments the world over have attempted to produce a social and economic climate devoid of wild gyrations. But their track-record speaks for itself. Now we are off on the last leg of the twentieth century, plagued with raging inflation, excruciatingly painful unemployment, social disorder on an alarming scale, and facing global conflict which could lead to a devastating war. Whatever a government claims, whatever the sophisticated political and economic tools, there is no answer. We continue to repeat the mistakes we have made through history, failing to learn from our predecessors. And it is quite obvious we are not in command of our destiny.

Still there is no reason to become totally fatalistic. Far from it. There are a great many opportunities for health, wealth and the pursuit of happiness. Most people fail in these pursuits because they are either unable or unwilling to perceive precisely how life on earth actually works. Those who are aware of the lemming tendency can prepare for the problems well in advance.

A fur trader, perhaps, should possess a knowledge of the rhythms of the lynx to prepare for the price fluctuations of lynx fur. Then he can maximise his profits.

Anyone with a passion for partridges may find it useful to know that every 22.7 years there is a peak and a trough in the partridge population. By using data accumulated between 1727 and 1909 on an old Bohemian estate in Kramau, Czechoslovakia, partridge hunting can be confined to periods when birds are abundant.

When Neanderthal man discovered that winter and summer alternated with a degree of regularity, he took a major step forward in adapting to his environment. He was able to anticipate that warm periods were better for hunting, and could store food and fuel for the cold periods to come.

Given the advent of computer technology and the tremendous ability we now have to store and correlate data, we can now make use of other phenomena with regular patterns. In many ways, we plan our lives on the assumption that what has happened before will always happen. Our lifestyle involves working, playing and sleeping, linked to the regular rhythm of a twenty-four hour day. We purchase a home on a twenty year mortgage. We are now able to make the repayments on that mortgage. We see little reason why that may not continue. In our twenty-four hour day, we have many thousands of years of repetition to convince us that night will follow day at reliable and regular intervals. Yet, the data we rely on for our continued ability to repay the mortgage is likely to be far more subjective and far less reliable.

We assume that what has happened for the past five years will happen over the next five years. If we watched the lemming population grow for two years, and assumed the lemming population would always grow, we would be totally unprepared for their mass suicide every 3.86 years.

If we studied the salmon for five years and concluded that since the salmon population had been growing for five years, it would continue to grow forever, we would not be prepared for the peaks and troughs in the salmon population which occur every 9.6 years on average. If our standard of living has been improving for the past fifteen years, it would certainly be wrong to assume it will continue to improve without some evidence to support that assertion. It would be downright dangerous to enter long term financial commitments by supposing that the future will always follow a straight-line projection of the past without investigating whether it makes sense.

As history has repeatedly demonstrated, the future is certainly not a straight-line projection of the past. Dramatic changes take place at fairly regular intervals. We seem perfectly content to anticipate the future on the basis of an historical repetition of the past. But there is a primary weakness in our ability to anticipate the major changes which are also a part of historical repetition.

The economic recession of 1973–1975 was the most severe depression since the 1930s. The recession was believed to be attributable to the oil crisis, and was considered the underlying cause of considerable worldwide dislocation. During the fourth quarter of 1979, the global economy began another recession. At the beginning of 1983, that recession was still raging, but still no one actually believes we could experience a depression on the scale of the 1930s. Guess what? During the 1930s that was exactly how people felt about the depression of the 1870s. During the 1870s they felt the same about the depression of the 1820s. Historical accounts of the 1820s demonstrate conclusively that no one believed that economic dislocation on the same scale as the 1780s could ever happen again.

'Our leaders will save us'; 'Governments of today know much more than they did in the 1930s and are better equipped to handle the problems'; 'economic planning is now far more sophisticated'. These are the clichés and platitudes we cling to so that we may convince ourselves that this time around history will not repeat itself. This time around, we say, we will be spared. We dismiss the repetitions of history as coincidental quirks based on suspect statistics. But what evidence do we have to indicate the situation will be any different this time around? With unfailing regularity, we have had inflations, deflations and depressions, each spread about 50 years apart.

For 200 years and more, our leaders have attempted to smoothe the periodic dislocations in our economic lives, and failed. All the evidence indicates that we are going to continue to fall into the same traps we have fallen into for thousands of years.

The Long Waves of Economic Life

There was a depression in the 1780s. There was another in the 1830s. Most of the historical data on these great depressions has faded from memory. Our great grandfathers may recall the depression of the 1880s during their childhood. Most people alive today need no reminder of the Wall Street crash which precipitated the depression of the 1930s. In the latter part of 1979, one of the most detailed chronicles of the era was published, 'The Day the Bubble Burst' (Gordon Thomas and Max Morgan-Witts). It followed J.K. Galbraith's superb account of that time, 'The Great Crash', published in the 1960s. There was a television series in 1982 entitled 'The Great Depression', which punched out the horrors of the 1930s. The era will not be forgotten easily . . . at least not until the next period of prosperity. Then the depression of the 1930s will join the historical remnants of previous depressions.

You may by now have come to the conclusion that during the 1980s we are due for an action replay of one of those nasty scenarios. Don't jump the gun! These periodic depressions are merely one component of the wheels within wheels and circles within spirals in the complete framework of economic life. There are many many factors which contribute to our lemming-like existence. That we have had a depression every fifty years or so, and have not had one for the past fifty years, may suggest that a depression is now due. By the time I have finished presenting the evidence – that idea will be more than mere suggestion.

Every fifty to sixty years, we build our metaphorical beehive, tear it down, then build it up again. The building process is a socio-economic one, described by economists as the 'upwave'. The demolition process is called the 'downwave'. In between, there is a lot of messing about, but that is relatively unimportant. As a common denominator for measuring the building process and the tearing down process we use raw material prices. These are the nucleus of our social and economic existence.

During the 'upwave', or building the beehive, raw material prices move up at an ever-increasing rate until we reach the trend of exponential growth – like the growth trend of the lemming population. Our economies are not sufficiently productive to meet the demands which cause those rising prices. So, we get a series of financial crises and a nasty recession.

But the big bang comes later on. When it comes to prices, nothing ever goes up and down in a straight line. There are periods of advance, and periods of contraction. During the 'upwave', when prices are rising, there are minor skirmishes and recessions. After each recession, the economy resumes its uptrend. Life could not be better. A recovery follows the recession.

But the situation is not so rosy any more. We have already entered the downward phase of the long-term economic wave. That phase coincides with the price peak. Instead of an ongoing economic recovery, as in the 'upwave', we have a financial calamity at the end of the first recession in the 'downwave', like the 'Crash of 1929' or the 'Panic of 1873'. The house of cards comes tumbling down. It's brother-can-you-spare-a-dime time, with the apple sellers appearing on street corners, and remaining on the street corners for possibly a couple of decades.

Essentially, our economic beehive and lemming-like existence consists of a long wave of fifty to sixty years. Of that fifty to sixty years, twenty-five to thirty years are spent building the beehive. When the beehive is finished, we spend about eight to ten years stagnating. After that, we spend about twenty to twenty-five years tearing the beehive down so we can start building it again.

Figure 1 is an impression of the idealised long wave of economic life taking you through the period of rising prices. Then there is the initial period of falling prices. The first fall in prices coincides with a severe recession, which is followed by recovery. The recovery is usually quite shallow, ending with financial catastrophe, unemployment, bankruptcies, general mayhem and depression.

The 1920s Revisited

This cycle of 'upwaves and 'downwaves' has been going on for about 200 years. You would think by now we would have enough sense to prepare, but we never do. Rollicking and frollicking during the roaring twenties, people may have had a vague recollection of the depression of the 1870s, but that was far from the mind's eye amid the bootleg booze, short skirts and sexy flappers. Prices were falling in the early 1920s and unemployment was rising, but a man with a steady job had little to worry about. He might have had little chance of a rise in wages, but the fall in the prices of food, housing and clothing meant his purchasing power was rising. Prices always rose in war; then fell in peace as the war machine switched to production for peace and consumption. It had been that way since the Industrial Revolution. There was no reason why the average man should expect any change in the 1920s. What did he know about history? History was for the historians.

The Industrial Revolution demonstrated many things. It brought one of the most dramatic and dynamic changes in lifestyle and the family unit since the beginning of Christianity. The Industrial Revolution was built on improving the means of production, using fewer people to produce a greater abundance of goods and services. The fewer the people and the more the goods, the lower the price and the greater the spread of goods and services for all, provided society remained in relative equilibrium, which it never does. As the effects of the Industrial Revolution worked through the global economic system from the eighteenth century to the twentieth century, there were periods of disequilibrium, temporary dislocations and hardship.

Immediately following World War I there was such a time. At the start of the 1920s unemployment was high. For a while, people felt totally disillusioned. Soldiers returned from the front to discover they had no jobs to go to. But peacetime output began to grow, and so did demand for goods and services. The number of jobs grew, and the number of unemployed fell.

Throughout the industrialised world, the 1920s was a decade of prosperity, powered by the commercial application of the internal combustion engine and the electric motor. The average man believed

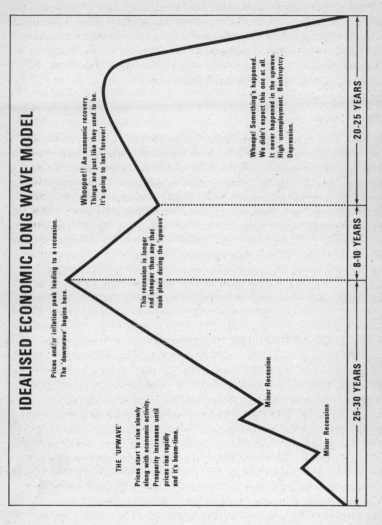

Figure 1 The Idealised Economic Long Wave Model

that prosperity would last forever. His dad may have been alive in the 'great depression' of the 1870s and 1880s, but only as a youth. Our twentieth century Neanderthal *knew* that the prosperous days of the 1920s were quite different from all the other prosperous times which had collapsed before. Governments and economists were so much wiser in the 1920s than ever before . . . ça va?

As we now know, that proved drastically wrong. Remember what happens in the economic beehive? Prices reach an unsustainable peak and then decline. After that, we get a recession. After the recession, there is economic recovery. Then everyone thinks everything is just as it used to be . . . but it is not. The beehive is being destroyed. It has already reached its optimal level of growth.

The calamity of the 1870s was repeated following the Crash of '29. The secondary prosperity of the 1920s went up in smoke, and a multitude of businesses were wiped out. It is highly probable there would have been no depression if the assumptions about continued prosperity had not been so widespread. There may have been no World War II, if fewer people had assumed it could not happen again.

200 Years of Economic Repetition

It is the early 1930s. A stooped emaciated figure trudges in chains through the dreary Siberian landscape and disappears into history – one of the hundreds of thousands who die in Stalin's prison camps. His name, Nikolai Dmitrievich Kondratieff. Occupation: Economist. Crime: Thinking for himself.

'Forbes', November 9, 1981

I neither discovered nor invented the long wave of economic life. I wish I had. But the discoveries belong to several great economists. One of them was N.D. Kondratieff. He died in a Siberian concentration camp for what the Communists believed was a heretical and danger-ous view of economic developments. His theories were deemed a threat to the Communist regime.

Kondratieff studied the work of several economists who were attempting to discern a pattern of rhythmic regularity in the ebb and flow of international and domestic trade. While most economists of that time were concerned with trade cycles of three, five and fifteen years, Kondratieff noticed a much longer term business cycle repetition. While John Maynard Keynes was sipping champagne in well-appointed Edwardian drawing-rooms, formulating an economic policy for manipulating our way out of the depression of the 1930s when that depression was nearing an end, Kondratieff was thinking in much grander terms.

He was pondering the long sweep of economic history. He questioned the nature of the waves of prosperity and adversity ebbing and flowing in price sequences spanning hundreds of years. These upswings and downswings seemed to persist throughout the period following the Industrial Revolution in all industrialised nations, regardless of political party or economic policy. Kondratieff concluded there was a supreme order in our economic affairs, an uncontrollable order involving great tides of economic activity capable of humbling economists and plundering politicians.

Kondratieff's theory was originally published in German under the title, 'Die langen Wellen der Konjunktur'. His paper first appeared in 1926 in the *'Archiv fur Sozialwissenschaft und Sozialpolitik'*. Kondratieff said:

> The upswing in the first long wave embraces the period from 1789 to 1814, i.e. 25 years; its decline begins in 1814 and ends in 1849, a period of 35 years. The cycle is therefore completed in 60 years. The rise in the second wave begins in 1849 and ends in 1873, lasting 24 years. The decline of the second wave begins in 1873 and ends in 1896, a period of 23 years. The length of the second wave is 47 years. The upward movement of the third wave begins in 1896 and ends in 1920, its duration 24 years. The decline of the wave, according to all data, begins in 1920.

Kondratieff never lived to see the startling conclusion to this third wave. The price cycle actually peaked in 1920. It led to a downwave lasting 20 years, involving the Great Depression, and the completion of another long wave lasting 44 years. Our current position within the long wave cycle is just about where it was when Kondratieff's work was terminated about fifty years ago.

I have applied the idealised long wave economic model to our global experience over the past 200 years. Figure 2 shows three distinct repetitions of the long wave tendency from 1789 to 1940. The horizontal grid on the chart is a time scale. The vertical grid on the chart represents a raw material price relationship.

My intention is not to cloud your mind with facts and figures, but to demonstrate the consistency of the long wave economic model. Its shape and the timing of the peaks and troughs correspond to peaks and troughs in the price indices of several countries. This is not peculiar to the United States and Britain. The crests and troughs of the waves do not repeat themselves at any precise time. The actual highs and lows of the price level are distorted. There is, however, a marked tendency for periods of extreme strength to follow each other at forty-five to fifty-five year intervals. Such time spans are separated by periods of weakness. Although the precise time relationships may be somewhat obscure, in no way does this undermine the forecasting value of this phenomenon.

The First Wave

The world was in deep depression through the 1770s and 1780s, after a boom and collapse in England. France also suffered under the guidance of John Law, who was responsible for the invention of fiat money and the ill-fated Mississippi Bubble. The South Sea Bubble, a speculative orgy in England which sparked an economic slump, and the Mississipi Bubble in France, both produced a series of economic dislocations throughout Europe for most of the eighteenth century. European economies were severely squeezed, and raw material prices fell. Wheat, the backbone of the global economy during the eighteenth century, was especially hard hit.

The depression of the 1780s hit bottom in 1783. European economies slowly began to pick up. By 1789, prices were beginning to rise again. After the outbreak of war between Britain and France in 1793, the gradual rise in prices turned into an explosive upsurge. A further surge in prices took place between 1798 and 1801, and again after the War of 1812. But, by 1814, prices and economic activity had reached an unsustainable peak. The crisis of 1809–1810 demonstrated the underlying weakness at the tail-end of the boom. There was a sharp fall in prices, and deep recession during 1814–1815.

The period 1815–1816 brought a post-war boom. England's exports to Europe and the United States far exceeded all possibility of sales. In 1819, there was a sharp fall in the price of wheat. Six years later, canals and South American government bonds and mines joined the collapse. British exports plunged. Cotton sales collapsed; so did land sales in the United States. As railroad mania began in the States, the mid-1830s took an economic nosedive. Except for a brief period between 1815 and 1819, there was a seemingly endless series of financial panics from 1814 to 1843. They brought the deep depression of the 1820s, 1830s and early 1840s. Between 1814 and 1843, prices fell by 59%, so severe was the contraction in economic activity.

The Second Wave

A new upwave began in 1843, just 54 years after the trough of the depression in the late 1780s. (Fifty four years is the perfectly regular time frame of the long wave.) The 'lemmings' left on the shore after the depression of the 1830s and 1840s began to build anew. As they did, sections of European economies began to recover. Industrial production picked up, exports increased, wheat leapt again. Between 1852 and 1854, this price surge mirrored what had happened in 1798–1801. Consumer prices jumped by 33%. Just as the 1812 war produced an upsurge in prices, so did the American Civil War and the Crimean War. Just as the crisis of 1809–1810 warned that all was not well within

FOUR LONG WAVE CYCLES 1780 - 2000

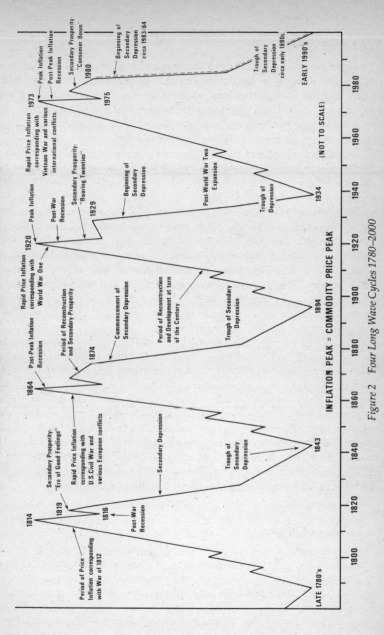

Figure 2 *Four Long Wave Cycles 1780–2000*

the economic beehive, the panic of 1857 brought warning before the final peak in economic activity in 1864.

After that, prices topped out. The recession had begun. It was steeper and sharper than anything between the 1840s and the 1860s. The system was eventually unable to sustain itself. A series of financial panics began in Germany in May of 1873, and spread to America four months later. Economic activity contracted. Prices fell, and again the world was plunged into depression. A second long wave was completed from 1843 to 1896, just under 54 years. A coincidence? A freak? Two repetitions . . . maybe. But three? Most unlikely!

The Third Wave

In the late 1890s, prices inched up again. From 1896, right through to the late 1930s, what had happened twice during the preceding 150 years, happened again. The lemmings were still at work. Prices rose steadily until 1920. Business was booming.

In 1920, prices peaked and the commodity market crashed. Hundreds of small investors in Britain went bankrupt speculating in Argentine companies and a host of new private companies of dubious merit. The financial crisis in a speculative market led to the recession of 1920, which lasted two years. There was enough strength left in the system to produce one more meaningful recovery. That brought the 'Roaring Twenties'. But they were not strong enough to withstand the 'Great Crash'. For the third time since the 1780s, the world plunged into deep depression.

The Current Wave

Probably the most important economic sequences over the past 200 years are happening now. We are all well aware that prices have been rising since pre-World War II days. Less obvious is strong evidence to suggest that we are now at a price peak similar to those in 1920, 1864 and 1814. According to the Consumer Price Index, inflation continued to rise in Britain after the global recession of 1973–1975. The global Consumer Price Index and the global Wholesale Price Index actually peaked in 1974. The *'Economist'* Dollar All Item Commodity Price Index peaked in 1973. World domestic credit expansion and world monetary growth also peaked in 1973. In early 1980, silver prices collapsed. So did gold.

A period of secondary prosperity began in late 1974, with a renewed upsurge in commodity prices and inflation. Both have now peaked again, well below the previous peaks of 1974. Commodity prices have fallen across a broad front. So have the prices of many finished products from the factory gate. And the price of oil, which many believed

COMMODITY PRICE INDEX

(Economist Dollar All Item)
1964 — 1982

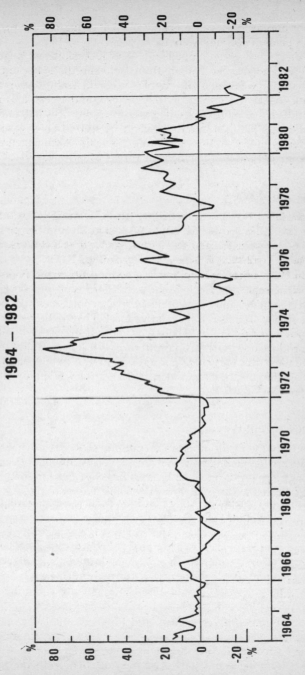

Figure 3   Commodity Price Index

would never fall, is doing just that. So are property prices.

The normal long wave pattern involves approximately 54 years from peak to peak. In 1920, commodity prices peaked. In 1974, commodity prices peaked again, 54 years from the previous top.

As we have seen, the peak in commodity prices is followed by a recession. This recession is followed by a recovery which involves a gradually declining plateau of economic activity. The recession, recovery, and gradually declining plateau last about a decade. The recession which began in 1973, and lasted until late 1975, was the worst since the 1930s.

The trigger which aggravates the recession and seems to coincide with the peak in the price cycle, is some form of financial panic. In our current cycle, this financial panic came as a second-line banking crisis, hot-on-the-heels of the global prices peak. The bell was rung, and the warning signal was given, just as it was in the past.

The economic recovery which began after the second-line banking crisis was typical in every respect, conforming to the precise nature of the type of recovery called for in the normal long wave pattern. In both Britain and the U.S., there was a brief spurt in economic improvement, beginning in late 1974, but petering out in late 1978. Economic activity throughout the recovery was sluggish. The gradually declining plateau of economic activity began in Britain and the U.S. in the fourth quarter of 1979. The model calls for a completion of the plateau period in 1982, followed by a secondary depression. You are there!

The prospect of depression perhaps only a few months away may be frightening. But it need not be. During the 1930s, 25% of the workforce may have been unemployed. But that meant 75% of the workforce was employed. Falling prices brought an effective wage rise with every fall in price.

There were several boom industries during the 1930s depression. The film industry was at its height. The Stork Club and the Copacabana were packed every night. Most of the get-rich-quick millionaires of the 'Swinging Sixties' are now defunct. Those who began making their fortunes during the 1930s still have their millions, and many more to boot. More self-made millionaires came from the ruins of the 1930s than from any other time over the past fifty years.

If the long wave cycle of economic life repeats itself, those who are unprepared will suffer hardship. So will anyone who is unable to prepare for the crunch. But anyone who can anticipate what lies ahead, and plans accordingly, could gain the opportunity of a lifetime.

Chapter Two

THE UPWAVE . . . LIFE AS WE KNOW IT

By the Law of Periodical Repetition, everything which has happened
once must happen again and again – and not capriciously, but at regular
periods, and each thing in its own period, not another's, and each
obeying its own law . . . the same Nature which delights in periodical
repetition in the skies is the Nature which orders the affairs of the earth.
Let us not underrate the value of that hint.

Mark Twain

Modern economic theorists revel in the trivia and minutiae of contem-
porary history. They treat any economic event before World War II as if
it was prehistoric. To understand and use the patterns in the long
wave, you do not need an IBM 1264 with 2,000 megabytes and a
daisy-wheel printer, or to understand alphas, betas, sigmas and diffe-
rential calculus. The principle is simple enough. It is based on the idea
that there is a strong interaction between political and social developments, wars and the long term price cycle, all of which come to a peak
at 50–60 year intervals. The complete economic sequence involves four
basic components: first an upwave, then a recession. Then there is
secondary prosperity, and finally, secondary depression. The cycle
then starts all over again.

The Components of the Upwave

Recently I have been giving a series of lectures entitled 'Personal
Survival in a World Turned Upside Down', so-called because all of the
things people have been doing correctly during the upwave, everything that currently seems normal and natural, will soon have poten-
tially disastrous consequences. We are now heading downwards in the
long term economic scheme. Social, economic and investment worlds
for the past thirty years are being turned upside down.

An understanding of the four components I have mentioned will not
only help you shift your emphasis and lifestyle in the future. It will also
demonstrate conclusively that the upwave which began in 1939 has
come to an end.

The long wave pattern of economic life is based on a model of prices, the foundation of economic behaviour in the capitalist and pseudo-capitalist system. The price model carries with it some definitive and seemingly unalterable implications. They will affect your finances, and your way of living in tomorrow's world. The price of money, or interest rates, is an important element during the expansion phase of the long wave. When you negotiate a mortgage of, say, six per cent in one part of the upwave, and fifteen per cent at another, you will feel the effects at firsthand. These long waves of economic behaviour may at first glance seem rather esoteric. But if you were among the unemployed or made bankrupt between 1930 and 1940, your plight would have been more than just a passing interest. All the more so, because your plight could have been predicted fairly accurately several years before it happened. What lies ahead during the next two decades is no less predictable.

Inflation During the Upwave

We have lived through nearly four decades of inflation, and many people think inflation is a permanent part of our existence. They believe that prices will rise because prices have always risen. History shows that this is not true, but preconceptions die hard. Inflation is now considered 'Public Enemy Number One' by most governments. Politicians love to promise to control inflation. In the mid-1970s, Britain was cited as a nation on the brink of becoming a 'banana republic'. Now it is thought that inflation must be conquered at all cost. This fear that something horrible will happen if inflation is not conquered and obliterated – leads us into the same trap as other governments in other countries during periods of high inflation.

If there is one thing to be learned from studying these long waves of economic life, it is that rising prices are certainly not a permanent part of the economic system. Wheat prices from 1295 to 1980 show that clearly. Long waves of economic life ebbed and flowed well before the first observable wave began in 1798. French price indices beginning in the 1850s verify this. So do English and American prices back to the close of the eighteenth century, and British prices back to the thirteenth century. It seems the British have a penchant for keeping records.

The upswing in the first long period of rising prices, or inflation, goes from 1789 to 1814. In those 25 years, prices advanced, slowly at first, building in momentum with the increase in business activity. After war between Britain and France began, the gradual increase became an explosion. At the time, the 'Gayer Index of Domestic and Imported Prices' was the standard inflation index, similar to the modern Retail Price Index. From a pre-war trough of 88.0 in 1792, the Gayer

The Long Wave of Commodity Prices
(1901-10 = 100)

UNITED STATES ······· ENGLAND ——— FRANCE ----------

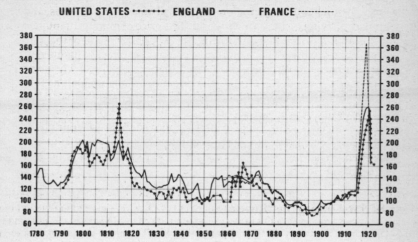

Figure 4   The Long Wave of Commodity Prices

Index reached 107.9 in six years. In the following three years to 1801, the price increase was much more spectacular, leaping from 107.9 to 155.7. It reached a peak of 168.9 in 1813.

According to the Gayer Index, prices soared by 92 per cent from 1783 to 1813. In just three years, from 1798, they shot up 44 per cent. Such a massive gain over a comparatively short period is not unusual. History shows that it is characteristic of practically all inflations.

Prices did not go straight up from 1783 to 1813. There were peak years in commodity prices in 1799, 1805, 1810, and 1814. There was no dramatic fall in prices between those years, merely an easing back. But, after 1814, the downward trend had begun, the turning point had been reached.

The second upwave began in 1849, and lasted 24 years. Inflation again returned after an absence of 35 years. Prices began rising slowly at first, duplicating the pattern of the upwave of five decades earlier, then suddenly surged. From 1852 to 1854, prices increased 33 per cent, quite something for people accustomed to falling prices for 35 years. This price rise was almost identical to the huge jump between 1798 and 1801. Over 90 per cent of the price rises during the 1849 to 1873 inflation took place in two years (1852–1854).

The world was free from inflation again until 1896. In the mid-1890s prices drifted upwards, as they had during the 1780s and 1850s. And just as there had been big price rises over relatively short periods before, (1798–1801 and 1852–1854), the steady increase from 1893 to 1918 saw a similar pattern. Half the total increase in prices was crammed into the three years 1897 to 1900.

History repeated itself elsewhere. Inflation during 1893 to 1920 was largely the result of gold-mining, war and cyclical expansion. The same combination was responsible for the inflation of 1849 to 1873. It was not until the crisis of 1920, another turning point in the upwave, that prices stopped rising.

About 19 years passed between the end of inflation in 1920 and the beginning of the fourth upwave. Once more, prices rose gently at first. Then World War II broke out, and produced another price convulsion. The Korean War played its part. So did the war in South East Asia. But the Middle East War sparked off the biggest price explosion. Oil prices quadrupled, and inflation produced just the kind of phenomenon as in other upwaves – an explosion in prices over a relatively short period.

The mind often plays tricks on people, and the most recent difficult experiences often appear to be the most painful and intractable. The inflation of 1939–1974 was, of course, the historical legacy of the previous depression. During the 1920s, inflation was perceived as the common enemy; an excruciatingly painful enemy as demonstrated by the horrifying German hyperinflation of the early 1920s. The depression of the 1930s left a lasting impression with the policy-makers of the time. But, by the end of the decade, the problems of inflation were all but forgotten. Nothing could ever again be as painful as the depression the world had been forced to live through. High unemployment and queues of people on breadlines seemed a far greater evil than anything ever produced during the inflationary times.

So the policy-makers embarked on measures to curb unemployment and provide sustenance for the unemployed. They also sowed the seeds for the inflation of the 1939–1974 era, in precisely the same manner as the economic policy-makers in the wake of previous depressions. The measures of the late 1930s, 1940s and 1950s may have differed in detail, but the objectives were still the same. What had happened in the previous 150 years meant nothing.

The economic theories of John Maynard Keynes provided the foundations upon which the inflation of the past four decades was built. If it had not been Keynes, somebody else would have provided the philosophy which appealed to policy-makers who were totally preoccupied with averting another depression, and blind to the inexorable forces within the social and economic fibres of a nation. Keynes' theory said that economic recovery could be induced by government spending. During periods of slack demand, the government could create

The Price of Wheat in England: 1259-1975

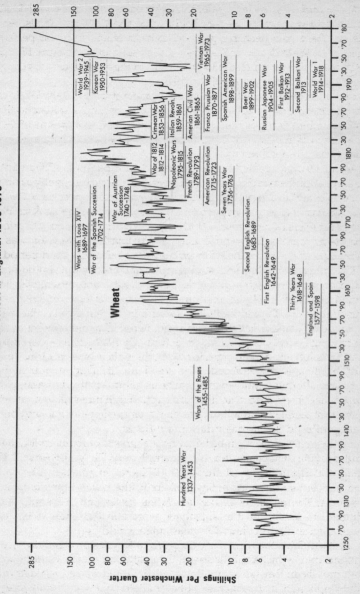

Shillings Per Winchester Quarter

Figure 5   Wheat Prices

new demand by its own social expenditure programme. In turn, this would result in an overall increase in demand for goods and services throughout the entire economy.

President Roosevelt's 'New Deal' was based on the Keynesian doctrine. So were the policies of the British administration during the tail-end of the depression of the 1930s. Keynes, of course, recognised the dangers. He knew his principles could cause high inflation and was quite emphatic that if high inflation, and deficits, were to be avoided from government-induced economic stimulus during bad times, governments would have to make every effort to maintain budget surpluses during boom times. In other words, recessions could be prevented from deepening through government stimulation. But since the government was likely to be paying out more than it was taking in, a deficit would result. Deficits, the result of living beyond our means, are inflationary. Keynes believed the inflation could be mitigated, provided the government cut social spending once the economy picked up again. What Keynes did not foresee, or perhaps turned a blind eye to, was that once politicians commit themselves to buying votes with promises of a 'chicken in every pot', a 'car in every garage', and a 'Henry Moore on every public building', there is no turning back. Social spending grows, and keeps on growing.

Governments always tend to underestimate inflationary forces, preferring to accept the more optimistic of any two estimates put forward. They fear that otherwise they will be replaced by another government more willing to feed the public with a political plethora of pusillanimous piffle. Political considerations allowed policies designed to ease the depression of the 1930s to fuel the fires of inflation through failure.

The depression of the 1930s, the depression of the 1890s, the depression of the 1840s, and the depression of the 1780s, shared another common denominator: countries imposed high trade tariffs to protect their domestic markets once demand contracted. Soon, currencies became debased, and inflation was fuelled. Soon high trade tariffs failed to protect vulnerable domestic markets. Major industrialised nations had to abandon the gold standard as a basis for fixing currency relationships. The next step was to abandon fixed parity and float exchange rates. That inevitably led to instability. History has repeatedly shown that floating exchange rates gain only temporary relief. Ultimately, the major currencies will always gravitate right back to where they were before floating exchange rates were introduced.

In the 1940s, floating exchange rates achieved little success. So, post-war planners put their heads together and came up with the Bretton Woods Agreement. This worked magic during the late 1940s and 1950s, and world trade expanded considerably. But it also allowed the United States and Britain to live far beyond their means for nearly two decades, and, in doing so, pushed up world inflation.

For twenty years after the war, great chunks of the world underwent a dramatic rebuilding programme: first Europe, then Japan, and Germany. Since the U.S. was never devastated by war, there was nothing to rebuild. But it certainly profited by selling the tools that others needed to rebuild their countries.

The 1950s and 1960s also saw the victors of World War II surrendering control over Third World countries. Britain gave independence to India and several other colonies. France was ousted from Indochina. Holland severed its relationship with Indonesia. These were the kind of empire liquidations witnessed during the early 1800s and 1860s. These emerging nations were in no position to cut the financial umbilical cord with their Mother countries. This meant that poor people in rich countries were taxed for the benefit of rich people in poor countries. Huge debts began piling up among Third World countries. The outcome? You guessed it . . . more inflation.

The list of factors contributing to the inflationary upwave of 1939–1974 is virtually endless. But all that is important now is to recognise the nature of inflation and its relationship with previous periods in the long waves of economic behaviour.

Inflation is a common enemy, just as it was in the past. But it is an enemy few people actually understand. At first glance, having no inflation might seem ideal. Yet the inflationary forces in Britain seemed to improve the quality of life, except in recent years when it appeared to be out of control. Compare this with Switzerland, one of the few countries with virtually no inflation for most of the current upwave. Price stability has made very little impact in improving the material quality of Swiss life.

Today, a lot of people are re-examining their material goals. 'Is it worth it?' they ask. The answer is 'yes'; provided that inflation and its incumbent problems can be avoided. These people would be quite content to dispense with growth. No growth is suddenly becoming desirable and acceptable in many quarters. Inflation is a monster; anything must be better than inflation.

This attitude is a fallacy. The upwave and its inflationary counterparts have provided prosperity which otherwise would never have occurred. More people own their own homes in Britain and the U.S.A. than ever before. The standard of living worldwide is higher than ever. Most people in industrialised societies today demand an improved standard of living. Labour unions preach that an increasing standard of living is their inalienable right, regardless of what they produce. Most people would strongly resist any measure to halt the long wave economic upwave if they were aware of it.

The problems associated with inflation are not characteristic of inflation itself, but are a product of the type of inflation experienced as we near the end of the upwave.

Like the lemming population, whose growth exceeds the supply of vegetation for its sustenance, the demands made of the industrialised economy near the end of the upwave are too much for the economy to bear, so it self-destructs. The rise in prices reaches a point where inflation is no longer an asset, but a severe penalty. One which is likely to lead to an economic holocaust, perhaps even worse than any we have known before.

The battle against inflation begins in earnest when that massive bulge occurs during the latter stages of the upwave. It came in 1920 and 1974 with peaks in commodity prices, followed by peaks in wholesale prices, and then in retail prices. This final price bulge usually occurs when a fully extended economy is forced to battle it out with an event such as an energy crisis, a banking crisis, a war, or a combination of them all.

The economy will start to falter, unemployment will start to rise. The government is then forced to spend massive amounts while unemployment is rising and production is falling. Shortages caused by falling production, combined with expansive monetary growth, force prices to skyrocket. This, in turn, puts pressure on workers. They demand bigger wage increases to maintain the standard of living they have been virtually guaranteed by government. This is obviously frightening and confusing to people who misunderstand the root cause of inflation.

Contrary to popular belief, prices do not rise because of increases in subordinate areas such as labour. Labour is used as a political scapegoat. During the final stages of expansion, prices rise because of the imbalance between supply and demand for goods and services. Demand continues to increase, while supply contracts.

The combination of rising prices, sizeable industrial over-capacity, and a labour force which cannot be used, is formidable. It certainly cannot go on for any appreciable period. We have simply reached the end of the upwave.

One important way of spotting the final inflationary spurt is to note when it happens during the upwave. The majority of price increases occur within a relatively short period. During the first upwave, the price index rose 92 per cent from 88.0 to 168.9 between 1792 and 1813. From 1798 to 1801, prices rose from 107.9 to 155.7, a gain of 44 per cent. Nearly half of those price gains over 21 years were achieved in just three years. During the second upward cycle there was a similar pattern. Between 1852 and 1854 prices rose by 33 per cent. That was more than 90 per cent of the total gain from 1843 to 1864. In the third upwave, the big jump in prices took place during and after World War I. During the current wave, inflation did not really become chronic until 1974. Two years later, the inflationary spiral reached the peak of its exponential curve. Most of the price rises occurred between 1973 and 1976, although high rates persisted. This is further evidence of an inflationary spiral which has spent its force.

The rate of inflation in OECD countries began falling appreciably towards the end of 1980. Until then, inflation had climbed steadily during the recovery from 1975 to 1980. But they never reached the levels recorded earlier in the upwave. Many modern retail price indices are inadequate and imprecise. Prices may still appear to be rising because of an 'echo' effect that reflects monetary excesses of previous years working through the economy. These monetary excesses were originally generated by the energy crisis, and supplemented by the burden of social benefits during a recent period of lacklustre economic activity. When the 'echo' dies, there will be no other big noise to replace it. When the money spent on energy is redirected for use in the private sector, capacity will increase beyond current excessive levels. But there is little to stimulate demand. The mutually exclusive conditions of recession and inflation of recent years will disappear. The effect of falling prices will be more pronounced, and will bring far more devastating consequences than inflation ever could produce. Deflation is *much* more difficult to control than inflation.

Technology . . . Further Fuel for the Upwave

The 'star' of the upwave is inflation, but several other characters play extremely important supporting roles. Inflation is certainly not confined to raw material, wholesale and retail prices. It includes interest rates, wages, foreign trade, music, fashion, and the production of industrial bell-weather resources like coal, pig iron, steel and lead. All of these appear related to, or dominated by, overriding natural economic forces within the long waves of economic and social life in industrialised societies.

Dynamic phases of technological achievement seem inexorably linked to long wave behaviour patterns. These long waves are characterised by sharp gains in economic activity which peak, and are then separated by long valleys of stagnation. Prices and inflation follow this path, and the same seems true of technological development and achievement.

The first period of major technological achievement took place during the early part of the nineteenth century, soon after the first observable upwave began in our long wave scheme. A new form of society was built on the invention of the steam engine and the spinning wheel during the Industrial Revolution. At the beginning of the nineteenth century, British trade, as in other countries, was dominated by the cotton industry. Steam was the new source of power. The spinning wheel was the revolutionary tool. Both significantly boosted production. Both brought boom times for cotton. They also fuelled the upwave that began in the 1780s. And when technological momentum in cotton waned, so did economic activity.

The second major technological advancement came in the early 1840s, coinciding with the beginning of an upwave. Railway transport began in Britain, and opened a new era of expanding British coal exports. The train was a powerful catalyst during the second upwave. Railways lowered transport costs, brought new areas and supplies into national and international markets, and helped to generate export earnings. They, in turn, permitted the whole process of expansion to move faster.

Railways also accelerated new technologies in coal, iron and engineering. Their expansion altered and modernised the institutions of capital formation during the middle to late nineteenth century. This new transport system also accelerated the pace of urbanisation. It has been estimated that the railway alone lifted national income in Britain by more than 10 per cent. Almost a quarter of the growth in Britain between 1840 and 1865 can be attributed to the train.

During the third upwave, many new technologies made their début. The third wave gave us the automobile, propellor driven aircraft, and the wireless. New methods of steel production were introduced in 1902. Over the next three years, alloy steels, such as stainless steel and non-ferrous alloys, and new methods of aluminium production came into being. The electric furnace technique was introduced between 1903 and 1906. Modern methods of tin canning came in between 1905 and 1918. Diesel engines for large ships started in 1912. Many new products and processes completely transformed the distributive trades.

The fourth period of technological innovation started just after the Great Depression of the 1930s, before World War II. It was about 45 years after the beginning of the third period of major innovation and the third upwave. The fourth upwave provided a host of new products and processes – television, penicillin, synthetic rubber, radar, DDT, nuclear power, jet aircraft, antibiotics, agricultural chemicals, microcircuitry with transistors, 'the chip' and electronic computers.

While many marvel at the wonders of the silicon chip, genetic engineering and bio-technology, none of the recent developments actually involves new technologies, merely an extension of existing ones. Over the past ten years, technological innovation has virtually come to a halt with the end of the upwave. Global markets are no longer expanding fast enough to encourage the investment or to absorb new technologies.

Between 1930 and 1950, however, there were great strides in new technology. We now have artificial satellites and missiles. There have been commercial spin-offs from jet aircraft development and fuel technology. We have word processors, a spin-off from the micro-circuitry developed during wartime. Whatever product you can imagine, investigation will show it to be merely an extension of what has already been achieved, rather than a new area of development.

At the beginning of the upwave, we find dynamic technological achievement and new innovation. This continues throughout a large portion of the upwave. When we embark on transferring and using existing technologies, instead of coming up with something new, we know the upwave has ended. It is unlikely we will see a new era of technological innovation much before the 1990s.

The Patterns of War During the Upwave

Every upwave produces two major wars, one at the beginning and one at the end.

War at the beginning of an upwave lands on an economy with unused resources, deflated prices, reduced debts and reasonably low interest rates. The increased production and new demand for war goods assists the subsequent business recovery of the upwave.

War at the end of the upwave has a negative impact. Inflated debt, high prices, high interest rates, under-capacity, and full employment tend to accentuate the inbuilt distortions of an expansion which has run out of control. War at the end of the upwave adds to the underlying forces which terminate the upwave.

War is not the cause of variations or extensions in the economic scenario. It is the effect of a series of negative forces caused by many other deep-rooted factors, most of which have psychological origins. War is a symptom of social and economic pressures which build up in the system, at the beginning and at the end of the upwave. Wars at the end of the upwave are due in part to the same social tensions associated with hyper-activity during high inflation, generating exceptionally strong emotions. Wars at the early stages of the upwave are far less popular and are more or less accepted as a fait accompli by the electorate.

The war at the end of the first upwave was the War of 1812, which generated strong emotions on a global basis. It was a period of unusually excessive social tension. Not only was there a major international war, but civil wars were being waged the world over. Rebellions against the Napoleonic regime broke out, along with a series of revolutions to free Latin America.

At the peak of the second upwave, two major wars were being fought simultaneously, the Civil War in the United States and the Crimean War. They took place against a background of strong public feeling. The Civil War in the U.S. was a direct result of President Lincoln's refusal to allow the southern states of the Union to secede peacefully. Strong emotions were aroused between black and white

Americans. In July 1863, there were bloody riots in New York City by objectors to conscription. There were race riots. It was reported that as many as 50,000 people had been roaming the city streets without stopping for four days, burning, looting and killing negroes. Lincoln's move to free the slaves was a central issue of the war, arousing racial tensions and prejudices in a society already burdened with the problems associated with the end of an upwave.

The issues in the Crimean War were much more dispersed, but they did arouse public feelings. There was a growing trend toward imperialism. One of the issues was the demand by the United States that Japan open her doors to trade.

World War I occurred at the end of the third upwave. The emotive element for America was the supposed violation of the rules of war by Germany. It was claimed that illegal German submarine warfare was responsible for killing Americans at sea. Germany had shown herself the major aggressor with her attack on Russia and the invasion of neutral Belgium. The spirit of the Allies was particularly easy to arouse.

Like other wars at the tail-end of long prosperity, World War I began as a crusade for America. But the public soon became disillusioned, and mass rioting followed. There were frenzied May Day riots in 1919, and a series of terrorist bombings in the financial district of New York.

The typical tensions, frustrations and excitement following a long period of rising prices and social unrest resulted in the cluster of wars at the end of the most recent upwave. The Korean War, the Vietnam War, and the Middle East War combined to produce the same conditions that were prevalent at the time of World War I, the U.S. Civil War, and the War of 1812. The three wars of the upwave that ended in 1974 overlapped. The Vietnam War, instigated to stem the spread of communist aggression, produced student rioting and demonstrations as people became disillusioned when the objectives were not being achieved. In the Middle East War, Europe was outraged by the transfer of wealth from the west to the east, bringing a blow to western pride. The conflicts of the 1970s ultimately brought bitter disillusionment, and the feeling that people had been put to great expense with very little gained. Essentially, the wars near the peak of the upwave reflect the emotional climate created by the two decades of increasing prosperity. It seems people are no longer able to cope with the mounting complications of their lives. They lose their stamina and their ability to keep up with the accelerating rate of change.

The War of 1812, the U.S. Civil War, the Crimean War, the Vietnam War, and the Middle East War, all lost public support as they became larger, more protracted, increasingly difficult to manage, and progressively more costly to win. The three wars of the fourth upwave led to the economic troubles which normally occur when an economy has become grossly over-extended. They also generated the kind of public discontent and disorder typical of the emotional state at the end of the long wave pattern of social and economic life. Resistance to wars or the political system responsible for them is common at the end of an upwave.

Wars at the beginning of the long upwave are totally different. Then people are still relatively calm, waiting for the wounds of the down-wave to heal. Following the long austere years of the downwave, a war at the beginning of an upwave falls on a people who are primarily concerned with their own well-being, and less interested in inter-national affairs and military crusades.

The world was at war in the 1780s and 1790s when the first upwave is seen. Except for the French Revolution in 1789, there was little national spirit behind global conflicts at the time. England was at war with Spain. There was conflict between England and Holland. Russia had invaded Turkey. Sporadic battles were breaking out all over the world.

Similarly, the Mexican War, at the beginning of the second upwave, and the Spanish-American War at the beginning of the third upwave, both failed to generate public excitability equal to that in wars at the end of the upwaves.

World War II was horrendous and brought severe hardship. Yet, the character of the war and the people's response fitted the type of war which follows a depression rather than prosperity. At the end of a war following prosperity, there is disillusionment and resentment, public disorder and rioting. At the end of World War II, there was peace and rejoicing. The 'secondary depression' at the end of the downwave is long and tedious, involving painful upsets for most people. The initial response to the first glimmer of light at the beginning of the upwave is of cautious relief. The depression appears less intense. Few recognise that a major recovery lies ahead or that a permanent change has taken place.

Historical evidence suggesting there will be no return to the 'secon-dary depression' for at least four decades is not obvious to many when the upwave begins. Problems associated with depression may ease, but most people continue to believe that the depression will be part of their lives forever. War at the early stages of the upwave diverts attention from the problems at hand, temporarily. This does not last. People remain preoccupied with keeping their jobs and staying above the poverty line. They live in fear of another depression.

World War II began five years after the last upwave started. It was not a war of public issue or national pride. It was forced upon a people who had no choice. As the upwave which began in the late 1930s approached a peak, there was a steady increase in the number of military conflicts associated with a period of mass excitability fought over matters of public issue. This was the case with the Korean War, the Vietnam War, the Middle East War, and the Falkland Islands crisis early in 1982. Polls then show the British people screaming for blood and battle.

The timing of war as evidence to support the completion of an upwave and beginning of a downwave is overwhelming. It confirms that the upwave was completed in 1973–1974, at the commodity price peak, duplicating the sequence for the fourth time in 200 years.

There is little evidence of major international conflict during the downwave, according to the social pattern of the long wave. There need be no fear of a nuclear war or any other type of major conflict, at least until the downwave is over. War is usually the last of several attempts to reverse the deflationary cycle that follows five to ten years after the trough of the 'secondary depression', punctuating the transitional phase from downwave to upwave.

There appears to be a move away from wars involving open combat and mass death and destruction. Recent conflicts have been far more localised, not unlike those of the eighteenth and nineteenth centuries. The combination of wars near the terminal phase of the most recent upwave resulted in the same type of financial problems associated with the 1914–1918 war, but were limited to localised conflicts. While another major war can be expected during the 1990s, after the beginning of the next upwave, that war is likely to be localised, probably in the East. The damage will be mainly financial, not physical with the destruction of people, goods and property.

Aside from offering clues to the possibility of international conflict and mass destruction, the long wave tendencies governing war-like attitudes also help to establish our current place in the economic sequence. Wars in recent years appear after a period of prosperity. The response of the population to recent military conflict is further evidence to support the long wave thesis. We have passed the final phase of the upwave.

Chapter Three

LIFESTYLES DURING THE UPWAVE

The masses will not support any government in the near future that puts the control of inflation ahead of full employment and continued prosperity.

T. Rowe Price

The economic life of the western world, and your personal future, hangs by a single international thread. That thread is monetary policy. I have treated the period of rising prices and inflationary prosperity as the 'upwave'. Rising prices are not the cause of the 'upwave'. They are the effect of underlying forces which can be traced to the actions of politicians. They, in turn, reflect the demands of the electorate.

Take a hard look at inflation. What is inflation, precisely? The root of inflation is, of course, 'inflate' . . . the way you would inflate a balloon. When it comes to the inflation we know so well, the supply of currency is being inflated. Who controls the currency we have in circulation? You guessed it . . . the government! And the government benefits handsomely from inflation through substantially increased revenues which provide the illusion of prosperity.

To understand why prices rise, you must grasp the concept that rising prices, mistakenly referred to as inflation, are simply caused by more money chasing fewer goods, or the same amount of money chasing fewer goods. In the classic quantity of money theory, there is a balance between the amount of money in circulation, the amount of goods and services available for consumption, and the price of those goods and services. The government creates money through various means. When the amount of money in circulation is increased, but the quantity of goods does not increase proportionately, the further injection of money is used to bid up the existing prices of goods and services. That is what happens during an 'upwave', and that is why prices rise during the 'upwave'.

There is another fundamental cause for rising prices. If the amount of money in circulation stays the same, but falling production creates fewer goods and services, then we have a smaller number of goods and services competing for the same amount of money. Again the result is rising prices.

Government can reduce the money in circulation with the same ease as it can be expanded. During the early stages of the upwave, money tends to increase faster than the volume of goods and services, until severe shortages occur, and people begin hoarding, sending prices rocketing. During the latter stages of the upwave, production begins to fall, but the money in circulation continues to rise.

The power of various cartels and self-interest organisations increases with the upwave. As the upwave develops, people tend to group together like the lemmings. Labour is the most powerful cartel. It exerts an ever-increasing influence on government. If labour cartels exert their muscle for higher wages 'to keep up with inflation', the result is inevitable. Unless there is a corresponding increase in productivity, the money to pay the wages will have to come from the money creation pool within the banking system. Higher prices will result. Rising wages are believed to be a further cause of inflation. But they are the effect of rising inflation, since wage demands 'to keep up with inflation' would not occur if there was no inflation to start with. Rising prices cause rising wage demands, which lead to further price rises, leading to further wage demands, ad infinitum.

At the early stages of the period of prosperity, increased money in circulation leads to a reduction in unemployment, and full employment in the middle of the upwave. As the upwave becomes more mature, the only way to break spiralling wage and price increases, and to reduce labour costs, is for employers to start economising on labour, increasing unemployment.

A fall in demand for goods and services follows, once again leading to higher prices and higher unemployment . . . a self-feeding spiral down and down. At the end of the expansion phase, a severe recession becomes unavoidable. Prosperity and full employment raise the expectations of the electorate so that a recession becomes intolerable. The resultant mounting confusion cannot be solved in a democracy. When peak prices combine with a lull in business activity, and higher wage demands are rejected and met by higher unemployment, an untenable disillusionment occurs. Uncertainty and confusion become unbearable. The government is blamed for mismanagement. It is voted out of power, and political instability, uncertainty, and rapid changes in government peculiar to the final stage of a prosperity all follow.

Political Trends During the Upwave

There is a distinct interaction between political trends and the long wave pattern of economic behaviour. At the beginning of the upwave there is usually a shift from right wing to left wing politics. At the end of the upwave, there is a shift back to the right, before a period of political disarray and uncertainty. This has led to the demolition of the democratic processes in some societies during the downwave.

During the upwave, the correlations between political preferences and prices appear unreliable. During the latter stages of the upwave, there is a distinct tendency toward left wing politics. At the end of the upwave, the left is ousted and a right wing government usually takes over.

The upwave begins following a long period of austerity. The depression; lack of business opportunity; the absence of war for several years, all tend to leave the nation in a rather tranquil, subdued state, with little taste for politics. A major shift in political parties is likely to have taken place towards the end of the downwave. The political party in power at the time would have been held responsible for the depression. As living conditions begin to improve in the early stages of the upwave, people are primarily concerned with their day-to-day existence.

The first major socio-political shock during the early stages of the upwave is the outbreak of war. This starts the adrenalin flowing again. There is a rapid pick-up in economic activity and employment as the economy moves into wartime production. Expectations begin to rise as the economy becomes more prosperous, and then even more prosperous when there is a conversion to peacetime economic activity. During the transition phase at the end of the war, there are fears of a slump. To keep the economy moving and to avoid a post-war slump, the government will usually launch a peacetime spending programme to maintain wartime demand levels by encouraging consumption. This sows the seeds of the ultimate inflation. Social spending increases. Welfare payments increase. The government prints more and more money, and the balance of payments moves steadily into deficit. As the upwave progresses, expectations are heightened. The common enemy is believed to be recession, as the depression remains fresh in the minds of the electorate. Booms during the upwave create excesses. Recessions reduce excesses. Government policy prevents the elimination of excesses throughout the upwave, leading to an over-extended economy ultimately doomed to extinction.

As the upwave progresses, it becomes fashionable for the 'haves' to make demands on behalf of the 'have nots'. Trade union membership and power increase. The government is lobbied by more self-interest cartels whose demands must be met if they are to retain office. The political strategy is to placate the electorate. Whether the economy can meet the demands made of it is of little importance.

As the upwave continues, consumers are encouraged to consume. The more they are encouraged, the more they want. Consumers are not economists. The more the government promises, the more people will expect. When government rhetoric encourages people to believe that a steady increase in the standard of living is an inalienable right, they will demand that right.

The upwave is a period of more . . . more . . . more . . . more, more, more, more. Any political party promising more than the party in power will gain popularity. Towards the end of the upwave, no political party can satisfy the heightened expectations of the masses. The electorate is not prepared to accept the slightest sacrifice or inconvenience. At the first sign of economic trouble at the end of the upwave, the government is ousted, having failed to provide the unprovidable. Complete political disarray follows, with changes in party, sometimes leading to a coalition government or a dictatorship.

Long term political trends show several converging factors at the end of the upwave coinciding with a shift in the political cycle and leading to turmoil, economic deterioration, and the kind of instability seen all over the world during the past five years or so. The breaking down of political parties into separate factions is a warning of the political disarray to come. In Britain in the 1980s, we find the Conservative Party sharply divided between those who support the government and those defined as "Wets". Britain's Labour Party is divided into right and extreme left. In addition, Britain has the Liberal Party, the Social Democrats, the Communist Party, and the National Front. Instead of the normal two-party system, with the winner having a majority, in Britain, France, Italy and Germany, we see a three, four and sometimes twenty party system.

In the past, this has led to coalition governments. They upset the majority since only a small minority could possibly be represented by such a government. The realisation that minorities are actually dictating the course of a nation causes increasingly explosive reactions. During the depression years of the 1930s, a coalition government was formed in Britain. The U.S. elected President Roosevelt, a man considered to be an extreme radical. Following World War I, at the end of the upwave, Hungary provided a classic example. Bela Kun, chairman of the tiny Communist Party, was released from prison to head a coalition government to bring order out of confusion. The minority Communist Party ultimately took over the nation.

When political parties start to split into separate factions, this often leads to a new political system built around a cult of the individual with appeal increasingly outside the normal party structure. This has been happening in Britain since the end of the upwave in 1974. It has also been happening in the U.S.A. Historically, the individual who finally emerges as the major political force, the saviour, the knight in shining armour, often becomes a dictator.

Political disunity, and a break-up of the party system, merge with economic factors which also have political implications, at the end of the upwave. Productivity falls against seemingly intractable inflation. Government finds it difficult to collect taxes. There is an explosion in the subterranean economy. The amount of goods and services produced by workers steadily falls. All of these factors have been operating in Britain for quite some time, and the electorate has been unwilling to acknowledge the root cause of the problem, preferring instead to blame government.

Another factor leading to a sharp swing in the cycle of political stability can be found in the urban problems during the last days of the ancient city of Rome. The focal point for most of the havoc caused by inflation at the end of the upwave is the cities. There is a flight of capital out of the cities, causing urban decay, increasing crime and violence. These, in turn, accelerate the flight of capital. Dissatisfied city dwellers trigger forces leading to mob rule, riots and civil unrest. For a very brief time, mob rule is prevalent. Every mob seeks a leader. The chosen leader often turns out to be a dictator, threatening local democracy, undermining the national political system.

If we superimpose the political cycle onto the long wave patterns of economic behaviour, we find a period of relative stability during the early stages of the upwave. The party in office tends to hold office for relatively long periods. There is a tendency toward left wing politics as the upwave matures. In the later stages of the upwave, the strong move to left wing politics remains, but the promises of politicians are insufficient to meet the demands of the electorate. At the beginning of the downwave, the left wing party is ousted, leading to political turbulence for about a decade. The turbulence often involves several changes in government, or political philosophy. The mid-decade covering recession and secondary prosperity brings the greatest number of shifts in political preferences. Then many new parties emerge, all with proposals for solving the problems of the mid-decade.

Downwave politics move to the right until the 'secondary depression' gets underway. At the end of the 'secondary depression' there is a shift back to the left and democracy is most vulnerable. Whatever party was in office during the 'secondary depression' is naturally booted out. The incoming party usually has left wing leanings but, sometimes, the result has been a dictator.

Three factors must be considered when relating the political trends to the long wave. The first is the public support for right wing or left wing politics at various stages of the long wave model. The second is the general level of interest in politics. The third is the 'overlap' between political parties.

During the eighteenth century, interest in politics was low in Britain. It was difficult to distinguish whether the Whigs were more 'right' than the Tories, or vice versa. In later years, political philosophies became more definable. Yet there have been conservative governments whose policies were more 'left wing' oriented than some of the so-called 'left wing' Labour governments.

Sir Ivor Jennings, in his marvellous three-volume work, *'Party Politics'* (1960), provides records of poll turnouts dating back 200 years. The accuracy of poll turnouts as a percentage of the voting population at the time can be questioned. Political relationships during the long upwave and the downwave are difficult to measure with the same precision as prices. Nevertheless, specific political moods are particularly marked at the beginning and end of the upwave.

In the U.S., there are recurring shifts between liberal and conservative dominance. U.S. Presidents in office at the end of the upwaves reveal a distinct link between politics and the long wave economic pattern. There is additional evidence to suggest that an upwave has recently ended. Without exception, every U.S. President in office approaching the long wave peak, or immediately thereafter, favoured 'left wing' politics. Each of those Presidents was ousted from office immediately prior to or slightly after the end of the upwave.

At the peak of the first upwave in 1814, James Madison was President. He was elected in 1808, re-elected in 1812, and voted out in 1816, two years after the peak of the first upwave. James Madison was a liberal or 'left wing' politician by today's definition. James Monroe, who succeeded him, would have been described as right wing.

At the peak of the second upwave in 1864, Abraham Lincoln was President. He could have been called left of centre. In 1868, Ulysses S. Grant took office, 4 years after the peak of the second upwave. President Grant was a right-wing politician. .

President Woodrow Wilson, another public administrator with liberal leanings (or left wing politics in the metaphoric sense) was in office during the peak of the upwave in 1920. He was succeeded by President Harding, a right wing conservative, in that year.

Jimmy Carter was President during the peak of the upwave in 1974, an advocate of public spending, liberal monetary growth and probably the most socialistically left wing President the U.S. has ever had. He has been followed by Ronald Reagan, an exceptionally conservative right wing politician.

In Britain, the pattern is not quite so well defined. Yet there is support for a defined relationship between political influences and the long wave pattern.

The Tories held office for a particularly long period during the first upwave, spanning the period 1807 to 1830. There was a change in leadership just after the peak of the first upwave. In 1817, George Canning took over as Prime Minister from the Earl of Liverpool, who held office for six years. The politics of the nineteenth century were basically the politics of foreign policy. There are vague historical references, however, which suggest that, although a Tory, George Canning was less liberally minded than the Earl of Liverpool. The inferences are somewhat ambiguous, but there is an indication of a shift from left to right in British politics around the peak of the first upwave.

The shift from left to right is far more recognisable at the peak of the second upwave. Gladstone, a decidedly liberal Prime Minister, held office in 1864. Benjamin Disraeli, a conservative, followed in 1874.

The shift from left to right is even more apparent at the peak of the third upwave in 1920. Lloyd George was heading a coalition government at that time. In 1922, A. Bonar Law, a conservative, took office. Here again we see another shift from left to right as the first change following the peak of a long period of prosperity which precedes the peak in the upwave.

The top of the upwave in 1974 came while Labour Prime Minister, Harold Wilson, held office. In 1979, history repeated itself again. The upwave peak led to a shift from left to right when James Callaghan, Labour Prime Minister, was succeeded by the Conservative, Margaret Thatcher. The shift from left to right following the peak of the upwave appears to span two continents over 150 years.

Political relationships in the upwave provide further evidence that the fourth upwave has been completed, and a secondary depression is a strong likelihood in the early 1980s. The long term sequence suggests the Conservative Government is likely to hold another term in office, winning a small majority in the General Election in the mid-1980s. A major change in political parties is not due until the late 1980s or early 1990s. Then a strong left wing leader is likely.

Personal Values During the Upwave

The government we get is the government we deserve, because it is the government we ask for. That has become a hackneyed cliché. Nevertheless there is a distinct relationship between the change in personal values and our choice of leaders during the sequences of economic life in industrialised societies.

Economic hardship will produce an emotive response. When people experience pain or hardship they often become subdued, retrench, and seek some type of solace to avoid further discomfort. When people see their friends and relatives suffer a depression, and see the world as a risky place to live, they feel helpless. Individuals lose faith in their own powers. Most people believe they are in complete control of their own destinies, but during periods of severe economic dislocation, this belief is openly challenged. People become cautious, introspective, and unwilling to accept risk. They attempt to shelter themselves from uncertainty wherever possible. Their feelings run counter to the principles of individualistic capitalism where the risk-taker reaps the greatest rewards. The upwave begins under such a psychological atmosphere.

As the upwave progresses, and signs of prosperity appear, people become more willing to assume risk. They become more outgoing and gregarious. The pleasure principle takes over, and people become more prone to hedonistic behaviour, seeking fun and excitement. They indulge in their quest for pleasure and leisure. There is a move to abolish any form of censorship imposing intellectual or physical restraint. People want to stand on their own as individuals, and express themselves freely.

During a long period of prosperity, people will favour a government whose policies allow maximum permissiveness, self-indulgence with minimum restrictions. They see the world as relatively risk-free. When people become carefree and begin to assume the prosperity of previous years will go on forever, they once again feel they control their own destiny. They no longer need the strength of 'big brother' trade unions behind them. They start businesses, borrow money to increase their living standards, begin playing the stock market and engaging in speculative ventures. There is greater interest in politics, as people feel that not only do they have the power to solve their own problems, but also the problems of society at large. Endless prosperity is taken for granted. Capitalism and laissez-faire economics reign supreme during the final stages of the upwave. There is increasing competition and a move toward freeing all markets, and reducing trade barriers. This behaviour appears during each upwave of the long term economic pattern – including those of the eighteenth century.

The peak of the last upwave in 1974 brought the 'Age of Aquarius'. From the mid-1960s to the mid-1970s, there was a tidal wave of social and economic legislation the world over. World leaders promised to cure all the miseries of the human condition at the stroke of a pen. It was supposed to be the dawn of a new era, when people would be less concerned about achieving success, their inalienable right.

New found values meant people should be more intent on having fun, 'doing their own thing'. Women's skirts became shorter and shorter until 'hot pants' turned hemlines into crotch lines. The female form was emancipated. Promiscuity was fashionable. Women could take the 'pill', and enjoy the sexual freedom long enjoyed by men. Sex was fun, not filth. Millionaires were made in the pornography industry. 'The Happy Hooker', the story of an illustrious prostitute, became a best seller. 'Deep Throat', the adventures of a fellatio expert, was a notoriously successful film. It was fashionable for single people to live like married people, and for married people to live like single people.

The final stages of the upwave promised a period when the human spirit would liberate itself from the discipline and authority of repressive social and political institutions. Instant gratification was the primary objective. Liberation meant glue-sniffing, acid rock, mind expanding drugs, hippie communes, group sex, wife swapping, abortion, and an alarming deterioration in the family unit. During the 1960s and 1970s, the divorce rate soared. Following a cluster of inflationary wars that led to public resentment, the tranquility of the 1940s and 1950s came to an abrupt end as black ghettoes in Britain and the U.S.A. erupted. Extreme political groups sent shivers down the spines of the middle classes. Bombings, hijackings, kidnappings, and terrorism throughout the world became almost routine.

As inflation moved up and public morality went down, many felt they were entering a period of civilisation without precedent. Of course, this was untrue. During the early 1900s, a new upwave began, characterised by the same type of public attitudes, peace and tranquility, as were prevalent during the emerging prosperity of the 1950s. But, like the 1960s and 1970s with the peak inflation wars, the period surrounding World War I bears a strikingly close resemblance.

The third upwave began shortly before the death of Queen Victoria in 1901, and marked the beginning of changes that were felt with broadening impact all through the early twentieth century. There was a swing away from Victorianism. As the economic improvement gained momentum, and prosperity began to be taken for granted, the same type of idealistic hopes prevailed as in the late 1960s. Following World War I, a new era was believed to be underway. Fifteen years of prosperity convinced people that a depression on the scale of the 1890s could never happen again. It was generally assumed that people were again in control of their destiny, and it would always be that way.

A social revolution began in the period after World War I. People began adopting attitudes totally different from anything at the turn of the century. The period from 1919 to 1929 was a time of abundance. A taste for the good things of life: home ownership, motoring, foreign travel, previously the preserves of the rich, came within the purchasing power of the lower middle and upper working classes. The £300 a year man could afford a foreign holiday. The latter stages of the third and the fourth upwaves shared a curious blend of soft-option idealism on public issues with a desire to evade private responsibilities.

The post-World War I younger generation was as rebellious as the generation of the 1950s and 1960s, for much the same reasons. Affluence and irresponsibility bred a hell-raising revolt against discipline and parental authority. They wanted fun, thrills and living for the moment. The end of the war ushered in the 'Jazz Age', hip-flasks, flappers and the Charleston. It was a time of alcoholic abuse and a decline in moral values. Hedonism blossomed, as it did in the 1960s.

During the fourth upwave, women got the pill. During the third upwave women got the vote. What followed was a form of women's liberation that took the world by storm. Women took off their corsets. They smoked and drank alcohol in public. They bared their knees, their backs and bosoms, and began painting themselves with lipstick and rouge. The woman's place in the world was being aired as never before. The Establishment was forced to move into line. The House of Commons gave women equality with men on divorce. There was a vast increase in the divorce rate. In 1910 the divorce rate was 8.8 per cent. By 1928, it had nearly doubled to 16.5 per cent.

In the 1970s, homosexuals were given equality. For the first time homosexual acts between consulting adults were no longer illegal. The gay liberation movement flourished.

The upwave leaves its mark on many areas of industrialised society. In addition to the economic, political and social aspects, there are also decided trends in fashion, music, literature and religion.

Cultural Trends During the Upwave

The central cultural characteristic of the final stages of the upwave is the consumer mentality. During the upwaves of the eighteenth and nineteenth centuries, the West rejected two kinds of authority: the authority of the king to tell us what to do, and the authority of the church to tell us how to think. Freedom came to be understood as the absence of external constraint. In the 1920s, the Freudian gospel appeared, interpreted to mean that repression was harmful to the individual. Not only external constraints, but also internal constraints with their inherent moral codes, were seen as illicit restrictions upon personal freedom.

At the latter stages of the upwave, society becomes so preoccupied with consumption that even religion becomes a commodity to be ruled by the whims of shoppers in a religious marketplace. Alternative religions spring up like weeds, since the repressive status of the traditional religions, which can cope with the social mores of the early stages of the upwave, are incompatible with the freedoms required during the later stages of the upwave.

Fashion, music, literature, theatre and dance all fall under the influence of the upwave. The years of rising excitement can be heard clearly in the increasing excitability of the music. The 1950s and 1960s gave birth to rock music. It grew, slowly at first, but ultimately captured the entire 'pop' idiom. Rock became progressively more frenetic, reaching the epitome of musical discord with 'punk rock' in the late 1970s. Rock symbolised the mood of the final stages of the upwave in the 1970s, just as jazz symbolised the period of increasing affluence prior to World War I, and continued into the 'secondary prosperity' of the 1920s. The pre-World War I jazz, and the 1950s rock were joyful, a unique release from the traditions of the early stages of the upwave. But they were totally inappropriate for the heightened excitability later in the upwave. Action music is a product of the final stages of prosperity, relieving the tensions generated at a time of mass excitability in many areas.

Action dances are invented to accompany action music. During the 1940s and 1950s dancing was a peaceful romantic experience to be shared by a man and a woman. They held each other gently, their bodies touching, swaying to the rhythm of the sweet lilting strains of an orchestra. Just as the Charleston and Blackbottom were the action dances of the third upwave, our recent upwave produced the Madison, the Mashed-Potato, the Twist, the Frug. Ultimately they led to free-style narcissism, where young girls and middle aged women jerk their bodies at mirrored discotheques, oblivious to the problems of their sometimes less than loose-limbed male companions who often take on the unfortunate appearance of spastics.

The 1970s was the fashion age of the male peacock. Middle aged men wore tight trousers with navel-level waistbands and see-through paisley shirts. Jackets were thrust aside. Jeans and open necked shirts became as acceptable at establishments previously only open to those wearing a lounge suit and tie. During the final stages of the upwave, clothing followed the mood of the young . . . excited, rebellious, defiant. Whatever the style was previously, it had to be changed. The change had to be noticeable, exaggerated. Above all, clothes served as a uniform of identification, signifying the wearer was 'with it', a member of the new movement. His clothes told others he was 'letting it all hang out'. He was 'together'. The attire of the young was a statement of open rebellion against the constraints imposed by parents. But, the adult population also becomes ensnared by the excited tempo of steadily increasing prosperity. And, as adults began adopting the fashions of the younger generation, rebellious youth had to adopt even more outlandish styles to remain at arms length from the adult world.

Women's fashions are linked to the upwaves and downwaves with even greater clarity. The amount of feminine charms on display during periods of growth as opposed to periods of contraction is especially striking. According to James Laver, of the Victoria and Albert Museum in London, there was no such thing as fashion in ancient Greece, or the Roman Empire until the middle of the fourteenth century. From the fifteenth century onward, fashion trends can be seen quite clearly, inextricably linked to economic conditions. As armament in the fierce battle for masculine attention, the woman of the court during the fourteenth century adopted some of the most effective weapons known, even today, displaying various amounts of decolletage combined with tightly laced corsets and elaborate hairstyles. During the fourteenth century, necklines were high, corsets loosely tied, and the feminine form well covered.

The following century brought a complete change in the fortunes of nations, and a change in women's fashions. Bosoms were exposed by low-cut bodices, and derrieres were thrust outwards through tightly pinched wasp-waisted corsets. During early Tudor times the wealth of nations declined. Bosoms were covered again, corsets were loosened, and the feminine form was removed from display. Then came Elizabethan times and prosperity, and out came the bosoms and bottoms. The same pattern could be seen in seventeenth century America, as fashion shifted from the modest Puritan styles to the lively exposed style of the Restoration.

During the upwave that followed the French Revolution, women's fashions were light and near-transparent. Legs came into diffused view, sometimes suggested under dresses of such diaphanousness that pink tights had to be worn beneath the skirt. From 1814 to 1843, legs and bosoms vanished again.

In fashion, there is the thesis of 'erotic capital', by which the effectiveness of women's fashion depends on its newness to men. When concentration is on the legs for a considerable period, fashion will then shift to bosoms and bottoms. Following the display of legs during the upwave that began in the late 1780s and ended in 1814, it was not until the upwave of the 1840s to 1860s that bosoms and bottoms appeared once again. Early Victorian styles permitted horizontal lines of decolletage, revealing not only breasts, but shoulders, a new zone of 'erotic capital'.

The downwave of the nineteenth century sent necklines back up to the neck. Hemlines fell so low that skirts had to be lifted when a lady walked.

During the prosperity of the upwave beginning at the turn of the twentieth century, 'erotic capital' achieved its grandest exploitation in history by revealing the feminine form. Necklines opened up into a long V. Hemlines moved up until knees appeared. The female back emerged with evening dresses, and some daytime clothing opened in the back down to the waist.

During the downwave of the 1930s, ladies covered up again. Hemlines dropped to the ankle, bosom lines rose to the neck, and backs were covered.

It would appear that by the time of the fourth upwave, there was nothing new to display. But never underestimate the ingenuity of fashion designers. Our recent prosperity brought the hemline up to the crotch, the neckline down to the waistline. Bras were discarded, and nipple erections were outlined under outergarments. Some young women were having their pubic hair tinted and permed for purposes best left to the imagination.

Trends in women's fashions and their link with economic activity have been so consistent that an investment analyst devised the 'Hemline Indicator', supposedly to help predict the course of the stock market. If skirts went higher, the stock market would go higher. If hemlines fell, shares would fall.

The increasing desire to shed social mores and rid ourselves of

The Cycle of Fashion through the ages

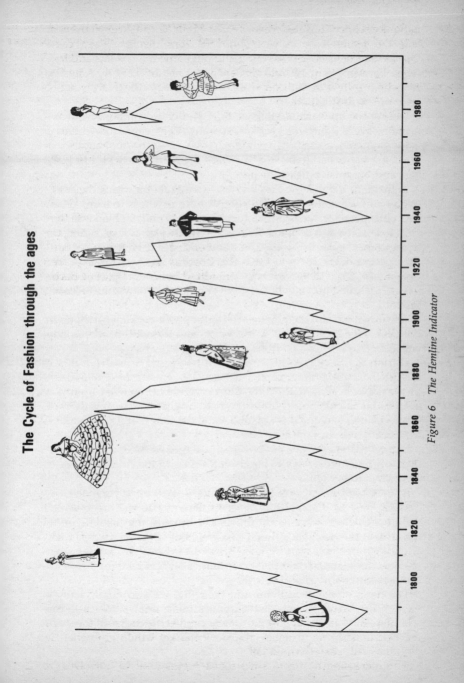

Figure 6   The Hemline Indicator

constraint as the upwave progresses also has its influence on literature and the theatre. 'Oh, Calcutta' and 'Hair', with full frontal nudity on stage, were the hit shows of the 1970s. During the 1940s and 1950s, the cinema code would not permit a man and a woman to be shown in bed together, even fully clothed. During the 1970s, filmgoers were treated to a varied diet of male and female copulation on the screen involving men and women together in bed, unclothed. The film, 'Caligula' released in late 1979, featured homosexuality, sodomy, fellatio, cunnilingus, rape (the male and female variety), and a scene where the mother of the roman emperor was having a sperm bath while a group of centurians masturbated into the bathing vessel to keep it topped up.

This was an action replay of the terminal stages of the previous upwave during the 1920s. The 'Roaring Twenties' was also a time of sexual permissiveness. Outlandish behaviour was accepted and tolerated. There was a proliferation of sex magazines. Lewd pantomime and lascivious sitcoms kept the burlesque houses packed. Men and women ogled at spinning tassels which whirled clockwise, then counter-clockwise, around pendulous bare breasts. The five foot giant penis strapped to the buttocks of a clown was a standard prop which assured a good laugh.

A Mr. Avery Hopwood was jailed in November 1921 for producing a farce, 'The Demi Virgin'. The charge was 'promoting an immoral, impure play with an intentional appeal for box office profit to lustful, licentious, morbidly erotic, vulgar and disorderly minds'. Frederick Lonsdale was castigated for elevating a fallen women to moral superiority in 'Spring Cleaning'. Somerset Maughan was scourged for flaunting 'vice, naked and unashamed, through three acts of glittering immorality' in 'Our Betters'. Noel Coward was damned for 'shovelling up ordure on an unprincipled smart set' in 'The Vortex'.

The 1960s and 1970s were a time of a new morality, but that new morality certainly was not an invention of that period. The term was used as early as 1922 by May Eddington, co-authoress of 'Secrets'. The 'new morality' was taken several steps further by Mrs. Bertrand Russell's book, 'Hypatia', described as the handbook of the new morality. Dr. Marie Stopes' book on birth control excited enormous attention in the 1920s and was a record bestseller. The counterpart in the 1970s was 'The Joy of Sex', followed by 'More Joy'.

The nature of the upwave permeates practically every conceivable area of society. Public psychology is the driving force behind the upwave . . . and the downwave.

Opponents of the long wave theory claim that it lacks a motive. Many say a long wave may exist but, in the absence of evidence to demonstrate why, deep suspicions have been aroused. It is my firm belief that the causes lie deep within the psyche of our human race. We can look at inflation, wars, political trends, speculative manias, etc., but these are not causes. These are the effects of mass psychological phenomena involving long term swings of pessimism and optimism that occur in short term rhythmical patterns within a longer term rhythmical pattern and within a still longer term rhythmical pattern thereafter, like the wheels within wheels, and circles in a spiral. According to L. Peter Coogan, there are well-defined correlations between patterns of pessimism and optimism and sequences of share prices, major business contractions, business indicators and other economic phenomena. In his extensive work on the subject, 'The Rhythmic Cycles of Optimism and Pessimism', Coogan states:

> Monetary and fiscal policies do not appear to be the primary causes of the business cycle, but appear to modify the amplitude and, to some extent, the timing for better or worse, depending upon the correctness, liquidity and ingenuity of lenders, borrowers, and spenders. It would appear that 1929–1932 would have been a major turning point regardless of who had been President. Despite the importance of the influence of military and political decisions upon the economy, the business cycle and the private sector persists.

The upwave spans a period of psychological desolation to a period of excessive optimism, covering the full spectrum of people's greed and fear.

Chapter Four

WHEN THE BUBBLE BURSTS

Financial genius is a short memory in a rising trend
J.K. Galbraith

In the beginning God made morons. He did that for practice. Then He got down to the serious task of making total imbeciles. And on the dawn of creation, He placed a group of people upon this planet who shared the profound belief that wealth could be created in a vacuum, and who went forth among the populace, entrusted with the task of such wealth creation.

The King's alchemists, many centuries ago, tried to create wealth by attempting to manufacture gold by combining horse manure with goat urine. They failed, of course. The job was turned over to the King's chancellors. They invented counterfeiting.

If the kingdom had 1,000 gold coins and one gold coin was required to purchase one bushel of wheat, then only one thousand bushels could be bought – unless more gold could be found to make more coins. As long as 1,000 bushels of wheat was sufficient, there was no problem. If the peasants suddenly became greedy and demanded more wheat, then more gold had to be found to buy it. The King ran the risk of an uprising, or possibly exile, if he did not produce the goods. Normally, the way to get more gold was to make goods in the kingdom and sell them outside at a profit. But, if the peasants wanted more wheat and did not want to exert themselves by producing more goods, the chances of accumulating more gold were slim. That was when the King turned to his alchemists. When they failed, he turned to the chancellors. They advised the King that if the edges of the gold coins were shaved off, just a little, more gold coins could be made from the shavings. The chancellors believed no one would notice the gold coins were just that little bit smaller.

Coin-clipping led to a little dilution with base metals, which led to a major dilution. Gold value became a silver value. Silver value became a paper value. Paper money acted as a certificate entitling the holder to claim its value in gold, then in silver, then the paper of a different country, known as foreign reserves. This process evolved because of the ease with which paper wealth could be created compared to real wealth. It is far easier to clip coins, dilute gold with base metals, and print paper money than it is to produce goods. And that brings us to the massive expansion of currency in circulation during the 1970s.

Britain was hit by a recession early in 1969. It lasted for two years and claimed Rolls-Royce and the Vehicle & General Insurance Group as victims. By the spring of 1972, that was all forgotten. A few businessmen and speculators were damaged by the recession; a few workers lost their jobs. Most people in Britain sailed through it, unscathed. Throughout the late 1960s, right into the recession, people continued to demand higher wages. They felt it was their inalienable right to a higher standard of living. And, under Harold Wilson's Labour Government, they were getting what they demanded. No matter how much the Labour Government promised, it was not enough to satisfy an electorate which had experienced prosperity for over two decades. Although few people were seriously affected by the 1969–1971 recession, and living standards rose steadily, it still caused a public outcry. A recession was not considered part of the scheme of things.

In June 1970, the Labour Government was pushed out. The Conservatives took over under Edward Heath, and were lumbered with meeting the inexorable demands of the electorate. The Heath Administration, which ultimately brought a new dimension to the meaning of mediocrity in national government, promised to 'Go for Growth'. The fact that 'the kingdom had very few gold coins' and very little to grow with, was certainly no obstacle to the Heath Administration. If you couldn't earn money, print it! After all, that is precisely what Keynes had been telling governments to do during the 1930s. Keynes may have murmured something about surpluses and deficit financing, but the Heath Administration had little use for such economic esoterica.

The business community demanded more paper money and the Heath Administration duly obliged, aided and abetted by the 'demon Barber', then Chancellor of the Exchequer. The Heath Administration created more paper mini-pounds through the traditional methods of cutting taxes and increasing government spending. In addition, a money boom was generated in the banking system and, supplemented by the creation of second-line and fringe banks, even more mini-pounds were created.

Ladies lifted their skirts and bared their bosoms. The Beatles held consultations with the Maharishi. Nudes came out on stage, and then mingled with the audience. The final stages of the fourth upwave were underway. For two years until November 1973, property speculators and financial manipulators more than quadrupled their bank borrowings. These two groups actually owed more to the banking system than the whole of British manufacturing industry combined.

Private individuals trebled their bank borrowings in an orgy of self-indulgence and personal consumption. And rampant speculation on the stock exchange further stimulated bank borrowings. A flood of new companies appeared. They were often highly dubious, unseasoned and under-financed, and were eagerly leapt on by 'gamblers' hoping to make a quick fortune.

The economy seemed to be improving during the latter stages of the upwave. In Barber's April 1972 Budget, taxes were cut by £1,800m. He announced that the money supply, which had been growing at an annual 20 per cent, would continue to expand at a rate which was supposed to ensure growth in output. Public expenditure, which had been cut in 1970 by £960m., was raised by £500m., then a further £1,200m., in 1972. On the surface, the plan to secure additional growth seemed successful. Output rose by 9.1 per cent between the second half of 1971 and first half of 1972.

Beneath the surface, there was a deep malaise. Imports were rising faster than exports, and Britain's competitiveness in international markets was rapidly deteriorating. In June 1972, there was a run on sterling. Over one billion pounds of speculative funds were withdrawn from British banks and placed in other currencies as overseas investors lost confidence. The Bank of England was forced to purchase £356m. worth of government securities from the banks to help maintain their solvency.

The mini-boom of 1971–1973 had several other flaws. The boom was concentrated primarily outside manufacturing. Profits for manufacturing industry rose by a mere 6 per cent in those two years. In the service and construction industries, profits rose by 30 to 55 per cent. In insurance, banking and finance, profits rose by 122 per cent. The low rate of improvement in manufacturing industry had little to do with availability of credit, supposedly its life-blood. The biggest explosion of credit in the history of U.K. capitalism occurred between 1971 and 1973. By the second quarter of 1972, the money supply (M3) was growing at an annual 31 per cent. Manufacturing investment fell by 10 per cent between the first quarter of 1971 and that of 1972. Investment in the finance sector rose by 42 per cent. It was an extremely speculative and inflationary mini-boom. Prices began to accelerate rapidly, while much of the machinery for industrial production continued to lay idle. By the first half of 1973, prices were rising at $7\frac{1}{2}$ per cent per annum worldwide. Gold and property were the first targets for speculators. But other areas soon fell prey to speculative dealing, including primary products. Between the summer of 1972 and the autumn of 1973, industrial materials prices almost doubled.

The speculative boom soon began to make an impact on unemployment in Britain, providing further evidence of the underlying problems. Unemployment rose steadily until the very last stages of the boom. In the winter of 1971, the number of unemployed reached one million for the first time since the war.

As the boom approached its terminal phase, many individuals knew the situation was becoming progressively more unhealthy. But, each in his own way wanted to squeeze the last penny out before the final day of reckoning. Practically no market remained immune to rampant speculation. Office workers, sales assistants, clerks, porters, even the unemployed, were all dabbling in stocks and shares without even knowing the business of the companies in which they were dealing. All sorts of companies were changing their names to include the word 'finance' or 'property'. They were immediately the subject of speculative sponsorship, merely because of their new name. Yet, stock exchange speculation paled into insignificance compared to the property market, where even inexperienced operators were making fortunes overnight.

What followed this speculative euphoria and blind optimism of the early 1970s has been heavily chronicled elsewhere and requires little further elaboration. The first 'bubble' to burst was on the stock market. The Financial Times 30 Share Index reached an all-time high in May 1972; then plunged by 78 per cent of its value over the next thirty months.

This debacle looked like a Sunday-school picnic compared to property and banking. The collapse of the second line and fringe banks, which were heavily committed to financing the property boom, shook the foundations of the entire British banking system. The first of the fringe banks to collapse was London & County. The crisis snowballed when depositors rushed to take their money out of these second-line banking institutions. The Bank of England stepped in and organised the 'lifeboat' scheme. By the end of 1974, lifeboat loans had escalated to £1,285m. as the property boom collapsed and banks suffered severe losses on a worldwide basis and had to be rescued. Millions were lost by shareholders in banks and property companies which either went bankrupt, or were merged with other companies after tottering on the brink of near-bankruptcy.

Historians will argue for decades about the cause of the financial holocaust of the early 1970s. There is no single cause. The only common thread, historically, is the rhythmic sequence of greed and fear which has dominated the upwaves and downwaves for centuries. As one area of economic activity after the other began to crumble, it was obvious the cycle was again approaching the same calamitous decline seen so many times before, although no one knew when the hour would strike. The stock market crashed first, then the banking system, then the property market. Commodity prices peaked in 1974, then plunged. The quadrupling of the oil price in October 1973 added to the chaos. The downwave had begun.

Anatomy of a Speculative Orgy

When the upwave comes to an end; when prices peak and the final burst of economic activity in the upwave takes place, the speculative bubble bursts and sets the downwave in motion. During the early 1970s, this happened in the British stock market and in commercial property, and brought a banking crisis. It was an exact repetition of what has occurred after every long period of prosperity throughout history. The force propelling the speculative mania at the end of the upwave is growing optimism, born out of long periods of prosperity.

Increasing numbers of businessmen and individuals adopt the view that business contractions will be minimal, and that prosperity will continue indefinitely. This leads to over-confidence and a willingness to assume ever-increasing risks. According to economist, Hyman Minsky, the events which lead up to the end of a speculative boom and subsequent financial crisis begin with some sort of 'displacement', an exogenous event which acts as a shock to the macro-economic system. The exact nature of the 'displacement' has varied from one speculative boom to another in different countries at different times. It could be the ending of war, a bumper harvest, a new invention which boosts economic development, an improvement in production methods or transport, a sudden financial success by an individual or group of individuals. That 'displacement' could be a dramatic change in the political arena sparked off by war, revolution or a major shift in public attitudes. All of these factors have served as the vehicles for speculative orgies in the past. Any event or series of events potent enough to alter the perception of profit opportunities within a nation's economy could set the speculative ball rolling.

Without exception, every boom throughout history has been fed by an expansion of credit. It is endemic to every upwave. Easy money enables people who would normally never have participated to join in the boom. Easy money also encourages many to speculate well beyond their means. The credit conditions preceding the Wall Street crash of 1929 were cited as the major reason for the collapse. Then it was possible to buy securities for a mere 10 per cent of their market value. Many borrowed to obtain that 10 per cent. Some held many thousands of dollars worth of securities, all on borrowed money. But, of course, the money had to be paid back.

As the long period of prosperity continues and risk seems to diminish, the desire to make a quick profit grows in diametric proportion. The 'displacement' is the harbinger of newly-perceived investment opportunities which astute businessmen attempt to exploit at the incipient stages of the upwave. The urge to speculate gets stronger, and the upwave continues.

Eventually alarming numbers of individuals are speculating without any real understanding. The rational profit potential of investments which attracted more astute investors is exhausted. Speculation for profit, and profit only, leads people away from the normal investment criteria prominent in the early stages of the upwave. Marginal ventures emerge, along with imitations of ventures that were previously profitable. Frauds and swindles proliferate. What has been described as 'mania' and 'bubble' is the final result. Says Minksy: 'the word mania emphasises the irrationality . . . bubble foreshadows bursting'.

Obviously those who fall prey to mania in the later stages of speculative euphoria pay the highest prices. They also incur the highest financing costs, since there is a much greater demand for credit at that time. So, late participants are the most vulnerable when the 'bubble' bursts. Two-thirds of the participants in a speculative orgy are drawn into the stampede in the final stages. And the price of the speculative vehicle usually loses about 80 per cent of its gains, made during the previous upswing, when the 'bubble' bursts.

Anatomy of a Bust

In the past thirty years of my investment career, I have never been the victim of a speculative orgy. I have a perverse nature: I become an enthusiastic buyer after a severe price decline, then become extremely anxious after a long period of rising prices and rampant speculative activity. I attribute that to my early career as a Wall Street stockbroker, where I was guided by astute and successful operators. One event I recollect took place during the 1960s stock market boom in America. For several years I shared a desk with Charlie Meyer, one of Wall Street's old-timers. He had been around during the Wall Street crash, and had witnessed the events leading up to it. Charlie was an instinctive stock market operator. He would gauge the investment climate by the tempo of speculative activity. Without balance sheets and other popular investment aids, he managed to acquire several million dollars just by watching the prices as they travelled across the New York Stock Exchange ticker-tape, and by monitoring the expressions of greed and fear on the faces of his fellow investors.

One day, Charlie spun around in his chair, slapped me on the back and said, 'Beckman! Too many dummies are getting rich. I'm getting the hell out!' Charlie telephoned the firm's floor broker on the New York Exchange, and sold every investment he had within the hour. That was two days before shares peaked and began tumbling. Charlie reckoned the stock market craze had turned to insanity, and that share prices had reached a level beyond any realistic measure of value.

Towards the end of every speculative boom, the more astute investors who got in on the ground floor, take their profits and sell out. When the speculative 'bubble' reaches a peak, prices hesitate as new gamblers to the speculative mania are balanced by the smart money crowd who are then heading for the exits. When the speculative mania's slowing tempo becomes more obvious, latecomers are more reluctant to participate. Existing players increasingly decide to turn paper profits into cash. And so the gradual move out of the speculative counters accelerates into a race to secure the best prices before they fall further. The rush to turn paper into cash becomes a stampede. Many who borrowed heavily are late in turning paper into cash; others are forced to cash in their paper by worried lenders. The steep decline in values is self-feeding. Proceeds fall below the amount borrowed, and an entirely new set of problems is created.

The trigger which turns a speculative orgy into a financial crisis can take as many forms as the initial 'displacement'-which starts it. It could be the failure of a bank heavily committed to financing speculative activities, such as London & County. It could be the failure of a large company in the industry which attracted the most speculation. Sometimes it has been the unfolding of massive swindles, one sufficient to reverse speculative mania into financial panic and distress. Frequently, it has been the combination of things occurring simultaneously. Whatever the reason, individuals who have been financially over-committed are forced to reduce their speculative holdings and raise cash.

For example: You own a property and your bank agrees to advance 95 per cent of its value. Should the value fall by 20 per cent, however, 15 per cent of the banker's loan will be unsecured. A nervous banker is likely to want an additional 15 per cent to maintain his margin of security in a falling market. If you don't have that 15 per cent, your banker will often have the right to a forced sale of the property. It was precisely this situation which led to the collapse of second-line banks and many property companies in Britain during 1974.

Forced sales land on an already intensely vulnerable market, leading to an even faster fall in prices. The number of forced sales increases, as do commercial and private bankruptcies. The orderly liquidation of speculative holdings at the early stages degenerates into a full-blown panic. The panic feeds on itself after the speculative bubble bursts, a mirror image of the emotions that fired the speculative orgy. Greed subsides, and fear becomes the dominant force.

Bubbles and Panics of Periods Past

Speculative manias are virtually identical to each other in their basic form and in their place within the long pattern of upwaves and downwaves. An early example was known as the 'South Sea Bubble', which forced England's entire financial system to its knees. During the early 1700s, wild speculation in the South Sea Company sent the shares rocketing. A number of satellite companies which were mere imitations, also cashed in. In one scheme, promoters sold one million pounds worth of shares to the greedy and gullible in a company to produce a wheel for perpetual motion.

Speculation was so rife that other promoters did not even bother to inform prospective investors what the funds would actually be used for. A typical financial prospectus might simply have announced the formation of a company whose purpose was to 'carry on an undertaking of great advantage'. One such prospectus added, 'every investor who deposits £2 per share is to be entitled to £100 per annum'. Within five hours, that absurd prospectus had attracted £2,000. In the sixth hour, the director absconded with investors' funds, no doubt headed for the South Seas.

It has been estimated that £300m. was ploughed into various speculative investments during this eighteenth century mania. It reached such a dangerous level that the so-called 'Bubble Act' was passed in 1720, making it illegal for companies to raise funds without a Royal Charter. All too quickly, the Act proved counter-productive. No one really knew which of the 'bubble' companies were legal or illegal. When the 'bubble' burst, every company became suspect, and a potential victim of a selling stampede. The torrent of forced liquidations and distress selling affected the South Sea Company itself. It went bankrupt in 1720. Many banking institutions were heavily committed to financing the company, and many individuals had pledged the shares as security. Company after company went into bankruptcy, leaving all who had financed or invested in them in a total financial disarray. Before the bubble burst credit was easy to come by. After the 'bubble' burst, the English credit system was taken to the brink of collapse; commercial ventures lay strewn in the financial wreckage throughout London, testimony to the ravages of post-speculative mania.

1720 was quite a memorable year for the speculative bubbles and attendant financial panics. The Mississippi Company had a trade monopoly on French possessions in North America. It was in a unique financial position, thanks to the wizardry of John Law. He was among the first who would be described as a monetarist today, introducing our current concepts of credit. In one paper he submitted to the French Government, Law wrote, 'The workings of trade revolve wholly about money . . . the more you have the more people you can keep employed. Credit will take the place of money and will have the same results.' The creation of money by government decree was born.

In 1716, John Law formed the General Bank in France, which became the Royal Bank in 1718. The sole shareholder was the French Government. The Royal Bank was permitted to issue paper currency. It was not backed by gold or silver, or any other tangible with a fixed price. Instead, the Royal Bank's – and France's – currency was backed by shares in the Mississippi Company. As long as the company's shares were strong, so would the currency be. The converse applied when shares in the Mississippi Company were weak.

The Mississippi 'Bubble' caught on, and spread like wildfire. People pledged their homes, jewellery, livestock, whatever they had. The demand for credit reached explosive levels. As in England, bankers scrambled to satisfy the demand for credit which appeared to be well-secured. After all, the Mississippi scheme was apparently being promoted under the auspices of the French Government itself.

A nation's currency cannot possibly be linked to shares whose value can fluctuate violently. The Mississippi Company crashed in 1720. With it the entire credit and banking system of France was swept away. People were staggered: after all, the French Government had been party to the scheme; the French Regent had patronised it. Members of the French Government had grown rich on the scheme.

The average French investor did not fare quite so well. Over one million families in France held bank notes issued by the Royal Bank. They were investors in the Mississippi Company without actually wishing to participate in the speculative orgy. When the company crashed, those bank notes became valueless. England had just managed to survive the crash in the South Sea Company. The French were not so fortunate with their Mississippi Company. The monarchy tottered; it took 100 years of rule under the Bonapartes for the French to get back on their feet. Any government official who even dared mention the prospects of a bank issuing money related to an item which could fluctuate in value ran the risk of a swift encounter with Madame Guillotine. The desire for the French to hold gold is a hangover from those earlier years.

The South Sea Company and the Mississippi Company both had totally different objectives, and were sold to greedy investors for entirely different reasons. Both were spurred by an over-extension of credit which produced an unreal property, an illusion, a bubble where expectations went beyond the wildest dreams of avarice. When the normal laws of economics come back into play, these bubbles burst.

The upwave which ended probably around 1760 was accompanied in its final stages by heavy speculation in commodities, especially sugar. In Holland, heavy speculation in sugar was being financed by 'Wisselruitji' in Amsterdam, involving a chain of accommodation bills. In addition, there was a speculative mania involving the East India Company, fuelled by credit advanced by the Bank of Amsterdam. In England, there was a speculative boom in housing, turnpikes and canals. A lot of the money to support the boom in England was provided by the Ayr Bank, and a number of independent provincial banks. The speculative orgy reached a crescendo in the early part of

1763. Sugar prices peaked, wobbled, then fell. The same thing happened to wheat. The East India Company collapsed. A host of English companies heavily involved in the Dutch East India Company tumbled after it.

When a speculative bubble bursts, the fall-out soon extends across international boundaries. The collapse of commodity markets and the East India Company in Amsterdam brought the collapse of the speculative boom in construction, housing, turnpikes and canals in England. The Ayr Bank, which was primarily responsible for financing the boom in England, also collapsed, taking with it a host of smaller provincial banks. Thousands of investors in England and Europe lost their savings. The end of the upwave in around 1763 led to an extremely severe recession and the beginning of the new downwave lasting until the late 1780s.

The secondary depression of the 1780s followed a financial collapse around 1772. After that, the first observable upwave in the long wave economic pattern began. In the early 1800s, England was enjoying robust trade with Brazil and Scandinavia. Credit was again extended by various provincial bankers in unregulated fashion. The usual formula nurtured the boom which eventually collapsed, leading to financial panic. Greedy British businessmen sold more goods than they could possibly produce or acquire to Brazil and Scandinavia, who were importing at record levels on the back of rapidly growing economies.

While the British were selling goods from production facilities which had been mortgaged for years in advance, the Brazilians and Scandinavians were purchasing them with credit facilities they had little hope of repaying. The entire affair produced a totally false prosperity. The boom came to an abrupt end when British exporters were cut off from their Baltic outlets by a naval blockade set up by Napoleon. Many exporters went bankrupt.

A delay in payment means default. As exporters began to default, many of the financing banks failed in their obligations, leading to a chain-reaction default called the 'domino effect'. The crisis in England reverberated, spreading to Hamburg and New York, where banking institutions were also financing British export trade. The domino effect soon became an international phenomenon. A global recession followed the Panic of 1814. It was deeper and more severe than anything from the beginning of the upwave in the late 1780s. The bursting of a speculative bubble, financial panic, and a deep recession, confirmed existing evidence that the first observable downwave had emerged in the long term economic pattern.

The speculative mania which snowballed in the early 1850s was halted by the Commercial Crisis of 1857–1858. It marked the end of the second observable upwave, and set the stage for a series of worldwide panics. The upwave in the price structure did not actually end until

1864, when the series of financial crises which began some seven years before reached epidemic proportions worldwide.

The 1850s brought the railroad bonanza, new gold discoveries, speculation in wheat and other commodities. Once again it was a period of runaway credit inflation. In spite of the series of financial crises around the 1850s, the upwave was carried on by the Crimean War and the Civil War in America. Speculative bubbles were popping one by one before the end of both wars. After the Civil War, the entire international financial structure seemed to break apart at the seams. In August 1857, there was a panic in America. Two months later it had spread to England. The following year it hit Europe. By 1863, France had become the major victim of financial panic. In May 1866, the Overend Gurney Company collapsed, triggering the stock market crash in London. America, England, France, Italy, Germany and Austria were all in an international financial panic and banking collapse of horrendous proportions between 1864 and 1866. It would appear that each financial crisis in the final stages of an upwave contains deep roots which extend throughout the entire international financial structure. Charles P. Kindleberger, in his book 'Manias, Panics and Crashes' (1978), reflects upon the experience of one Parisian banker:

> Alfred Andre, a Parisian banker with major interests in Egypt, spent an 'exhausting week' in London looking after the interests of his firm at the time of the Overend Gurney crisis. He returned to Paris on May 17th, having concluded that the finance companies were ruined and that business was paralysed in Italy, Prussia, Austria and Russia, with France standing up pretty well, but only momentarily. The speculative mania that led up to the series of financial crises involved heavy speculation in cotton and shipping companies in France, England and Italy.

In 1864, another sequence was completed. It was a period of panic, collapse and deep recession, brought about by excessive credit stimulation and speculation. Another upwave ended and a downwave began. The recession of 1864–1866 was reckoned to be worse than anything since the depression of the 1840s.

Following the end of World War I, the inbuilt monetary excesses of financing a war were combined with financing the monetary expansion common to a long period of prosperity. The prosperity which began in the late 1890s had minor hiccups, but always managed to bounce back. By the turn of the decade of 1920, most were thoroughly convinced that prosperity was forever. As usual, such an attitude culminated in intense speculation in various forms of business, commodities, and the stock exchange.

During the post-World War I boom, most people believed that rising prices were no less permanent than continued prosperity. The only variable was how fast prices would rise from one month to the next. Wild buying took place in all sorts of items. Businessmen ordered more than they needed from several different sources, hoping for delivery of at least as much as they needed. As prices escalated in 1918 and 1919, many orders were left unfulfilled.

Consumers were the worst hoarders of all, fighting and clawing over goods in the shops. There was a frenzy to buy everything and anything. The higher prices rose, the more consumers wanted. When sugar rose to 1s 2d. a pound during 1920, there was a nationwide shortage. In many shops, sugar was limited to one pound per person. Shoppers often left a standing order for one pound a day. Others went from shop to shop buying as much as they could before prices went higher again.

A surefire way to increase profits was to buy or produce goods, then delay sales. That way, traders could get top prices as prices moved up. There was continual thirst for credit as prices spiralled. Sales were so profitable that the creditworthiness of borrowers was virtually ignored by lenders, who were booming as the cost of money escalated. There was also heavy lending to businesses and individuals outside of Britain who wanted to join the speculative binge.

The suggestion that the boom could ever end was inconceivable. Everyone tried to beat inflation by using it. Comparisons with previous eras and price declines were thrust aside. Britain and the world was embarking on a new era of prosperity, according to most commentators. It was believed that the American banking system, the Bank of England, and the other central banks would ensure that panics and financial crises would never occur again. Very few actually realised that the banking system itself ensured future panics were possible. Why? Because of one major weakness. Bankers are homo sapiens, just like those responsible for previous booms and panics.

Another popular notion around 1920 was that workers would never be willing to work for low wages again, that they would insist on a continually rising standard of living. It was argued that a steady rise in wages would mean that consumer demand would always be buoyant, and that prices would continue to rise. What seemed to have escaped detection was that prices at which goods can be sold, not the demands of organised labour, determine whether or not workers are employed.

Workers produced a multitude of reasons why wages would rise; employers retaliated with as many reasons why costs would continue to rise. And bankers explained why interest rates would go on rising. Their combined explanations produced an irrefutable equation; there would be no foreseeable end to the boom.

The 'bubble' burst in May 1920. Commodity prices were the first to plummet. When prices began to fall in one area, businessmen were quick to explain why it was impossible for them to cut other prices.

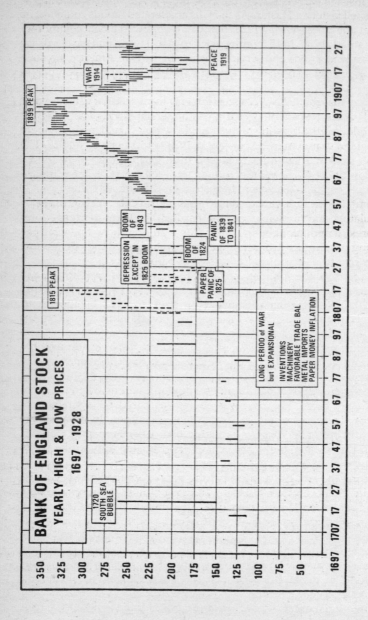

Figure 7   Bank of England Stock

They insisted early falls were only temporary. All were confounded as prices fell faster and faster. As the falls accelerated, goods could not be sold at any price. In May 1920, the widely followed global commodity index stood at 260. In 15 months, it fell to 115. It was a half-price sale for practically all goods and services the world over. In America, no such drop in prices had been experienced since the American Revolution in 1776.

To say that the 1920–1922 recession was the worst since the upwave began in the 1890s would be a gross understatement. The recession that followed the bursting of the 'bubble' was savage. Unemployment in England soared from 2.5 per cent in 1920 to 15.1 per cent in 1922. The British stock market index collapsed from its 1920 high of 161.0 to a 1922 low of 104.0. The value of foreign trade fell from £73.7 per capita to £38.5 per capita in two years. Industrial production fell by just over 20 per cent. Those who were unable to liquidate quickly, such as property speculators and farmers, were the hardest hit. Farm mortgage foreclosures soared, along with bank failures among those financing the farming community. Conservative companies passed their dividends. Many had to re-organise. Several went bankrupt.

The cause of the speculative mania, the bursting of the 'bubble', and subsequent collapse of the system, was the same as always. From 1916 to 1920, U.K. bank deposits just about doubled while banking clearances nearly trebled. There was a corresponding improvement in the level of industrial production, but not as much as the growth in monetary expansion. The amount of money flooding through the economy, not backed by equivalent output, fuelled inflation. There was also a 174.3 per cent increase in wages. This virtually guaranteed that an excruciatingly painful recession would follow when the 'bubble' finally burst. The post-war boom was based on a scramble to replace stocks exhausted by war in most countries. In Britain there were the brighter prospects of taking over German export markets. When the 'bubble' burst, the echoes reverberated around the world and markets collapsed everywhere.

During the late 1930s, another long period of prosperity began. By the late 1960s, another 'bubble' was being blown, the property 'bubble'. That eventually burst in 1974, bringing down large sections of Britain's financial sector. In the four years up to the collapse, very little of the monetary expansion found its way into industrial production. In 1974 the Organisation of Petroleum Exporting Countries levied a 50 billion dollar annual tax on oil. These proceeds were hoarded and were not used to offset the expansion of investment anywhere in the economic system.

Now, as we enter the decade of the 1980s, there is little to suggest that government, businessmen or individuals have learned very much from the history of over 200 years, and the things which have happened with unfailing regularity. It would not be unreasonable to assume we are likely to repeat history once again.

Chapter Five

THE DOWNWAVE . . . A WORLD TURNED UPSIDE DOWN

Until human nature changes materially, there is not likely to be abandonment of the law of expansion and contraction in business or its effects on the prices of stocks.

Charles H. Dow.

There is substantial evidence to pinpoint the beginning of the long downwave in our economic life. When a 30 year expansion crumbles and the 'bubble' bursts, panic follows:— financial institutions fail, companies go bankrupt, corporate profits decline, losses appear in large sections of industry, commodity prices start falling, output plummets, unemployment escalates, world trade slows. Confidence gradually gives way to fear. And, as we stumble into the 1980s, a variety of patterns are emerging.

The downwave is likely to span two decades or so, according to the historical pattern. Economic life as we have known it during the upwave will be turned upside down. The best personal and financial strategies in the upwave will become inappropriate for the downwave. Prudent actions during the upwave will be tossed to the winds, becoming imprudent and irresponsible in the downwave.

Most people were afraid to borrow money during the early 1930s and 1940s. They remembered how their homes were lost when mortgages were called, and how families were bankrupted when the debts of a failing business wiped out everything they had. They remembered the burden of instalment purchases, and the repossession of goods when monthly payments could not be met. But time eases painful memories. All too soon people forget. By the 1970s, people were eager to borrow, many taking as much as they could lay their hands on. In the 1980s, fear of borrowing has been all but obliterated. We live in a society geared to consumers. It is all too easy to consume today, and pay tomorrow.

During the upwave, people on fixed incomes watched helplessly as the value of their cash was eaten away by rising prices. Those who refused to save, who borrowed dear money, and purchased lots of goods which were eventually paid for with cheap money, were rewarded. Savers and lenders were penalised throughout the upwave, while borrowers and profligate spenders benefitted.

In the early 1950s, you could get a home mortgage in Britain at an interest rate of 4 to 5 per cent. A 6 per cent rate was considered usurious. After tax allowances, the mortgage cost dropped to between 2 and 4 per cent. But, to rent a property would cost 10 to 20 per cent of the capital value. Anyone with their head screwed on could see it was far better to buy a home with cheap money than to rent at 15 per cent per annum of the value of the home, with nothing to show for it at the end.

That is no longer the case. Mortgages do not cost 5 per cent. They cost 10 per cent. Rents are no longer 10 to 20 per cent of capital value. They are 5 to 8 per cent, and falling. Property will no longer be a good investment: buying a home during the downwave could be one of the most costly and dangerous commitments anyone could undertake.

Employment is another area to go topsy-turvey. During the upwave, job-hopping was popular. Workers rented their time and skills to the highest bidder. Strikes were widespread during the upwave, and workers usually triumphed, largely because labour was in high demand. When the downwave comes, those who demand the highest wages are among the first to go. Job competition is fierce. Workers often lower their sights merely to get a job . . . any job!

During the upwave astute businessmen expanded stocks and increased prices as speedily as they could. During the downwave, the businessman who delays expansion plans and harbours cash is in the strongest position. The businessman who builds a factory, or opens another shop, in the early stages of the downwave finds himself at a disadvantage to those who waited until later in the cycle. If he postpones plans to expand, he will eventually find that purchasing premises and materials, and distributing goods, will be much cheaper than for others, who expanded too soon and found themselves lumbered with higher costs and financing charges. The financing mechanism is reversed during the downwave. In the upwave, businessmen attempt to borrow dear money, and pay back with cheap money. Any attempt to repeat this during the downwave can be catastrophic. The borrower will be borrowing cheap, and having to pay back with much dearer money. Sir Freddie Laker discovered this when he borrowed thirty million cheap dollars and was asked to repay with far more expensive dollars in 1982. Laker Airways collapsed.

During the upwave, the *price* of money rises, but its *value* falls faster by comparison. For example, if interest rates are 15% but prices rise 20% it costs 15% to borrow money which will purchase 20% fewer goods. The money you borrow is, therefore, progressively less valuable and usually quite easy to come by. During the downwave, the equation is reversed. The *price* of money may fall, but its *value* is likely to increase faster than the fall. If interest rates are 10%, but prices are rising at only 5%, the money you borrow becomes progressively more valuable and is likely to be more difficult to obtain. When money begins to lose its value, there is a flight away from money into 'things'. When money appreciates in value, people hang on to it, and are less prone to reckless spending.

The prudent and cautious investor of the 1930s and 1940s purchased gilt-edged government securities. The return on British Consols was a mere 2½%, but many investors were willing to accept the low return in favour of the safety that such stocks offered. Soon people began to see how rising prices eroded their savings, while the purchasing power of money was being squeezed. Investors who insisted on playing safe were heavily penalised during the upwave. The government securities market in Britain went into a decline in the late 1940s which lasted for 27 years. Anyone who had stashed his money away in a savings account, or an insurance policy, found that it bought in 1980 only a fraction of what could have been bought with the same amount when the saving began.

Many investors believe they have learned to protect themselves against rising prices. Large numbers believe they can beat inflation by using it. Fixed interest investment has been shunned. People have been placing their money in areas which they believe will be able to compete with prices. Investments in diamonds, gem-stones, works of art, antiques, and other speculative areas have found popularity. Such investments will suffer greatly during the downwave. Most people attempting to beat inflation will lose all or most of their savings. The global economy will experience deflation for the first time in five decades. Rising prices will no longer pose a threat. Falling prices will be the major worry. Government policy will be geared toward controlling deflation, rather than inflation. Speculators and manipulators will be wiped out during the downwave. The primary beneficiaries will be the prudent, the savers, the low-risk takers. Cash will be king as the downwave gains momentum.

Businesses which were successful during the upwave will suffer in the downwave. Lifestyles will change markedly. Fashions will change. Attitudes will change. The old social mores will be resurrected. Existing social attitudes will be buried. A sharper division between the 'haves' and 'have nots' is likely to develop. There will be fewer 'haves', and more 'have nots'.

Women will cast aside their banners of equal rights, put on their bras and return to the home. People will turn increasingly to friendship, and the comfort of the family unit for security. Alternative religions will fade. Alternative medicines will be discarded in favour of the bedside manner of the old family doctor. These dramatic changes in values, morality, fashion and culture will exert a dynamic influence on the economic background during the downwave.

The Nature of the Business Cycle

The nature of the business cycle is such that, at one point, businessmen become over-pessimistic. The goods and services produced fall well short of the nation's needs. Businessmen and entrepreneurs with foresight then reverse their strategies. Manufacturers begin producing more goods to compensate for society's demands. Those businessmen who spot the improvement in the early stages of the upwave begin their re-expansion programmes at the lowest costs for the goods, services, labour and money needed to increase production.

As business activity begins to turn upwards, profits soar for those who acted early. This restores confidence in the business community as a whole. Soon everyone is leaping onto the bandwagon of boosting production. And the effects spill over to the consumer.

Manufacturers begin re-hiring. Unemployment levels fall. More people have more money. Consumer demand improves. This leads to further falls in unemployment. Increasing numbers of workers go on overtime. Bigger and fatter pay-cheques result. People increase their spending. They borrow more and consume more as the tempo of activity spurs businessmen to even greater expansion.

As the nation prospers, and as confidence grows, more people are prepared to take risks. Those willing to gamble include individuals who simply live beyond their means, leaving little room for savings. No one believe this prosperity will ever end. This optimism is so strong that entrepreneurs steadily increase expansion plans, and ultimately take on commitments which once would have been considered irresponsible. Many new inexperienced entrepreneurs jump on the bandwagon. Those who remain employed borrow on the assumption that next year's income will be greater than this year's, and the income for the year after will be greater still.

The inevitable occurs. Everyone becomes recklessly over-confident. When too many people demand goods they cannot pay for, when too many are producing too many goods which cannot be paid for, the system becomes exceedingly unstable and collapses under its own weight. The downwave begins.

As the end of the period of expansion approaches, the price of money and the cost of labour has moved up substantially, bringing higher risks and lower profit margins. The growing demand for labour, especially non-productive labour, has cut productivity, amplifying risks. Businessmen who were late to expand become vulnerable to the slightest ripple. Some businesses begin to lose money; retrenchment becomes the order of the day; confidence is shaken.

When trade becomes sluggish, businessmen cut back purchases of goods and services for retail distribution, while manufacturers cut production. These reductions cut consumption, less labour is required, and businessmen lay-off workers.

In an effort to reduce unsold stocks, eating up interest on borrowed money, businesses cut prices. When demand drops off, prices fall, the need for more labour disappears, and the cost of labour is reduced as employees accept lower salaries to remain employed. Attempts to cut out labour-intensive areas and cut costs only exacerbate unemployment. Productivity therefore increases during the downwave, but is of little overall benefit since demand is likely to be falling faster than productivity is increasing. The increase in productivity, in effect, serves to push prices down and unemployment up. What was a self-feeding spiral of expansion during the upwave becomes a self-feeding spiral of attrition in the downwave.

The Deadly Decennial

The downwave begins following the interaction of several unsustainable phenomena:

the effect of war
a surge in prices.
a speculative 'bubble'
over-expansion by industry
profligate monetary policy.

All of these are superimposed on a community with abnormally high demands and expectations. Within a relatively short period, at the end of the upwave there is a massive, bursting, climax.

The upwave involves continuing prosperity, interspersed by minor contractions. But the downwave is more complex. Each downwave is characterised by two important financial panics. The first in the early stages of the downwave is accompanied by an abnormally destructive recession. Then a second financial panic totally collapses the system.

The bursting of the speculative 'bubble' at the end of the upwave does not bring on the depression. It is only a warning of far worse to come. There is still considerable resilience at the end of the upwave, which results in a short period of recovery. When the second speculative 'bubble' bursts at the end of the recovery phase, a 1930s style depression starts. The time between the bursting of the first speculative 'bubble', the recession, and the subsequent recovery leading to the bursting of the second speculative 'bubble', is about 10 years. Two of those years are in recession, eight in 'secondary prosperity'.

When studying the speculative boom in the 1760s it can be seen that the initial plunge in commodity prices circa 1763 was not the collapse that led to depression. There was a serious recession following the plunge in markets . . . but not a depression. After several years of speculation in housing, turnpikes and canals in Britain and heavy speculation in Amsterdam in the East India Company, another panic seized financial markets which was described as one of the fiercest financial storms of the century. This was the panic of 1772. It was that panic that ushered in the depression of the 1780s, nine years after the initial plunge in commodity markets. There was enough resilience in the system to allow for a 'secondary prosperity' following the crash of 1763. By the time of the panic of 1772 the system had been so weakened that a depression was inevitable.

Once again we see the pattern repeating itself in the 19th century. Although the recession following the financial crisis of 1815 was greater than any since the 1780s, there was sufficient strength in the global system to allow a fairly rapid recovery between 1815 and 1822 in Britain. But the wounds of the earlier crisis never fully healed. The international crisis of 1819 fell on a system where speculation had been rekindled; and the initial crisis had not been fully resolved. From 1816 to 1819, there was an export frenzy in Britain. It finally broke at the end of the Napoleonic Wars. In 1818 and 1819, there were financial panics on both sides of the Atlantic. A collapse in commodity markets sparked off a crisis in Britain in 1819. In America the Second Bank of the United States precipitated a panic by calling in pledges from a series of under-capitalised provincial state banks. The Second Bank of the United States then collapsed, and took smaller banks with it.

The straw that broke the camel's back in Britain was the Baring crisis in 1825. According to one of the chronicles of that era, 'A panic seized upon the public such as had never been witnessed before'. The panic of 1825 was a precursor to the depression of the 1830s. Once again roughly ten years had elapsed between the panic that terminated the upwave, and the panic that started the depression.

The period of 1864 to 1866 saw a series of financial panics. Heavy speculation in cotton and shipping companies led to a financial crisis in 1864 which originated in France, spread to Italy, and then to Britain. One of the worst financial panics on record in Britain was associated with the collapse of the Overend Gurney Company in May 1866. A fairly severe recession followed. Recovery came after the deep recession, and calm was restored. There were further extensions of credit and a new wave of speculation.

The system had not fully recovered from the first panic of 1864 which ended the upwave when a second crisis occurred. In the five years from 1868 to 1873, bank deposits in the U.S. increased by 43 million dollars, but bank loans rose by a colossal 283 million dollars. Debts rose 50 per cent, while circulating capital rose a mere $7\frac{1}{2}$ per cent. By 1871, the cracks were beginning to show. During that year, 2,915 businesses failed. In the following year there were 4,069 failures involving debts of 121 million dollars. In the early part of 1873, financial commentators were warning of the risk of crisis from the perilous debt structure in the U.S. banking system. Most of the problems were due to financing speculation in American railroads and homesteading. The big crunch came in 1873, when the New York Warehouse Company failed. Five days later Kenyon Cox and Company failed. Rumours spread quickly that several other large companies were in dire straits. On the 17th September 1873, the U.S. stock market collapsed and there was pandemonium on the New York Stock Exchange. The year ended with over 5,000 business failures, with liabilities a staggering 228,500,000 dollars.

America plunged into deep depression, and took the rest of the world with her. Losses from heavy speculation in American railroads were shared by the Germans. A crisis erupted first in Austria, where banking was more vulnerable than in Germany. When several Austrian banks failed, several moratoriums in weaker German banks followed. Italian banks heavily involved with German banks failed. Dutch banks financing both German and Italian banks collapsed. Dutch banks had borrowed heavily from Belgium banks. They too failed. The sequence was completed. The second collapse was essentially a crisis of confidence which was sufficient to topple the system in 1874. There were roughly ten years between the first panic and the second – just about the time it takes for people to forget the painful lessons they should have learned about financial panics in general.

The crisis following the collapse in commodity markets in 1920 was horrendous. Historians described the period of 1921 as 'the slump'. During the first few months of 1920, unemployment in Britain was rising steadily. By March 1921, 1,355,000 were unemployed . . . 11.3 per cent of insured workers. By December 1921, over two million were out of work, nearly 18 per cent of the work force. Christmas 1921 in Britain was bleak indeed. Unemployed ex-servicemen wearing medals could be seen rattling collection boxes in London's West End. Many businesses had simply closed down for an extended unpaid Christmas holiday.

In shipbuilding, the recession was exceptionally severe. Only one man in three had work. Nearly one in four engineers was out of work, and many others were on short time. In January 1922, 'The Labour Gazette' recorded that in the pig iron industry there were only 77 furnaces in production, compared with 274 the previous year. In cotton, employment was described as 'continued bad, even worse than in November 1921'. In woollen worsteds, conditions 'continued bad'; hosiery was 'fair'; jute was 'bad'. In boots and shoes it was 'very depressed'; in paper, printing and bookbinding it 'continued bad';

food preparation was 'only moderate'. Woodworking and furnishing 'remained bad'. The building trades were far more depressed than anyone remembered. A quarter of all seamen were out of work. Businessmen were totally demoralised. No one could remember a recession like that of 1920 to 1922. Unemployment was the worst for a hundred years. What lay in store was far worse.

By 1928, monetary growth and speculation were on the rampage once again in Britain. The 1920–1922 recession had become a distant memory. Britain's capital markets had been advancing for nearly six years. The nation was considered to be embarking on a new era of prosperity. By 1928, prices on the Stock Exchange were making new highs daily. But beneath this lay severe weakness. The downwave had begun in 1920. During the six years following the end of the recession in 1922, there was little to justify the optimism of 1928, other than self-perpetuating euphoria. People believed what they wanted to. During those six years of illusory prosperity, U.K. wage rates merely moved sideways. In 1925, U.K. foreign trade reached a peak of £50 per head, and then fell steadily up until 1928. Commodity prices recovered from 1922 to 1925, but began a renewed decline in 1926. By 1928, interest rates had nearly doubled from the 1922 trough of 2.75 per cent. On the surface, at least, the economy appeared buoyant. There were sharp rises in industrial production, and a few other economic aggregates, all of them fuelled by a renewed bout of monetary expansion.

As the final hours of the 'roaring twenties' approached, it was generally believed the old rules were dead. Anyone who didn't believe prosperity would last forever was either a madman or a heretic. Early in 1928, interest rates began a rapid rise. By the end of the year, they were excruciatingly high. They bit into business margins severely. Commodity prices were falling during the latter part of 1928, along with the rate of inflation. Higher interest charges could not be passed along in price increases. With the sharp rise in interest rates, there was a lull in business activity. New housing starts and commercial developments went into retreat, and the first signs of the recession began to appear.

Conditions deteriorated during early 1929. Some businesses went into decline while others increased profits quarter after quarter. Suddenly, during the fourth quarter of 1929, the New York Stock Exchange collapsed. It came quite without warning, and sent shockwaves through the global business community.

Some historians claim the pin that finally pricked the bubble came from Great Britain. Whatever the source, the destructive forces unleashed in tandem with the stock market crash brought one of the worst depressions the world has ever known.

At the tail-end of the 'secondary prosperity' that began in 1922, there was some speculation in Europe, but it was mild compared to that in the United States. Throughout the late 1920s, bankers in Europe became bitter over the hardships inflicted upon them by the headstrong rampage into American investments. England was unable to hold her gold in the face of high interest rates being paid by borrowers investing in the American boom. The government was forced to raise the discount rate from 5½% to 6½% on 26th September 1929. All available domestic credit lines were used up during the speculative orgy in the U.S., and European credit markets came under heavy pressure. This in turn aggravated the upward pressure on interest rates. Several European bankers began withdrawing credit lines, eventually strangling international money markets. When credit is withdrawn, the boom ends.

It still took one more major 'hiccup' in Britain to precipitate the Wall Street crash. Towards the end of 1929, the collapse of the Clarence Hatry Group, a rag-bag of companies in everything from grain to slot machines, was the catalyst which sent the spiralling downwave into motion. British businessmen who traded with Hatry and the banking institutions which financed Hatry were severely strained. Losses from the Hatry collapse were prodigious, and forced the sale of massive holdings of American securities. Sell orders went out to American brokers as European bankers rushed to restore liquidity depleted through bad debt write-offs from the Hatry failure. Within 24 hours, stock markets in America were wilting under heavy sales of stock from Britain.

The collapse of the speculative commodity boom in 1920 began in Europe, but took on global dimensions. Dumping from Europe on an already vulnerable U.S. stock market was the final straw. Many American businessmen were fully aware of the shaky U.S. economy during the latter part of 1929 and were ready to jump. Without warning the bell was rung. Something had gone terribly wrong. The chain-reaction ricocheted from country to country. Banks, businesses, individuals, all collapsed in a torrent. The commodity crash in 1920 left the system with considerable resiliance. There was little resilience left when the second collapse came in 1929, nearly ten years later. The deadly decennial had left its mark again.

After nearly three decades of prosperity, speculative fever returned to Britain in the early 1970s in the commercial property market. What commodity markets were to the European economies in the 1920s, commercial property was to the British economy in 1974. Then the 'bubble' burst; property companies and banks collapsed. A severe recession followed, greater than any since the 1930s. Yet, a strong 'secondary prosperity' began in early 1975. That has continued, at least in the consumer-oriented areas of the British economy, through the decade of the early 1980s. Of course, the 'secondary prosperity' will come to an end. 200 years of history, marked with strategic points,

TRADE CYCLES CHART

(ORIGINATED BY THE LATE JOSEPH KITCHIN ESQ.)

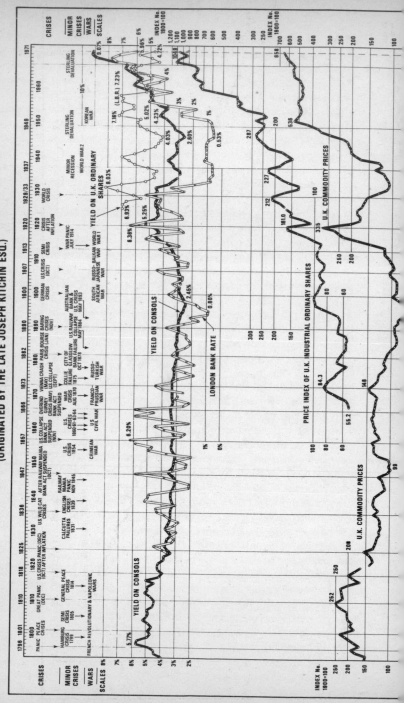

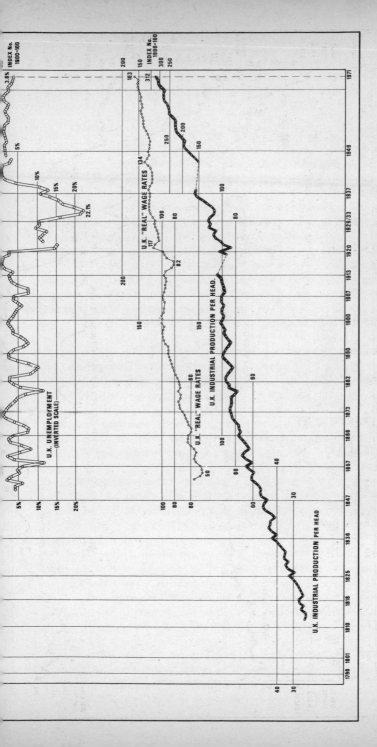

Figure 8   Trade Cycles

suggests a financial holocaust is due during 1983 or 1984. It will represent the second financial collapse of the downwave. The international system will not be able to absorb it without moving into depression.

'Secondary Prosperity' . . . Happy Days Are Here Forever

The reason that recessions, depressions and panics occur with such persistence is that few people ever prepare for them. If everyone took precautions to protect themselves as soon as there were signs of overheating in the economy, there would never be any collapses. The business cycle would merely look like a horizontal line across the page, as would our long wave patterns of economic life. The most treacherous part of the early downwave comes with a false sense of security from the secondary recovery which follows the first major move into the downwave.

During the recession there is a marked change in social, cultural, political and economic attitudes. An unsuspecting public invariably assumes the recession will be similar to the recessions in the upwave. Those are relatively shallow and brief. The first recession in the downwave is long and deep. When it ends and 'secondary prosperity' finally takes hold, most people believe that conditions will be exactly the same as they were before the severe recession. During the secondary recovery, which lasts six to eight years, almost the entire range of cultural and social change which took place in the upwave is compressed into this much smaller time frame.

During the recession, people become frightened, and thus more prudent. There is a change in dress. Styles become more conservative. Music is quieter, more subdued. Church attendances increase. Speculative activity drops sharply.

In the secondary recovery, hemlines start rising again. Music becomes more frenetic. Morals lapse. Labour disputes resurface. Speculative activity is rekindled. People start buying houses again.

It is not uncommon for the final stages of 'secondary prosperity' to resemble on the surface an extreme version of the end of the upwave. But, beneath the surface, there are very marked differences. Inflation at the end of the 'secondary prosperity' is much lower than at the end of the upwave. Business activity is appreciably slower. Monetary expansion is strong, but nowhere near as strong as in the latter stages of the upwave. The speculative 'bubble' which bursts at the end of the 'secondary prosperity' involves extremely high numbers of people. They are the principal victims. Members of the public are more easily seduced by the 'secondary prosperity' than the business community. Most individuals become even more reckless and spendthrift during the 'secondary prosperity' than they were during the upwave.

Many fortunes are made in business and in speculation during the upwave. But they tend to make only the rich richer. The 'secondary prosperity' of the downwave offers something for everyone. Prices rise far more slowly than in the final stages of the upwave. There is a plateau between the peak of rapidly rising prices and the abyss of their rapid fall. Often referred to as 'the plateau period', the 'secondary prosperity' phase represents a kind of disinflation, or no-flation.

The decade embracing the 'secondary prosperity' has been one in which the national budget has balanced more often than in any other decade in the five decade wave pattern. The three decades which follow inflationary peaks have, over the past 200 years, provided surpluses 23 times and deficits only 7 times.

There are indications that it has been easier for governments to cut borrowing requirements and run a surplus while inflation is declining. In general, the attitude of the electorate following an inflationary phase has always been one of complete resolve to eliminate the swollen debt. High public sector borrowing is blamed for inflation. But, as the 'secondary prosperity' continues and demands increase, memories fade. Hostility towards public spending also fades; determination to mop-up the debt fades, and tax cuts begin. Eventually, screams for reflation are heard at the first sign of discomfort when the 'secondary prosperity' nears its end.

Through four long wave sequences since the 1790s, tax cuts have appeared with rhythmic regularity during the 'secondary prosperity'. Each time, they seem to have the magical effect of increasing revenues when expenditure is falling and commodity prices are easing. The result is stimulation of the economy which deflates it at the same time. During 'secondary prosperity', tax cuts work because the economy had previously been over-taxed during the upwave, and the high level of deficit financing in the inflationary spiral. When the 'secondary prosperity' begins following deep recession, pent-up domestic demands are met by turning economic output toward the consumer.

Tax money is returned to the consumer to spend. The Conservative tax cuts in 1980; tax cuts by the Americans shortly before; tax cuts in France and Germany, could all have been forecast many years in advance, so consistent are they in the 'secondary prosperity' phase of the downwave.

As the period of 'secondary prosperity' gains wider public recognition, the atmosphere steadily improves. During the early years, most people are highly sceptical. After a year or so, scepticism turns to optimism. Wages increase faster than inflation during the latter stages of 'secondary prosperity'. The consumer feels a tremendous sense of well-being. Money is plentiful. Industrial output improves. Unemployment remains high. But those who are employed, never had it so good.

'Secondary prosperity' brings an entire change in the psychology of a nation. The crisis industry goes into a slump, and journalists begin to think positively again. They totally ignore cracks in the prosperity. They are oblivious to the vast differences between normal prosperity and 'secondary' prosperity. The 'secondary prosperity' is a time when the nation psychologically returns home to business, back to personal lives and careers which were disrupted by the previous recession. People turn away from labour strife, political unrest, soaring inflation and personal crusades.

The peak inflation around the world in 1974 also represented an emotional peak. Pent-up repressions gushed out in a kind of global catharsis. By the time the 'secondary prosperity' was into its second year in 1976, public feeling had changed considerably. Nations had rid themselves of considerable aggression and were returning to a state of equilibrium. Unfortunately, such a situation cannot last. The economy can never remain stable. It constantly fluctuates, as it has to.

During early 1975, a lot of people felt that a recovery could not possibly get started. Forecasts ranged from an oncoming depression to a period of hyper-inflation. Stagflation was a by-word. Some economists said we were having recessionary inflation. Others believed the City of London was about to witness the end of the capitalist system as we knew it. The Labour Government began pumping money into the economy again in 1975.

It is likely the economy would have turned up anyway, since the recession had run its course and too few goods were being produced. Industrial production began rising, and continued to rise strongly through 1977. Consumer trends usually lag industrial trends. There was little pick-up in retail sales until 1976 but, when it came, it was explosive. By late 1977, the monetary aggregates had been turned on full blast. The annual percentage change in M1 (the narrowly based measure of British money supply) had reached 25 per cent by early 1978. Government and private borrowing raced ahead. Mortgage lending was at record levels. So was lending for cars and hire purchase. The new era of economic recovery was plainly visible by 1978, and there was a stampede of eager participants.

Mass psychology takes an epicurean turn during times of plenty. 1978 was such a period. It ran parallel to the late 1960s and early 1970s, when public interest centred on consumption, sexual liberation, and drugs. Attention turned from convention and the work ethic much more dramatically this time. There was a greater proliferation of X-rated movies and sex shops, topless barmaids and waitresses, wife-swapping and group sex. Alternative religions were making the headlines. In Britain, there was a move to ban the Scientology sect. Parents of teenagers attracted by alternative religions were hiring psychological exorcists to effect debriefing and de-brainwashing. Divorce had reached record levels.

Waves of sensual excesses marked the peak in the Roman, Grecian and French civilisations. The downwave in the 'roaring twenties' (the 'secondary prosperity'), ushered in the speak-easy, bootlegging, university hi-jinks, and . . . as a mark of new sexual freedom demanded by the suffragettes . . . the rising hemline. It is no coincidence that, as we approach the final stages of the 'secondary prosperity' that began in 1975, we see a repetition of the social, cultural and moral patterns that foreshadowed the decline of these great civilisations.

Early in 1979, the Labour Government was ousted because it could not provide optimum prosperity with minimum inconvenience. The Conservatives, led by Margaret Thatcher, promised renewed prosperity, tax cuts and the like.

During the fourth quarter of 1979, flaws began to appear in the economy again. Unemployment rose sharply. Government policy was heavily criticised. In early 1981 the Conservative Government was one of the most unpopular ever to lead Britain.

The fourth quarter of 1979 produced the first signs of a recession that has, to date, been long and stubborn. In my opinion, it will lead to a secondary depression. As the recession deepens, ever so slightly at first, prices will tip toward deflation, crisis and depression. The shift will be subtle, and will go unnoticed by most economists. But the effects will certainly be felt. Almost without exception, the end of any 'secondary prosperity' has produced the worst economic declines in history. These depressions have always been the most unexpected. When the phase of 'secondary prosperity' is finally over, and the impact hits the consumer-oriented sectors, the economic aggregates do not simply move gradually from good to bad; they move rapidly from practically idyllic to total disaster.

Look at the current debt structure of individual economies, of our global industrialised society as a whole, and of the lesser developed countries. When the gradually declining plateau turns into a secondary depression, the financial Armageddon will be devastating.

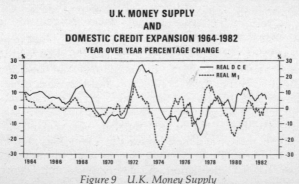

Figure 9   U.K. Money Supply

Chapter Six

SECONDARY DEPRESSION . . . A SCENARIO FOR THE 1980s

Only if you think the depression is now beginning could you say that the recession has now ended.

Malcolm S. Forbes

As the 1973–1975 recession took hold, almost anyone could have seen that something had gone terribly wrong and the world was building up to some drastic adjustment. Economists attributed the deep recession to the oil crisis. The oil crisis was a symptom of the underlying malaise, rather than a cause. The cause could be traced to several decades when everyone insisted on living beyond their means. By 1973, it was time to pay the piper.

Very few were prepared for the depth of the 1973–1975 recession, although the long wave pattern of economic life had been issuing warnings for some years. The supposedly oil-induced recession was far more severe than the most pessimistic expectations.

For some strange reason, economists and commentators continued to assess the economic background as if the nature of economic activity prior to World War II was of little consequence. For those with a knowledge of history, the 1973–1975 recession was certainly not without precedent. The global economic community had experienced similar recessions many times before, after the long upwave of prosperity had spent its force.

The 1973–1975 recession was indeed destructive. Banks failed. Property companies went bankrupt. Unemployment soared, and the British stock market crashed. Between May 1973 and January 1975 the Financial Times 30 Share Index had lost 78% of its value. Many likened this to the depression of the 1930s, but the similarities were merely on the surface. The stock market crash in London between 1973 and 1975 was worse than the crash of 1929–1931 in terms of share values, but the effect was far less devastating, thanks to help by the Bank of England to sections of the financial community which were most in trouble. During the recession of the early 1970s output fell, unemployment rose, bankruptcies increased, but not on the scale of the 1930s depression. That was still to come.

There were striking contrasts between the two periods. Unemployment in the United States rose from 0.9% of the labour force in 1929 to 23% by 1932. Industrial production dropped by 28% between 1928 and 1931. In 1932, one half of the total productive capital in America was idle and fourteen million people were unemployed. There was a crisis of dramatic proportions.

In the 1970s, falls in production were steep. Average unemployment for the OECD countries remained below 10%, even at the trough of the recession. Probably the most dramatic contrast was in prices and wages. In the United States between 1929 and 1931, wages fell by 39% and wholesale prices by 33%. During the early 1970s, in Britain and America, prices and wages continued to rise. The recession of 1973–1975 was typical of the severe recessions which punctuate the end of a long wave of prosperity, and usher in the downwave.

In early 1975, there was sufficient resilience in the system for one final phase of recovery in Britain and the rest of the world. Governments began increasing their deficits to prevent demand from falling too far, acting to contain the rise in unemployment and to limit the fall in output and the number of bankruptcies. The same medicine was used effectively in 1922, and worked again.

In the November 1974 Budget, strong measures were introduced to pull Britain out of the recession. The government reduced the corporation tax liability on stock appreciation, and previous price controls were slackened. Companies were allowed to pass on in price rises, 80% of the increase in labour costs, and 17½% of the cost of fixed investment. In addition, £1,000 million of loans were to be made available over two years for investment through Finance for Industry. Total financial benefits to the British corporate sector were estimated at £1.5 billion in 1975. The after-tax rate of corporate profits for 1974, jumped from minus 0.3% to plus 4.1% as a result. It was estimated that easing the price code would raise corporate profits by £800m., and the rate of inflation by 1 percentage point.

By late 1975, the first signs of recovery began to appear. Many people believed a return to normal was about to begin. Yet, although there was some economic recovery from 1975 to 1979, high inflation, instability, social disorder, continued disruption in the labour market and shortages were the price for this secondary prosperity.

A few months after the government plans to rejuvenate industry, both wages and prices could be seen to be escalating. During the first quarter of 1975, there was a settlement of 25–30 per cent for nurses, teachers, bankers and local authority workers. It was publicly defended by the TUC. In the April 1975 Budget, attempts at damping down consumer demand were made. Income tax was raised by 2 per cent. Excise duties were raised and the top VAT rate of 25 per cent, previously only applied to petrol, was extended to a wide range of luxury goods.

These moves fuelled inflation rather than eased it. By the summer of 1975, the deficit financing of late 1974 was beginning to show as the balance of payments deficit widened. Sterling was affected severely. By the second quarter of 1975, the value of the pound measured against a weighted average of other currencies had fallen by 29% since December 1971. The secondary prosperity had barely begun before Britain's competitiveness in international markets was sinking fast.

By the second quarter of 1975, retail prices were rising at an annual rate of nearly 38%, compared to 10% for Britain's major competitors. Wage settlements of 30% or so were still common during the second quarter of 1975. Average earnings were 27% higher than in the previous year, pointing to still higher rates of inflation. Pressure on the pound became intense. In the six weeks to mid-June 1975, the pound plunged by 4%. On the 30th June 1975, the pound fell 1.3% in a single foreign exchange dealing session. The government and the TUC manned panic stations and agreed that wage increases would be restricted to 10% in the following pay round. On the surface, the secondary prosperity continued. Beneath the surface there was little to check the headlong decline of U.K. capital markets, or to stimulate any long term growth.

Early in 1976, the Bank of England decided to engineer a devaluation of the pound to improve competitiveness in international markets. The idea was to reduce the price of U.K. exports and increase the price of foreign imports, making British goods more attractive, both domestically and internationally. With floating exchange rates, sterling needed to be eased down gently through Bank of England intervention in foreign exchange markets.

Unfortunately, the plan backfired. When dealers heard that the Bank of England was selling while the pound was falling, the market panicked. The pound plunged through the $2.00 for the first time in history. Within a week, it was down to $1.90. That was the original planned level, but the panic selling did not stop. The pound continued to fall through $1.80, then $1.75. By the time it reached $1.71, it was decided to apply for a 'standby' loan of $5bn. from a foreign central bank consortium until confidence had been restored. The 'standby' loan was agreed for six months.

The pound stabilised temporarily, but then began to fall again. By 9th September 1976, $1½bn. of the 'standby' loan had been spent and the pound was still falling. During the first two days of the Labour Party Conference in 1976, sterling had dropped by 7½%. Ultimately, Britain was forced to seek aid from the IMF, with all of the restrictive policies that entailed. Prior to the IMF loan agreement, sterling had fallen to $1.57.

The secondary prosperity suffered a severe hiccup between 1976 and 1977. The cost of living rose by 5.3%. At the same time, earnings increases had fallen from 13.9% in 1976 to 8.9% in 1977. The result was a sharp decline in living standards. This was partly a result of the government's wage restraint policy of Phase I and Phase II, but was more of persistently high inflation. Phase I involved a £6 pay limit for settlements between 1975 and 1976. Phase II involved a 5% norm, with a lower limit of £2.50 and an upper limit of £4 per week for settlements between August 1976 and August 1977. By the end of Phase II, real earnings were 10% lower than at the trough of the recession in 1974. Prime Minister Callaghan had intended to introduce Phase III with a 10% wage ceiling. At the 1977 TUC Conference, further restraint was rejected. There was an overwhelming vote for a return to free collective bargaining which the government accepted. The floodgates were opened, and the secondary prosperity began anew. Real take-home pay rose by 7% between July 1977 and July 1978, and the standard of living in Britain was improving once more.

The British people felt that their economic environment was returning to the way it used to be. In many respects it was, even down to the labour disruption which characterises the end of prosperity. The long wave of prosperity which began in the late 1930s did not really provide consumer benefits until the 1950s and 1960s. Similarly, the secondary prosperity which began in 1975, did not help the consumer until it reached a mature stage of development.

Bitter labour disputes are characteristic of the final stages of a long wave of prosperity, and of the final stages of a secondary prosperity. Bells warning the end of a secondary prosperity rang in August 1978 when the ever-hopeful Callaghan proposed a 5% ceiling on pay. By August 1978, British workers had once again enjoyed a high standard of living, regardless of their productivity. The TUC Conference again rejected wage restraint, and workers embarked on a wave of strikes in the 'winter of discontent'. Some 10 million working days were 'lost' between October 1978 and March 1979.

To all intents and purposes, 1975–1979 was a recovery period. But it was not the type of recovery normally associated with the long wave of prosperity, when recessions are brief and shallow, and recovery periods take the economy to new heights. At no time during the 1975–1979 recovery did the British economy reach growth comparable with the 1960s or the turn of the decade. Although the economy was deemed to be recovering from 1975 to 1978, unemployment increased from 600,000 to just under 1½ million in 1977 and 1978. The fundamental cause was the major slowdown in the growth of demand, and the rate at which industrial production was growing. The phenomenon was not just peculiar to Britain. It was worldwide in the secondary recovery period.

The lifeblood of any economy is company profits. The rate of corporate profits from 1975 to 1978 had risen only marginally above the catastrophic level of 1974–1975. U.K. company profits grew at 2.2% in 1975. By 1978, this growth had improved by a mere 0.7% to 2.9%, the peak during that so-called period of recovery.

Elsewhere in the British economy, the picture was similar. In 1973, Britain's share of world markets was 9.4%. By 1978, the improvement was a mere 0.1% to 9.5%. Maintaining Britain's share of world markets over that period was achieved at the expense of a more rapid rise in the foreign currency price of U.K. exports than in those of her major competitors. The actual volume of U.K. manufactured exports rose by 21% between 1973 and 1978, against a rise in world manufacturing exports of 30%. Attempts at maintaining Britain's share of world markets were clearly unsustainable by the end of 1978. The U.K. continued to import increasingly more goods. By the middle of 1979 imports of finished manufactured goods were 70% higher than in 1973, while total manufacturing output in the U.K. remained virtually unchanged.

Manufacturing investment in Britain was stagnant during the secondary prosperity of the 1970s. Whatever investment there was seemed to be directed toward the service industries, property and land, rather than manufacturing industry. Markets for British manufactured goods stagnated. Because profits were low in comparison to other areas, capitalists refused to invest. The stagnation of Britain's market for manufactured goods meant that U.K. capacity was even more underemployed than that of her international competitors. Productivity was low. Output per person per hour in British manufacturing industry rose by a miniscule 1% per year from 1973–1978. During the same period, output per man hour in manufacturing industry rose by 15% in the United States, 17% in Italy, 20% in West Germany, and 22% in Japan and France.

Signs that Britain's manufacturing base was steadily being eroded, even though the economy was supposedly in a period of global growth, could be seen in the unemployment figures. Employment in British manufacturing industry fell by 7% between 1974 and 1978. If the fall in employment in manufacturing industry had exceeded the fall in output by a reasonable margin, productivity would have risen. This never occurred. Output fell nearly as much as employment, with little productivity gain. Even before the recession began to emerge again in late 1979, sales for British manufactured goods were sluggish. Some old plants were closed, and equipment was sold to foreign buyers as the manufacturing base in Britain contracted.

As Britain approached the General Election of 1979, it was generally believed that the policies of the Callaghan Administration were incapable of stemming the economic decline, much less reversing it. Bankers, industrialists, capitalists and the electorate began to look for radical policies that might restore conditions for sustained economic growth. In time-honoured fashion, the British people punished the

Labour Government for failing to accomplish the unaccomplishable. In May 1979, the Thatcher Administration was elected by an overwhelming majority.

At the beginning of every year I prepare a programme of guidelines on the likely nature of business activity during the year ahead. In early 1979, I presented my programme for the year on my daily broadcasts over LBC and to readers of 'Investors Bulletin'. For the most part, 1979 looked a reasonably promising year for those sectors of the British economy with the most resilience, essentially the consumer sectors. There appeared ample scope for further gains in house prices. The stock market appeared capable of moving higher, particularly if there was a General Election and a Conservative victory. Commodity prices looked set for another rise, along with the rate of inflation. Consumer spending was going up steadily, and it looked as if the British consumer was ready for another spending spree while manufacturing industry languished. The U.K. Treasury was forecasting 2% growth for the economy during 1979. Consumer spending and exports were considered the main growth force.

The consensus of forecasters felt that 1979 was going to be a good year. So did I, until the fourth quarter. It was my forecast that, in the fourth quarter, a recession would begin. The recession would ultimately bring an end to the consumer boom, an end to the stock market boom, an end to the housing boom, and a fall in U.K. living standards. In other words, an end to the secondary prosperity of the 1970s. Time had run out.

It was clear that governments in the mid-1970s had no idea how to restore equilibrium to a system with a colossal debt structure, floating currencies, contracting markets and inflation that kept going up, up and up. The international monetary system remained out of control, with planners powerless in the face of natural economic forces.

Beneath the surface of what appeared a relatively buoyant economy in Britain during early 1979, there were severe cracks. As the year passed, warning indicators (new housing starts, share prices, the inverted series of bankruptcies, and the average hourly work week) were all showing serious deterioration. There was a brief celebration on the stock exchange following the Conservative victory in May 1979, but the economy was already deteriorating. A change in government was certainly not sufficient to alter the inexorable economic tide.

In 1979, industrial output resumed its precipitous decline, falling a staggering 13.8% between 1979 and 1980. In accordance with my forecast, the recession had begun in the fourth quarter of 1979 in earnest. Britain's Gross Domestic Product during the 1980–1981 fiscal year fell by more than double the Chancellor's Budget forecast of 2%. At the same time, seasonally adjusted unemployment continued rising at over 100,000 per month, yielding a raw jobless total of 2.42 million in

1981, equivalent to 10% of the labour force. By 1982, the jobless total had risen to 3 million, or 12% of the work force.

The recession which began in 1979, and has continued since, is certainly not peculiar to Britain. Its effects are global. The roots of the worldwide recession can be found in global commodity markets. They sounded the early warnings of global economic difficulties first in 1973.

Commodity markets are the nearest to reality. At the start of the economic production process, commodity prices give advance warning of changing trends elsewhere. Copper and tin are important indicators of future construction and manufacturing activity. Cotton shows the direction of consumer spending and retail sales, well in advance. Silver and gold reflect inflation and the possibility of approaching chaos, like wildcat strikes and international disruption. Corn and wheat prices give us a clue to the future price for goods in the grocery store, as well as the prospective rate of inflation.

The growth in commodity prices began its cyclical decline in 1973. By 1975, non-oil commodity prices were falling sharply. From 1975 to 1977, the growth in commodity prices resumed, along with the global secondary prosperity. Growth peaked in 1977, and never reached the levels of 1973, confirming a major terminal juncture in the long upwave of prosperity. In 1977, the growth rate of non-oil commodity prices began to decline again. There was a minor recovery from 1978 to 1980, but early in 1980 the secular downtrend in the growth in commodity prices was resumed. During the second quarter of 1982, commodity prices appeared at the incipient stages of a collapse. Gold and silver were plunging to new lows for the cycle. Tin had plunged from £9,000 a tonne in February to under £6,000 a tonne by May 1982.

A new phase in the long wave pattern of economic life was beginning. The upwave had been completed in 1973. The recession that followed the upwave had been completed in classic fashion in early

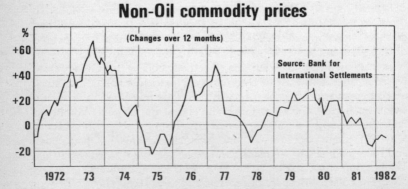

Figure 10   Non-Oil commodity prices

1975, just as at the end of each upwave for the past 200 years. In 1979, the secondary prosperity was completed, leading to a 'gradually declining plateau' of economic activity. It is being called a recession, but I believe it will lead to the great depression of the 1980s. In 1982, we began the phase of secondary depression that leads to panic and distress. The world is on the brink of monetary collapse, and western industrialised society is faced with the prospect of the worst depression of this century. That means . . . breadlines, fruitstands, bankruptcies, panic, riots in the streets, anxiety, business foreclosures, capital losses, bank failures, a collapse in the housing market, ruin, worry, joblessness, hunger . . . for 60% of the population, possibly more.

The Timing of the Secondary Depression

A recession or a depression does not happen all at once. It is not a matter of going to sleep one night feeling prosperous, and waking next morning to discover you are in a depression. A depression begins slowly in vulnerable areas and gradually spreads. It does not reach everything, even at its nadir. Many businesses will go bankrupt. Many banks will fail. Many individuals will suffer severe hardships, but not all. Neither Britain nor the rest of the industrialised West will disappear into oblivion, never to recover.

As the long wave pattern of economic life takes us into the 1980s, it is certainly not a matter of whether a depression will occur; it is a matter of how far and how fast the depression will spread. In many areas of Europe, there has been a depression for some time. Unemployment in Ireland is equivalent to that in the great depression of the 1930s. In Britain, several towns have become ghost towns, because there is no work available. The inhabitants of Corby know that Britain is in a depression. So do the people in Port Talbot.

The red light that flashes oncoming depression is often signalled in the stock market. In 1920, stock market prices rose to a peak and then crashed, signalling the 1920–1922 recession. Share prices recovered during the secondary prosperity of 1922–1929, and then crashed again. A depression followed. Some people actually believe the 'Great Crash' was the cause of the 1930s Depression. The idea is naive. The stock market crash was only one of many elements revealing an economy due for collapse. The recession at the end of the upwave, combined with the period of secondary prosperity, lasts for about 10 years. In May 1972, share prices on the London Stock Exchange reached a peak and then fell sharply, signalling the worst recession since the 1930s. The London stock market is due for a peak again somewhere around 1982. The collapse in share prices which follows should be worse than the collapse of the early 1970s.

I do not place much stock in these over-simplistic attempts at judging the future by fixed periodicity cycles from the past. Although they serve as guidelines, they can be dangerously inaccurate, particularly when dealing with a pattern of economic life over 50 to 60 years. Timing could be off by 5 to 10 years. Far more important are the economic markers that form the long wave pattern, and their course of development. They make a far more convincing case for the approach of a secondary depression.

Obviously, if we can determine whether we are facing a period of prolonged prosperity or merely a secondary prosperity, we can plan accordingly. It is vital to recognise the difference between a period of inflation and one of deflation. When that final stage of secondary prosperity ends, and depression, danger, crisis and acute panic threaten, it is vital to be able to make the correct economic moves. This can be done by placing emphasis on the shorter waves of economic behaviour within the 50 to 60 year framework.

The most serious work on business cycle synergy was carried out by Professor Joseph Schumpeter at Harvard University. Schumpeter combined the findings of three cyclical economists, Kitchin, Juglar and Kondratieff. The Kitchin cycle involves a period of approximately 40 months. The Juglar business cycle runs for 8 to 10 years, and the Kondratieff cycle approximately 54 years. In terms of the overall rhythm, there are three Kitchin cycles in a Juglar cycle, six Juglar cycles in a Kondratieff cycle, and eighteen Kitchin cycles in a Kondratieff cycle, involving a distinct interaction. Of greatest interest are those periods when all three cycles have moved in tandem.

To determine the type of environment immediately ahead, the Juglar cycle is most useful. Juglar, like Kondratieff, finds one primary cause for his nine-year rhythm: The fluctuation in commodity prices. According to Juglar, the prosperity that precedes a crisis always brings high commodity prices. As prices rise, exports become more difficult, the balance of payments becomes less favourable. Gold and then foreign exchange flow out of the country, weakening the internal financial position. The unique cause of the crisis, according to Juglar, is the ending of the price rise. In Schumpeter's magnum opus entitled 'Business Cycles' (1939), he refers to Juglar, stating:

> His great merit is that he pushed the crisis into the background and that he discovered below it another, much more fundamental, phenomenon . . . Henceforth, although it took decades for his new view to prevail, the *wave* ousted the crisis from the role of the protagonist in the play . . . The problem has changed its complexion. It is no longer a problem of the wave. It is the problem of identifying and, if possible, isolating the many waves and studying their interference with each other.

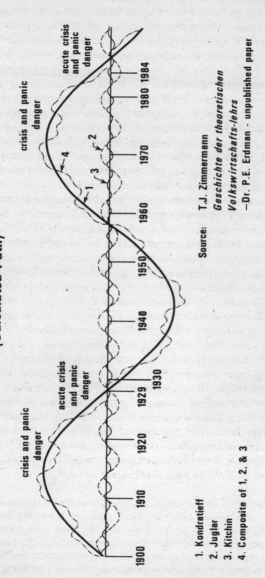

Figure 11   The 20th Century Business Cycle and Crisis Points (Calculated Path)

Schumpeter discovered these Juglar cycles in the economic life of Germany, England and the United States. The Bartels test of probability suggests that the recurrence of the nine year business cycle (which is in effect a 9.2 year business cycle) could not occur by chance more than once in 5,000 historical repetitions.

Combined with the 54-year rhythm, the 9-year rhythm of Juglar can often signal important events in the economic flow. The 1919 peak in the 9-year rhythm came when the longer term 54-year rhythm was also reaching its final peak at the end of the long prosperity. In the late 1920s, so long as the 9-year rhythm continued to rise, the momentum of the stock market was maintained. When this 9-year rhythm peaked again in 1928, and then turned down, after the 54-year rhythm had been falling for almost 8 years, the beginning of the great collapse in stock markets, commodity markets and the global economy was at hand.

Juglar divides the cycle into three periods: (1) prosperity, (2) crisis, and (3) liquidation. He emphasised the influence of bank credit on the development of crisis. After studying the accounts of the Bank of England, the Bank of France, and the leading American banks, Juglar deduced that there was a law of crisis and a recurrent periodicity. Juglar felt that wars, droughts, abuse of credit, excessive issue of bank notes, and even events such as the oil crisis, would not be sufficient to provoke an industrial crisis if the general economic situation did not warrant it. These events may hasten a crisis, but only when the economic factors make it inevitable.

According to Edwin Dewey in his marvellous book, 'Cycles – The Science of Prediction' (1947):

Inversely, it was after this rhythm had reached a trough in 1923–1924 that the economy started rising expansively to the peak reached in 1928. And it was after its trough in 1932–1933 that recovery began from the 1928 fall in commodity prices and from the subsequent 1929 crash in share prices. The well-known peak in 1937 followed. The next peak of the ideal wave was in mid-1946.

In 1867 there was a massive peak in commodity prices. It preceded the great depression of 1873–1878. Approximately 54 years later, in 1920, there was a further peak in commodity prices, confirming the continued presence of the long wave cycle which ultimately involved the great depression of 1929–1932. On both occasions, the peak of the 9-year cycle was close to the peak of the 54-year cycle.

In August 1974, I said in 'Investors Bulletin':

'Projecting this phenomenon into the future, assuming that commodity prices have peaked this year, we would expect a trough in the stock market cycle between late 1974 and mid-1975 leading to a secondary recovery which will ultimately lead to another great depression, likely to begin in the early 1980s . . . *but not likely to materialise this decade*.

The trough in the stock market cycle occurred on schedule in January 1975, when the Financial Times 30 Share Index reached 146, following a decline of 78%. The ensuing share boom took the FT30 up to 600 in May 1981, and the secondary recovery in the economy began as forecast. The 310% rise in share prices over the 6-year period more than vindicated the use of the 9-year rhythm. We are now 'in the early 1980s'. I have little doubt that the 9-year rhythm discovered by Juglar will prove no less valuable to those who heed its warnings.

Another major contribution to the work of Professor Schumpeter was made by Joseph Kitchin, with a business cycle lasting approximately 40 months. The cycle had manifested itself in industrial ordinary share prices since 1871, and was first discovered by a group of American investors in 1912. The original formula for the 40-month business cycle is attributable to the banker Rothschild, who reputedly had analysed British Consols and dissected the price fluctuations into a series of repeating curves, combing these curves and using them as a forecasting device. Some 10 years after the Rothschild discovery, Professor W.L. Crumm of Harvard University noted a cycle of '39, 40 or 41 months' in the length of monthly commercial paper rates quoted in New York from 1866 to 1922. Professor Crumm reported on this in the Review of Economic Statistics for January 1923.

At about the same time as Crumm's discovery, Professor Kitchin, also of Harvard University, discovered a business cycle which he claimed ran for approximately 40 months and involved six economic time series: bank clearings, commodity prices, and interest rates, for both Great Britain and the United States. The continued repetition of the rhythm was noted throughout the period 1890–1922. Professor Kitchin reported his findings in the same issue of 'Review of Economic Statistics' for January 1923.

Charles Hoskins, totally unaware of the previous work on the 40-month cycle, concluded early in 1935, as a result of a time-chart analysis of pig iron production and many other economic series, that a cycle of approximately 40.5 months seemed to be operating over a considerable period. The 40-month rhythm, first attributed to pig iron production, is also duplicated in scores, if not hundreds of other economic phenomena. These include bank debits, industrial production, commodity prices, and share prices. George Armstrong, a research analyst for the Bell Telephone Company in the United States, determined the length of general business conditions in America since 1885 was approximately 40 months.

Professor Schumpeter liked to refer to this 40-month cycle as the Kitchin cycle. Schumpeter noted that the long wave economic cycle should contain six individual Juglar cycles, and that each Juglar cycle would comprise three Kitchin cycles. However, Schumpeter clearly stated that expectation from the theory would be much less regular.

The work of these four great economists can be applied to the real world of the 1980s. Edwin Dewey, who has probably done more research into business cycle development than any man alive, claims that all cycles of the same length tend to turn at the same time. In other words, they act in synchrony. From this, there might be some clue as to the probable emergence of a financial crisis along with an international battle, because both cycles of crisis in Britain are 9.6 years. Dewey states:

> I suspended my personal judgment in regard to cycles for many years. It was only after we discovered that cycles persisted over hundreds and even thousands of years, and after we were able to make comparative cycle studies that showed that substantially all the cycles of any given length turn at about the same time, that I became convinced without any lingering doubts as to the significance of at least some of these behaviours.
>
> It is simply inconceivable that *all* the observed coincidences should have come about as a result of random forces.

Applying the synchrony of Schumpeter's three cycle schema involving the long wave Kondratieff cycle, the 9-year Juglar cycle and the 40-month Kitchin cycle, we find that the initial crisis, panic and danger occur when these three cycles turn down simultaneously. This occurred circa 1973–1974, with the collapse in the stock market and the secondary banks. The only time these three cycles turn down simultaneously during the upwave is in the very last stages of that upwave. When these three cycles are falling simultaneously during the downwave, then *acute* crisis, panic and danger develop, leading to depression. If we now apply the 9-year cycle, projecting forward from the 1973–1974 crisis, then a period of acute crisis, panic and danger is due for 1982–1983. If we attempt to pinpoint the timing by using the 40-month cycle, it is likely to have begun in June 1982 with the renewed collapse in commodity prices then.

The period begins with a crisis of confidence, where many believe that a decisive change for the worse is happening. In a relatively short space of time, a feeling of insecurity turns into expectation of possible catastrophe. The crisis begins after a psychological climax. Ironically, the ending of the Falkland Islands War could have been the trigger for the crisis which usually occurs at the end of a temporary period of euphoria. The mega-crisis feeds on itself until it turns into a mega-panic.

Panics develop purely out of human emotion. With a bang, the herd begins to stampede, dashing madly in all directions at once, fearing everything from left to right. Panics are, by definition, irrational. Instead of attempting to develop rational ways to deal with the oncoming depression, most people simply try to escape the future by running. People dump investments unmercifully, leave their homes and seek solace wherever they can find it. The nadir of the crisis, the panic, cannot be anticipated by any statistical systematic fashion. To a large degree, it is psychological. It can happen at any time during a crisis. The crisis period was entered in 1982. The evidence to support the high probability of an oncoming panic and depression, in my opinion, is overwhelming. Thus far, the evidence I have presented is of a statistical and cyclical nature. There is more evidence, much more.

What Makes a Recession Turn Into a Depression?

Jokers have said that when your friend loses his job, that is a business contraction. When you lose your job, that is a recession. When your wife loses her job, it is a depression.

The first use of the term 'depression' can be traced to Henry Vansittart. He used it to describe the slowdown in business during 1793. In later years, Professor John Kenneth Galbraith told us that the word 'depression' was resurrected as a substitute for 'panic'. Karl Marx preferred 'crisis' for 'panic'. Herbert Hoover, the U.S. President presiding over the chaos of the 1930s, adopted what he believed to be a much softer term, resuscitating 'depression' so as not to panic the crisis-prone.

When it was suggested to President Franklin D. Roosevelt that America was likely to remain in a depression for a considerable period, the President waggled a menacing finger and warned his opponents never to speak of rope in the house of a man who was about to be hanged. Since then, hard times have been euphemised as 'business contractions', 'periods of stagflation', 'inflession', 'rolling adjustments', and 'extended seasonal slumps'.

The difference between a recession and a depression seems to be a matter of degree. A severe recession may be termed a depression, and a mild depression might be called a recession. The National Bureau of Economic Research in the United States defined a recession as 'a recurring period of decline in total output, income, employment and trade, usually lasting six months to a year and marked by widespread contractions of the economy'. This definition was ultimately reduced to simply a decline in GNP for two consecutive quarters.

This definition has now received international acceptance. Obviously, there is a big difference between recession as it has come to be accepted and the panic, crisis, paralysis and unemployment from 1929 to 1933. Economist, Alan Greenspan, defines a 'depression' as 'either a 12% unemployment rate for nine months or more, or a 15% unemployment rate for three to nine months'. Richard Rahn, another U.S. economist, says, 'I would consider the country to be in a depression if there were a sustained, major drop in GNP for more than one year, combined with unemployment well into the double-digit range for an extended period of time'.

The level of unemployment appears to be the agreed common element in a depression and a recession. Any doubts that the western industrialised economies of the 1980s are heading for a depression on the scale of the 1930s, should largely be removed by serious consideration of the current unemployment problems.

As we continue into the 1980s, we are confronted with a double-edged sword. High technology offers the possibility of producing more goods at lower prices, while escalating unemployment means the market for these cheaper, more abundant goods is steadily diminishing. Since the late 1960s, the global economic environment has been experiencing a shift in emphasis which is no less dramatic than the Industrial Revolution, when an agrarian society became an industrialised society. In 1800, 95% of the British working population was employed in the fields. By 1980, the number had fallen to 2½%. High technology food processing and great strides in agricultural production mean that 2½% of the population in 1980 can do as much as 95% of the population in 1800. Food production per man hour of labour has increased prodigiously, while the Industrial Revolution opened new areas of employment to absorb the labours of former farm workers.

Over the past decade, we have seen the introduction of a vast array of labour efficient devices. We have robotics, where one machine can perform the work of ten men and more, untiringly and without over-time pay, holiday pay, redundancy payments, and without strikes. Micro-technology in business equipment is allowing the number employed in offices to be cut by as much as 50%. The cost of equipment has been falling rapidly, while the efficiency of new equipment is racing ahead. Today we have a pocket calculator that costs about £5.00 doing the work of a similar calculator costing £200 less than ten years ago. We have desk-top micro-computers with a storage capacity and output capability which would have required housing in a small ballroom fifteen years ago. Machines are becoming far cheaper to employ than men and women, at a time of peak labour surplus, with jobs being lost in manufacturing industry at an alarming rate, never to be replaced. Unlike the transition from agrarian to industrialised society, where the industrial base grew as the agricultural base declined, this time around Britain and others have failed to provide a post-industrial base capable of absorbing the surplus labour which comes from labour efficient technology and a global recession.

Britain appears to be the country singled out specifically as failing to integrate new technology. In May 1980, the Central Policy Review Staff reviewed three new books dealing with the tremendous challenge to Britain's creaking industrial empire posed by the technological achievements in micro-processors and other electronic systems. The reviewer seems to have severe doubts as to the potential benefits for Britain:

The danger is that Britain will stay well clear of the edge of this revolution. We seem to be good at buying micro-based television games and to some extent at developing new micro-based information services. But at modernising industry to compete in world markets . . .?

Coupled with the increasing number employed by government, a vast new class of service workers is being created, instead of workers skilled in mass production. In 1956, some 44% of British workers were in some form of service industry. By 1980, that figure had increased to 55%, engaging 14 million people. By 1990, the figure may grow to 18 million, providing those jobs survive . . . and that is one big proviso. As the service class has been expanding, the number of workers employed in factories where goods are produced is rapidly decreasing. The catastrophic aspect of the equation is that the new jobs in service industries have not been sufficient to absorb the number of workers leaving the factories. The closure of these factories is creating a vast reservoir of people who may be permanently unemployed.

From 1964 to 1974, approximately one million jobs were lost in manufacturing industry. In the three years that followed, Britain's industrial force was reduced to a mere $7\frac{1}{2}$ million people. The flight from manufacturing industry is likely to continue even faster in the years immediately ahead. At the current rate, by the year 2000, a further 2 million jobs will have disappeared, leaving one-tenth of the British population to produce goods for close to 60 million people.

In Britain and elsewhere, industries are collapsing just as the young people across Europe from the 1960s baby boom are seeking work. It is estimated that 8 million school leavers will be hunting jobs in Common Market countries alone during the first half of the 1980s. One in three currently have prospects of finding employment. Unemployment in Britain could reach 5 million by the mid-1980s. In the Common Market, there is likely to be at least 12 million officially unemployed by 1985. Taking the OECD industrialised countries as a whole, we are already two-thirds of the way toward the 35 million people some expect to be without work at the middle of the decade.

Most governments are deeply uncertain and divided about the job crisis. Their response has been to under-emphasise the seriousness of the problem, rather than to confront it. In France, during 1979, key forecasts indicating the growing problem were suppressed by government edict. The manner in which the British government has continued to suggest that a recovery was in the offing throughout the continuing recession of 1980, 1981 and 1982, completely refusing to acknowledge any forecast contrary to this prepared doctrine, is testimony to the way governments can deny credibility to those whose warnings are not welcome. Forecast feedback, an attempt to produce an economic recovery by predicting one, was the futile platform of the Hoover Administration during the Great Depression of the 1930s. Economic growth by rhetoric is the policy of the 1980s.

Burgeoning unemployment combined with industrial contraction and decay present an inexorable formula for depression. We are at what Professor Gerhard Mensch has termed a 'technological stalemate'.

We have transcended great cycles of change which are the product of new technology and invention. Minsky describes these as 'displacements'. Each of the distinct patterns has been marked by a technological revolution – steam power in the 1800s, electricity and the rise of mechanical transport in the 1880s, electronics and plastics in the 1950s. Each cycle of technological innovation has ended in a crisis of stagnation. Kondratieff believed that, during the upwave of the long wave pattern, invention resulting in increased productive capacity produced prosperity. But during the downwave, a technological crisis developed as a generation of productive capacity ran into obsolescence, leading to a secondary depression.

Professor Jay W. Forrester sheds considerable light on the technological sequence of the long wave pattern of economic life in an article entitled 'Changing Economic Patterns' in Technology Review, published by the Massachusetts Institute of Technology. Forrester has developed his 'System Dynamics National Model', which is essentially a computerised econometric model of the U.S. economy. Forrester claims his experiments confirm that there is a long wave cyclical pattern with a time frame of 45 to 60 years. Forrester also asserts that the U.S. economy is nearing another depression.

Forrester's model of the U.S. economy contains 15 industrial sectors, such as consumer durables, capital equipment, energy, agriculture, housing and building construction. He says, 'The Model is a translation into computer language of the knowledge people have about organisational structure and operating policies surrounding their daily activities. Such a model is designed to be a role-playing replica of the real economy. It should behave like the key economy, generating growth, fluctuations, shifts in population between sectors, inflation, unemployment, and other phenomena of the real world.'

Forrester's model includes three of the major business cycles, the short term (three to seven year) cycle, the medium term (15 to 25 year) cycle, and the long term (45 to 60 year) cycle. He believes that the longer term cycle is the most important in explaining economic behaviour.

The long wave manifests itself as a massive expansion of the capital sectors followed by a relatively rapid collapse in their output. It is usually described as a peak of economic activity followed by a 10-year plateau, then a drop into a depression period for about a decade, and a long climb over some 30 years to the next peak. Long wave behaviour seems to account for the great depression of the 1830s, 1880s and 1930s, and it may be of critical importance in explaining our present economic situation. Forces arising from the long wave seem to explain many present economic cross-currents, raising the spectre of another depression period in the 1980s.

Forrester, who developed the computer model used in the famous 'The Limits of Growth', sees the long wave pattern of economic life as a process in which the capital goods sectors grow to a size which cannot be sustained, and ultimately collapse. He traces the dynamics of long wave patterns from the industrial expansion in 1945.

Following the Great Depression and the Second World War, many industries were ravaged and there was a widespread shortage of capacity. The consumer durables sectors, housing, office buildings, factories, transport systems, and schools were also insufficient to meet the growing post-war demand. The need to rebuild the capital stock as quickly as possible meant that the growth in construction rose beyond real long term requirements. The limits to growth in capital expansion were believed to have been achieved in the middle 1960s, since when tremendous forces to sustain the process of capital accumulation have persisted. This has left an unbalanced economic system, with too much capital equipment and too much debt. Excess capacity in capital equipment has caused the upward trend to falter, while the need to liquidate debt has meant a dismantling of capital plant. The tendencies in Forrester's model go a long way toward explaining the current state of industrial degeneration in Britain.

Governments would like people to believe that if businessmen would get off their backsides and invest, our problems would be solved, and we would have renewed economic recovery.

Forrester says 'I don't share the widespread expectation that the resumption of business investment will solve existing economic problems. The current slowdown in investment is attributed by many to a lack of confidence. But that lack of confidence is produced by the underlying facts. Return on gross investment has been declining for the past decade and there is no longer a significant risk premium for investment. And, as you look around the economy, there is a strong tendency toward excess capacity; you see it in office buildings, in the steel industry, and in airline seats. New tankers have been coming out of shipyards and going immediately into lay-up. College graduates, who represent investment in human capital, find it increasingly difficult to get jobs.'

The economic conditions of the 1980s present amazing parallels to those following the peak of all of the long wave patterns of economic behaviour since the 18th Century. We are witnessing a decline in capital investment, rising unemployment, a levelling out of labour productivity, and reduced innovation. Similar conditions existed in the 1920s, 1870s and 1820s, and during the latter part of the 18th Century, when interest rates rose to historic highs as investment opportunities had diminished and heavy debts had been incurred.

Forrester sees the U.S. economy poised on the brink of a slump similar to that of the 1930s. Until such a depression takes place, imbalances in the system cannot be removed to pave the way for the new technological era that will follow.

In 1976, Ehud Levy-Pascall, of the International Functional Staff Office of Political Research, Directorate of Intelligence, Central Intelligence Agency in the U.S.A., produced a study entitled 'An Analysis of the Cyclical Dynamics of Industrialised Countries'. At that time, the study predicted 'especially troubled times lie ahead'. In 1979, Levy-Pascall suggested that energy problems might serve as the trigger for a downturn. Levy-Pascall believes in the 50-year Kondratieff cycle. Adding further dimensions to the long wave pattern of economic life, Levy-Pascall's model consists of five basic elements or phases, which together span approximately 50 years.

The first phase involves one or more major technological innovations which usher in new industries. The new innovations bring a dramatic uplift in the economy. From the beginning of the first phase to the end of the second phase, about thirty years elapses. During the third phase, a backwash of economic change revolutionises the system once again. Major changes occur in lifestyle, values and the social system generally. These changes first take place among the youth, later among parents, and generally after severe socio-political turbulence. During the fourth phase, politicians eventually switch to policies in keeping with the changed technological, economic and social system. A relatively calm period follows. The final phase involves the stagnation of economic, social and political systems, and optimism gives way to pessimism. Politically, there is a shift to right wing conservatism.

Prior to the election of President Reagan, Levy-Pascall believed the United States was ripe for a change of political leadership. Such a change took place in the U.S. in 1980, and in Britain in 1979. Levy-Pascall points out, and most economists would agree, that periods of economic expansion and contraction among western industrialised nations are becoming more closely attuned. The world economies are becoming increasingly synchronised. In 1975, virtually every western industrialised nation experienced an economic downturn of almost equal severity. Now a depression in the United States, with its $3 trillion economy, will be echoed in every corner of the globe. Levy-Pascall's model is darkly pessimistic. He believes the United States entered its 'fifth phase' in the early 1970s, pointing to the end of the upwave. He sees little hope of avoiding disaster.

The Shape of Things to Come

Writing in the New York Review of Books in June 1974, Professor Geoffrey Barraclough implied that the steep plunge into a depression could be expected sometime around 1979. In the 'Wall Street Journal' of October 1974, Alfred L. Malabre Jr. foresaw a deep secondary slump in the early 1980s. Walter W. Rostow, author of 'The World Economy', believed that if the price explosion of 1973 was, in fact, analagous to that of 1919–1920, then we might expect a second crash in 1983. Shuman and Rosenau foresaw a plunge in or about 1981. The work of Schumpeter's three cycle schema would indicate crisis and panic is due about now.

For quite some time I have been advising listeners to my LBC broadcasts and subscribers to my 'Investors Bulletin', that a depression was inevitable. If we use the definitions of Alan Greenspan and Richard Rahn, Britain is already in a depression. It now becomes a matter of how people should attempt to cope with what lies ahead.

The lessons of previous depressions suggest that we are currently only at the incipient stages of a depression. Over the next few years, we can expect to see unemployment increase, inflationary expectations will be shattered, and the biggest problem will be for businesses to survive. International tensions are likely to heighten, leading to protectionism and trade wars.

Some governments in Europe now fear that mass unemployment may lead to another major military conflict before long. Frank L. Klingberg carried out an examination of U.S. foreign policy dating back to 1776 and discovered what he defined as alternating phases of 'introversion' and 'extroversion' in U.S. international relationships. According to Klingberg, war-like tendencies are manifest during periods of 'extroversion'. These phases of 'introversion' and 'extroversion' are seen to average about 27 years. Klingberg believes that a fourth phase of 'extroversion' began in 1940 in the U.S., extending until 1967. In 1967, Klingberg cites opposition to the Vietnam War as the major politically potent element at the time. It is Klingberg's view that by 1988, when the memory of the Vietnam War has faded from the consciousness of most Americans, there is likely to be an even more vigorous involvement in world affairs which could plunge the U.S. and her allies into another great war. Quite clearly, the attitude of the electorate dictates whether or not a war is a politically desirable achievement. The popularity afforded Prime Minister Margaret

Thatcher in her waging of war against the Argentinians in defence of the Falkland Islands not only demonstrates that the electorate finds war politically acceptable . . . but actually desirable, at this time.

In domestic economies, debt has reached unsustainable levels. Many companies have been borrowing to survive, hoping for economic recovery. When lenders and borrowers realise that no such recovery is likely in the immediate future, lenders will become more prudent and borrowers will abandon hopes of survival. A wave of bankruptcies can be expected that will reduce debt burdens, and ultimately restore domestic monetary stability.

We have entered a period of intense global financial instability which will inevitably lead to an international financial crisis before the depression of the 1980s has run its course. Bank failures on a massive scale can be expected over the next few years. A 'bank holiday' similar to that in the 1930s must also be considered. Adding to the current financial chaos has been the stupendous growth of euro-currency, involving currencies outside the control of individual central bankers. The unregulated euro-currency market may be where the first clear signs of a major financial collapse appear. Euro-currency bankers have gone farthest in using short term deposits to finance long term loans to less than perfectly creditworthy borrowers.

It is my view that the depression of the 1980s will be far worse than that of the 1930s. During previous depressions, a far larger segment of the economy was in agriculture, and was largely self-sufficient in food. People are much further removed today from the subsistence agriculture which once provided for those who were out of work.

Consumer debt levels have been extended beyond anything ever seen before. As a result, many more people will be affected by the depression of the 1980s. People have been encouraged to live beyond their means for decades. The nature of a self-feeding debt liquidation, which comes with deflation, will mean that these debts will have to be repaid. Personal bankruptcies are likely to reach terrifying proportions.

Socially, the decline in the family unit will intensify the problems for many who will find themselves without a home and without a job. The far more closely knit family of the 1930s and the 1880s provided a cushion for many whose survival was assisted by friends and relatives. During the depression of the 1980s, the more introverted nature of society will mean that fewer friends and relatives can be counted upon to help.

People will turn to the government for help. If government was as powerful as people would like to believe, or as politicians would like us to believe, we would never have inflation, recession, or depression. It is likely that government itself will be unable to help much. Ironically, the very heavy pressure to 'take action' will in itself reduce the government's ability to function effectively. Washington and Whitehall could become two major battlegrounds for demonstrators and protestors of every description.

The major turning point in every depression involves the bursting of a speculative bubble. Historically, a speculative boom in the stock market, commodity markets, property markets, or anything else, was immediately followed by the 'bust', after which the forces of depression became all too obvious. The 'bust' phase probably poses the greatest threat to the largest number of people in the 1980s. Due to inflation and taxes, many people have put most of their savings into their homes. The decline in home prices has already begun. An extended decline will leave many with no assets at all. If they lose their jobs and cannot repay their mortgages, they will be homeless and destitute. More people in Britain now own their own homes than ever before. The irresponsible drive to provide credit for housing amongst lenders leaves the home owner with a high mortgage excessively vulnerable to a depression. With 60% of the homes in Britain owner-occupied, the effects could be catastrophic.

Individuals who face the implications and possibilities of the type of depression that I have described will be able to protect themselves from the disorder to come. Some may even profit by it. There are many who refuse to acknowledge the true nature of global economic developments, who will be content to believe what they wish to believe, who will cling to an unshakeable faith that a depression of the style of the 1930s can never happen again. Sadly, those individuals whose judgment is governed by complacency and unreason will suffer most, and provide the unpreparedness which is at the root of the self-perpetuating boom-bust cycle.

Chapter Seven

THE COMING PROPERTY CRASH . . .
A BUBBLE ABOUT TO BURST

Men at sometime are masters of their fates; The fault, dear Brutus, is not in our stars, but in ourselves, that we are underlings.
William Shakespeare, Julius Caesar

The lemmings are headed for the sea. They are on a stampede of mad unreason, determined to trample over anything or anyone in their path, intent on repeating the ritual of self-destruction passed down through their psyche over the ages. In Holland, during the 17th century, the human lemmings chose tulip bulbs as their vehicle for financial self-annihilation. In the 18th century, shares in the South Sea Company, the Mississippi Company and the Dutch East India Company were the self-destruct mechanisms. In the 19th century, cotton, wheat and railways carried financial holocaust. In the 1920s, it was American shares. During the 1980s, residential property is likely to be the grim reaper providing the mode of financial genocide.

Nothing is immune from becoming the subject of a speculative bubble. Intense speculation can break out in any country, in virtually anything. Silver, tobacco leaves, tulips, canary seed, pepper corns, salt, sea shells, orange juice, railroads, ships, gold, building land, commercial property and residential property, have all been the victims of frenzied speculation in the past. And just before they burst, practically all bubbles are accepted as safe and sound.

In retrospect, most people judge speculative booms as bordering on the ridiculous. Can you imagine a Dutchman being foolish enough to pay the equivalent of 100 acres of land for one tulip bulb? Sounds crazy, doesn't it? But that is hindsight. If you are to be objective in future decision-making, you must be acutely aware that when these bubbles were biggest they looked perfectly normal. No less 'normal' and 'respectable' than gold at $900 an ounce, or buying a home at today's grossly inflated prices.

Few people today would become enamoured with tulip bulbs, tobacco leaves, or canary seed as a safe place to keep money. Yet, most were readily able to justify and consider normal the over-extended prices of gold, silver and property not long ago. In early 1980, when gold was heading up to $1,000 an ounce, it was generally accepted that gold was undervalued. There were claims that it should be $2,000 or $3,000 an ounce. Some were predicting $5,000. At the time, it was inconceivable that gold could actually fall.

People soon discovered that its price could go down as well as up. It lost more than 50% in a few short months in early 1980, and continued to fall. The reasons why this could never happen, why gold was different, were not too hard to find. The financial pages were saturated with them. But gold collapsed, in spite of the multitude of so-called guidance to 'prove' it never could.

Could the same thing happen to residential property? Most people will answer 'No!' They will be no less emphatic than the many property operators who believed that commercial property could never fall in value before the collapse in 1973–1975.

Somehow, residential land, and the buildings on it, are looked upon as the one sure investment. Most people today have little doubt that their home will always hold its value. They feel that if there is a price decline, it will only be temporary. It is difficult to find anyone who is not totally convinced their property will protect them against inflation, the deterioration of currencies, and any political climate.

On the surface, these assumptions sound reasonable. Unfortunately, history shows that residential property has not always protected its owner against inflation. It has not been able to shelter its owner against political risk, and for long periods, it has been a very poor investment.

There have been times when the value of residential property has collapsed, and some property became unsaleable. The same factors which sent property tumbling in the past could easily happen again. You do not have to be a Rasputin of the ready-reckoner to work it out.

After a speculative bubble bursts, there is usually a decline of approximately 80% from the peak. It happened when commodity prices crashed in the 1920s. The Wall Street Crash involved a decline of almost 90%. When the London Stock Exchange crashed between 1972 and 1975, the Financial Times 30 Share Index lost 78%.

Residential property during the 1970s was far removed from merely being a home to live in. Homes became gambling tokens, and residential property took on all of the characteristics of historical speculative bubbles. Purchasing a property for its investment potential based on future assumption is speculation. As such, house prices are likely to respond to the same mechanisms as any other medium, once the 'bubble' stage has been reached. A fall of 80% from the peak would therefore not be inconceivable for houses in the future.

The History of Housing

Most people harbour the illusion that house prices in Britain only go up
. . . never down. A reporter in 'The Times' says, 'House prices always
move up, step by step, reaching a plateau, then moving higher'. This is
a total fallacy. Not only do house prices move up and down quite
vigorously, but in the past they have often fallen much faster than they
have risen, once the downwave gets underway.

A collapse in house prices is certainly not rare, or unusual. Crashes
in property values have been plundering speculators, property
developers and home owners for centuries. The reason falls in house
prices appear so elusive is due to the very long term cyclical nature of
property price movements. The peak and trough of the pattern of
property prices involves a span of 50 to 60 years. Actually, property
prices move in tandem with the long wave pattern of economic life to a
more exacting degree than any other capital market, with severe price
declines about once in every fifty years in different places around the
globe.

There is little evidence to reveal any significant decline in house
prices ever in Britain. This does not mean that such an event has not
occurred, or will not occur. House prices have only been documented
since the housing boom has got underway. In 1914, only one home in
ten was owner-occupied in Britain. Between seven and eight million
families rented their houses, or their bits of houses, from private
landlords. There was a strong revival in house building during the
1920s. Close to one million houses were built, most of them by private
speculative concerns. The more expensive homes cost about £2,000,
smaller ones as little as £600. At £600, an initial downpayment of £125
was required. It was considered that an exceptionally highly paid
worker, earning say £5 per week or more, was the only one who could
afford such a house. Individual home ownership played a comparatively small role in the British economy during the late 1920s. When the
National Government took office in 1931, less than one in five homes in
Britain was owner-occupied.

It is difficult to ascertain precisely how the Great Depression affected
house prices, although there is evidence that prices were falling. A
good deal of the fall in house prices during the 1930s can be attributed
to cheaper labour and raw materials. A third of the houses built in 1931
cost less than £600. By 1939, nearly half the houses cost less than £600.
Second-hand homes were £400 or £500. During the early 1930s, building
societies financed most of the sales. Owner-occupiers could obtain a
mortgage of 75% of the purchase price at 5% interest, repayable over 20
years. This meant a house of £500 would only require a cash deposit of
£125. With a struggle, many middle class and salaried people could
manage this, but not the average industrial worker or most clerical
workers.

It is likely that house sales were difficult during the 1930s, though speculative building was rife. Builders began moving down the social scale. They negotiated schemes with building societies where both would provide security. In return for a guarantee from the builder, the building society was able to advance not 75%, but 95% of the purchase price. The £500 house could be purchased with a deposit of only £25. These builders' pool arrangements enabled not only clerical workers, but also the better paid industrial workers, earning say, £4 a week, or more, to begin buying a home.

A home could cost as little as £480 in the mid-1930s, with a deposit of £24 plus 13s/6d. mortgage repayments over 20 years. Yet, the growth in home ownership remained lethargic. In the mid-1930s, two-thirds of the families in the country continued to rent from private landlords. As late as 1939, owner-occupiers were still in a minority. There were three million owner-occupiers, about one quarter of all families. Between 1939 and 1947, the figure grew to 3.36 million. It was not until 1953 that the boom really got underway. From 1953 to 1961 there was a jump from 4.02 million to 7.04 million, the biggest percentage rise in home ownership since the turn of the century.

It is difficult to determine the trend of house prices during the 'secondary prosperity' and the depression that followed. It is unlikely that there was a collapse in house prices, since there was never a boom to begin with. There is strong evidence to indicate that investment in housing is certainly not a one way street, as the 1930s show. Such evidence is sufficient at this stage.

If it is assumed that the price of land bears some relationship to the price of the houses on it, we can certainly see wild acrobatics in prices over the past century. E.A. Vallis in his paper 'Urban Land and Building Prices' published in the 'Estates Gazette', shows that the 1892–1895 price median is £130 per acre of residential land. This rises to almost £900 an acre by 1899. By 1904, the price had fallen back to £130 again, a decline of 85%, the usual fall after a speculative bubble bursts.

The upwave which began in the early 1900s saw residential land up to £875 per acre again by 1917. By 1922, it was back down to £250. Along with the sharp increase in home ownership between 1953 and 1969, there was a massive rise to £10,600 per acre in 1965–1969. That boom rivals any speculative bubble in history. The rise in residential land prices after 1969, which is incorporated in my study of house prices, would obviously make the increase even more substantial.

Residential land prices are fairly well documented, unlike actual house prices. The price of the house is unlikely to rise while the price of land falls. The 1930s clearly shows that the cost of housing was substantially reduced by cheaper labour and raw materials costs. If the price of residential land also falls dramatically, this too will enable builders to sell houses at lower prices.

E.A. Vallis shows that land prices and building prices run in fairly close parallel. Between 1905 and 1948, both were falling, with building prices actually falling faster than land. On an inflation adjusted basis, land prices turned in 1939. Building prices did not turn up until 1948, then both rose together in that explosive uptrend which many people believe will last forever. History suggests that there have been two distinct falls in British residential property prices. One was in the 1890s, and marked the collapse of a speculative bubble. Another was in the 1920s, and was not quite as severe. There is little reason to believe that the buildings on this land resist the type of collapse which has plagued land speculators over the decades.

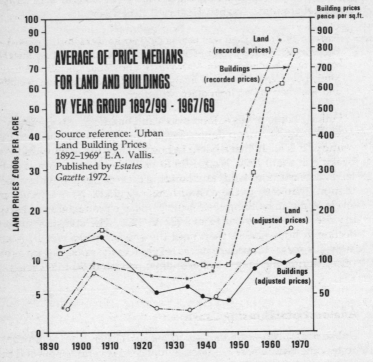

Figure 12   Average of Price Medians for Land and Buildings by Year Group 1892/99–1967/69

The dangers in residential property in the 1890s are hinted at in Noreen Branson's historical account of the 1920s, entitled 'Britain in the Nineteen Twenties':

The great housing boom at the turn of the century had been one of houses built for investment purposes. They had proved an attraction to the smaller investors such as retiring tradesmen, who had felt their savings would be safer in bricks and mortar than in less tangible stocks and shares. The boom has come to an end because it was often said Lloyd George's People's Budget of 1909–1910 had frightened the small investor away from land and property.

There was a strong recovery in residential land and in building costs after World War I. Christopher Addison, Minister of Health, ordered local authorities to build unlimited houses, and to let them at controlled rents equivalent to the 1914 level. The government automatically met, by subsidy, any cost over 1d. local rate. The way the 1920–1922 recession depressed the housing market is revealed in A.J.P. Taylor's historical account, 'English History – 1914–1945'.

Early in 1921, Addison was paying £910 for houses which a year or so later could be built at a cost of £385 each. There was an outcry against this waste of public money. In March 1921 Christopher Addison left the Ministry of Health. For a few months he was minister without portfolio and was then driven from office altogether.

Linking home prices to land prices and building costs generally, the records suggest a deep depression in house prices at the turn of the century. It is likely that a boom in house prices followed World War I, peaking in about 1920. From 1920 to 1922, the combination of a sharp fall in construction, land, and building materials costs, with a decline of more than 50% in the cost of housing, would have affected price levels. A rise in building costs is likely to have produced a corresponding rise in house prices from 1922 to 1926. The statistics suggest a decline in house prices then until the end of World War II. Accordingly, it appears that house prices respond to the same pattern as other prices during the long wave economic pattern of 50 to 60 years.

Anatomy of a Housing Crash

Unlike Britain, home ownership in the U.S.A. has been significant for quite some time. There has been evidence of several booms and busts in house prices over the past few hundred years. There are four distinct periods where American housing prices rose to fantastic heights, during the 1830s, 1880s, 1920s and 1970s. Each upsurge looked the same as the others, and the same as the house boom in Britain. So far, three out of the four have collapsed, with declines of up to 50% in value according to John Wesley English in his book 'The Coming Real Estate Crash'. The exception is the boom which ended in the 1970s. This 'crash' is yet to come, says English.

The collapse in property prices in Florida around 1926 serves as a perfect object lesson, and was compressed into a relatively short time period.

The period 1920–1922 saw the U.S. in the grip of recession along with Britain and the rest of the industrialised world. Late in 1921, the recession eased, and funds from sophisticated investors began flowing into Florida. Property developers decided that Florida was the land of opportunity. Soon, large property combines from the northern states began promoting the sale of Florida home land aggressively. In 1924, the strategy was starting to bear fruit. The U.S. economy was recovering, and disposable income was rising rapidly. It was the 'roaring twenties', and the good old illusion of bricks and mortar was quick to capture the limited imagination of the nouveau riche and the middle class. By 1925, the Florida land boom was running full force, fuelled by a widely promoted view that Florida was the most desirable state in the union, and the common notion that property prices could only go up, never down. It was the same old story.

Greed was undeflected by thought, a tendency not uncommon among bankers and mortgage lenders. The seemingly rock solid security of Florida land whetted the appetites of bankers. The Florida home buyer merely had to put down 10% of the purchase price, and watch his deposit propelled into the stratosphere. Immense paper fortunes were made quickly by people who never intended to live in the property they were purchasing. As long as property values continued to rise, profits could be compounded for virtually nothing, given relatively low interest rates.

A man or woman arriving in Florida with $1,000, could buy a home for $10,000, and sell it the next week for $15,000. That would mean a return of $3,500 on the initial $1,000, after the real estate agent's commission of 5%. With $3,500 in hand, the newly self-styled property magnate could buy a $35,000 property, and perhaps sell at $60,000 a week later.

Prices were spectacular. People were making profits beyond the dreams of avarice. John Wesley English refers to the city records of Miami. These showed that a plot of land which changed hands in 1914 for $1,500 was sold in 1926 for $1,500,000.

The mania for property in Florida prevailed throughout 1925 and 1926. Like many manias that came before, the price spiral took an explosive curve which usually signals the end of any speculative boom. During the final fateful days, it seemed as if people were willing to pay practically any price for a foothold in Florida, without the slightest consideration for value. Those who held back were thought ignorant.

At the peak of the frenzy in the late summer of 1925, the boom suddenly began to falter. Most people either never noticed, or refused to take heed. By early 1926, prices were marginally higher than in the summer of 1925, and some did notice that property was not selling so quickly. Prices continued to edge higher, but there was a distinct slow-down, and worry began to spread. In order to forestall panic, the U.S. government described the slow-down as a 'healthy breathing space' which would permit the boom to continue for many years to come.

During the summer of 1926, there was a proliferation of surveys and reports from mortgage lending institutions and so-called experts on Florida land. The nearly universal opinion was 'property was sound and the boom would last four or five years more'. As late as 1926, with property prices easing after two hurricanes had battered the State of Florida, the Wall Street Journal, America's principal financial newspaper, stubbornly insisted that the boom would continue. It did not.

By the autumn of 1926, the property crash in Florida should have been obvious to anyone who cared to look realistically. People with mortgages were defaulting in increasing numbers. In several cases plots of land with unfinished buildings found their way back to the original developers. In many cases, the accumulated taxes and property assessments amounted to more cash than was generated by the original sales. Practically everyone who had any property in Florida was wiped out unless they acted fairly quickly after the price peak of 1926. Many banks failed, and 26 Florida municipalities went into default.

After the collapse of the Florida boom, investment in property lost its lustre. The illusion of 'good old bricks and mortar' was broken. It would be difficult to convince anyone who had purchased property in Florida around 1925 that 'property prices could only rise . . . never fall'.

It was several decades before property prices in Florida returned to 1925 levels. During the early 1960s, prices were still well below the 1925 peak. Those who had decided not to sell during the crash, preferring to wait for the next boom, were still waiting . . . 35 years later.

The Post-War Housing Bubble

The average home in Britain was valued at £25,000 during the first quarter of 1982. This is by far the most valuable possession for most people. Britons consider their homes much more than just a place to live. The home has become a store of value, a medium for saving, the financial bulwark for the average man. Most people in Britain today are deeply concerned with house prices.

The best news most people can hear is that house prices will go on up for ever. Vested-interests in the property industry prey on this tendency, and estate agents, mortgage lenders, bankers, and the press all encourage it.

Day-dreaming has always been preferable to thinking amongst the masses. With shares, diamonds, gold or stamps, only a modicum of harm is done. A home, a necessity of life, bought on borrowed money, requires considerably more careful consideration.

The end of World War II called the turn for the post-war housing bubble in Britain. Just after the war, house prices were understandably depressed. Adjusted for inflation, prices were as low as they had been in 1919 or 1895. In the post-war reconstruction period, the baby-boom years of the upwave were just getting underway and the housing supply lagged behind demand. Prices began to rise.

Some economists say that prices never rise, the value of money just falls. This was clearly the case immediately after the war, when the pound was hopelessly over-valued against the dollar at $4.80. A series of devaluations followed, accompanied by a steady rise in the retail price index. By 1960, Britons could look back on 25 years of uninterrupted inflation dating from the mid-1930s slump. For the first time in British recorded history, every single year had produced an increase in the retail price index. Inflation was deemed here to stay, and soon the rise in house prices was linked to the prospects of a perennial rise in the rate of inflation. Between the 1940s and the 1960s, house prices had their fluctuations, but most believed that the peaks and troughs were always rising, faster in fact than other prices. The myth of inflation linked to house prices was born.

During the early 1970s, demand for new housing began to decline. The construction industry was in a recession, and the number of new houses being built slowed markedly. Yet, the rise in consumer prices accelerated in line with a less than frugal government spending policy. House prices were enjoying their fastest growth ever, rising at an annualised rate of 14% a year, a rate which would double the price in less than five years, multiplying it tenfold in 18 years.

By the early 1970s, most individuals felt it was foolish not to own a house, maybe even insane, since cheap mortgages were a-plenty, while mortgage interest rate payments were deductible from tax. Of course, interest rates were no longer 5% or so, as they had been in the 1950s. But even in 1974, the 11% mortgage rate cost only 7½% after tax. It was generally believed that house prices would rise faster than inflation. The retail price index was heading for a 38% leap in 1975. Buying a house at a cost of 7½% after tax looked a sure-fire winner at the time.

The principal mortgage lending agencies in the U.K., the building societies, competed to satisfy the seemingly endless thirst for mortgage finance. They are in business to lend, after all. Loans for house purchases were rising even faster than house prices during the 1970s. Although the rise in house prices was dramatic, it was nothing compared to the rise in house purchase finance. In the decade to 1979,

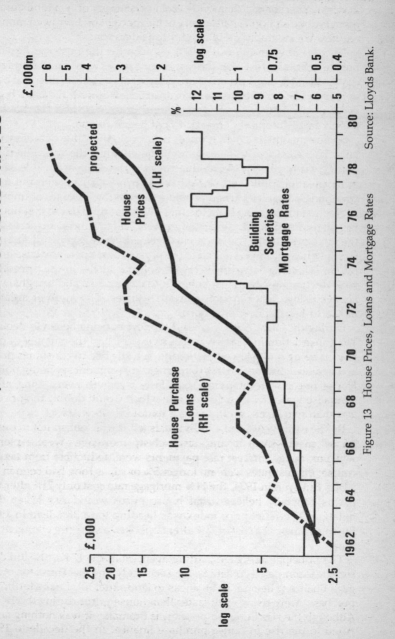

HOUSE PRICES, LOANS and MORTGAGE RATES

Figure 13   House Prices, Loans and Mortgage Rates

Source: Lloyds Bank.

annual building society advances rose nearly sevenfold to £6bn. During the 17 years from 1962 to 1979, building society advances had grown 15-fold. Their share of British residents' savings advanced from 20% to 41%. The house boom faltered briefly during the recession of 1972–1974 as the downwave began. During the latter part of the secondary prosperity of the 1970s, house prices made up for lost time. The two years, 1978 and 1979, brought an average increase of 60%, the type of explosive upward drive that usually precedes the bursting of a speculative bubble.

The manner in which building society advances have outpaced the growth in house prices gives ample reason for concern over the future of house prices. There is another factor. Between 1976 and 1980, the mortgage rate advanced from 11% to 15%, while the rate of inflation dipped as low as 8%. The equation favouring house buying when the after tax mortgage is $7\frac{1}{2}$%, and inflation is 28% is vastly changed when inflation is 8% and the cost of buying a home is 14% after tax.

A nominal 15% mortgage rate works out at a real actuarial rate of 16.3%. With local rates, water rates, insurance and repairs adding another $2\frac{1}{2}$%, the part of a house which is mortgaged is costing the owner nearly 19% before tax. This would work out at about 14% on borrowed capital after deducting tax at the standard rate.

Look at precisely how much it is costing the average individual to own his own home. In 1980, average house prices were about £25,000. Assuming the typical mortgage on a £25,000 house is £15,000, interest payments at 16.3% work out at £2,445 per annum. Rates add a further £625 and we must add the opportunity cost, the investment return which could be achieved safely on the £10,000 deposit locked into the house. Since 1980, a conservative 13% could have been earned in short-dated government securities, adding a further £1,300 to the cost of owning a home.

The total cost of a £25,000 house is therefore £4,370 per annum, before an additional £600 per annum capital repayment on the mortgage. The average income in mid-1980 was about £6,000 before tax and social security payments. There is a message in this equation. That message is that a great number of people will be unable to continue making mortgage repayments as the recession bites deeper into incomes, and the number who may consider buying their own homes will dwindle when they start adding up the costs.

This phenomenon is certainly not peculiar to Britain. William Baldwin, in 'Forbes Magazine' on housing in 1981 says, 'Given today's interest rates, less than 10% of American families can afford to carry a mortgage big enough to swing a median-priced new home. That translates into millions of young families suddenly – and, as far as they can tell, undeservedly – being forced to give up the dream, hang on somewhere as renters or double up with in-laws. An industry that finds 90% of its prospective customers priced out of the market is not a business but a disaster. When that industry customarily occupies 4% of the nation's economy, the disaster area is nationwide.'

Individuals with a mortgage tend to object to this sort of analysis. They say, 'Yes, but my mortgage rate and tax rate will come down'. They forget that mortgage rates and tax rates have spent more time going up than going down. They also ignore the fact that 'real' incomes are likely to come down if mortgage rates and tax rates come down. Individuals are extremely reluctant to make a serious effort to calculate the real cost. There is very little popular understanding of the real cost of home ownership. Resistance to reality is one of the standard components of a speculative bubble.

I have discussed the cost of home buying to the individual. What about the cost to the nation of billions of pounds tied up in residential property? The life-blood of industry is capital. The principal source of capital has always been long term savings. When these savings are lying dormant in property, industry must pay more for funds. If the borrowing cost cannot be passed on in rising prices, then industry is strangled. The massive increase in savings used for home ownership prompted an article in The Economist (17/11/79) entitled 'Feathering their nests – The British are stuffing too much money into house-buying and too little into industry'.

A government publication in 1979 stated that houses made up 40% of total personal wealth in Britain, against 19% in 1960. In other words, the combined value of private industry, commerce, service, agriculture, personal savings in banks and building societies, life insurance and the national debt comes to just $1\frac{1}{2}$ times the value of 54% of the nation's housing stock. There should be little doubt that house buying has reached an unmaintainable extreme in Britain and elsewhere.

Most will object to categorising house prices as part of a speculative boom. Yet, for all its respectability, the house buying spree has every characteristic of a speculative orgy. A speculative orgy begins with a 'displacement'. In the case of house buying, the 'displacement' was the depression in house prices during the 1930s and immediately following World War II, compounded by the series of devaluations in the pound.

Another aspect of a speculative orgy is the way it is fuelled by credit. Credit expansion for house buying has grown faster than house prices themselves. Credit has been freely available at rates enhanced by tax legislation. Before the 'bubble' bursts, we normally see emotional buying. The house buying during the 1950s was rational enough to start with, and perhaps only a little less rational during the 1960s. In the 1970s, many have been buying the most expensive property they could afford on borrowings. The most impecuniary individuals now own their own homes. They have been given 100% mortgages. Some building societies have advanced 'non-status' mortgages. As long as the deposit could be found, people on the dole queue have now been able to purchase their own home.

Any objective individual with a knowledge of finance will recognise the elements of a speculative orgy, and be frightened by the extent of borrowing to purchase homes. A speculative bubble bursts when the pinnacle of confidence has been achieved. The British market for residential property is now ruled by unquestioned confidence . . . who is left to be converted? If the answer is no-one, then the peak of confidence has been reached. History warns that the counterpart of a peak in confidence is high risk, probably peak risk. But, the peaks of confidence can only be perceived by hindsight.

The house price boom began to fade in 1979. Prices at the top end of the market in Central London, and in medium priced homes elsewhere were the first to suffer, offering what estate agents claim are 'exceptional buying opportunities ahead of the inevitable upswing'. Confidence in the housing market continues to reign supreme. Since 1979, house prices have been falling in Britain in 'real' terms. In other words, they have been lagging behind the rate of inflation. And they have been falling in absolute terms in many classes of the market.

There was a similar pattern at the beginning of the downwave. In 1973, in spite of the fall in prices in general, confidence was also unquestioned. So much greater was the extreme optimism in 1979, that individuals were prepared to pay twice 1973 prices.

The fourth quarter of 1979 marked the end of the secondary prosperity, and the beginning of a recession which I believe will plunge Britain and the rest of the world in deep depression and a further extension of the downwave, bringing a calamitous decline in house prices. During the secondary prosperity wages were growing rapidly in real terms, while real interest rates were low. This has all changed. Real wages are now declining, and real interest rates are excruciatingly high and getting higher. If the mortgage rate is 15%, and the rate of inflation is 20%, reflected in the growth of property values, you have made a profit on that money. If the mortgage rate is 10%, and inflation is 5%, reflected in the growth of property values, you have lost 5% on that borrowed money. This is the equation property owners are faced with while property values grow more slowly than inflation. Even if mortgage rates fall, there is little benefit to the house owner, other than lower repayments.

Risk in the U.K. housing market is currently very high, while potential reward is extremely low. The best working hypothesis is that the rewards are negative when set against the cost of credit. The cost of owning a home in Britain has never been higher. On the basis of average wages, that cost is prohibitive. Moreover, the process of home ownership has little room for expansion, given the current level of home ownership compared to the number of people who are willing or able to meet the existing level of mortgage repayments in Britain. It is now probably not worth borrowing to buy property in Britain, even with the tax advantages. It is certainly much less attractive than at any time in the last 35 years. Taking out a mortgage to buy a home could be an extremely serious and costly error. The conclusion is unpalatable: house buying is the speculative orgy of the long upwave that began about 35 years ago, faltered, but was revived during the secondary prosperity that is now ending. The bubble is about to burst. I do not know precisely what will burst it, but it will burst without warning.

The Crash That Won't Look Life A Crash

In January 1979, I told listeners to my LBC broadcasts that a recession would begin during the fourth quarter of 1979, and would ultimately lead to a depression similar to the 1930s. I also stated that a decline in property prices would lead to a crash in residential property prices. At the time, my forecasts were treated with scepticism. My views on residential property were considered absurd.

In March 1980, I restated them in a broadcast over Capital Radio. Again, I claimed that a collapse in residential property prices was imminent. An enormous controversy developed. It was generally agreed that my forecasts were irresponsible, and a severe fall in house prices could not possibly occur. As a result of my forecast, nearly two years elapsed before I was invited to speak on Capital Radio again.

At the beginning of 1981, the vested interest cartels in residential housing were engaged in a massive campaign to encourage people to buy houses, claiming there would be a spring rush for mortgage money and house prices would move steadily higher. At the time there were only faint rumblings among statisticians to suggest that house prices, although rising, were not keeping pace with inflation. Over the previous year, house prices had advanced by a mere 6 per cent, well below the rate of inflation. By mid-year, the rumblings were more than faint. There was no spring rush for mortgages. There was no spurt in house prices. A survey by the National House Builders Federation, showed that the number of companies reporting a fall in demand or no change had increased from 64.3 per cent to 86.5 per cent. 'Overall lack of purchaser confidence' was the most frequently quoted influence on demand for private houses.

By July 1981, there was further evidence that house prices were lagging behind the rate of inflation. That meant prices were falling in real terms. Figures compiled by the Abbey National Building Society to June 1981 revealed the average house price in Britain was just over £25,600, an increase of 2.8% during the second quarter of the year. The annualised increase was thus 11.2%, indicating house prices were falling in real terms (adjusted for inflation) by 2.8%. The year-over-year rise in house prices stood at 9.4%, an annual negative return of 4.6%. Money tied up in houses was depreciating faster than cash.

By September 1981, house prices were no longer falling in inflation adjusted terms alone. House prices were falling in absolute terms. Two surveys of house prices, The Times/Halifax and the Royal Institute of Chartered Surveyors, reported a static market at best, and falling prices at worst. The report from the Royal Institute of Chartered Surveyors, showed that for the fifth consecutive month, there were no price increases in 75% of all deals. More than a third of the estate agents in the survey reported falls.

By October 1981, house prices were virtually at a standstill, and falls were reported to be accelerating in certain areas. Property prices had risen by a meagre 2 per cent on the previous year, the smallest rise for 20 years. Tim Melville-Ross, assistant general manager of the Nationwide Building Society, said: 'Up to around £40,000, people are shopping around for good value. 'Beyond £100,000 buyers are not much affected by the recession. But, in between, and in the £50,000–£75,000 range, there are some pretty hefty reductions.'

In October 1981 the Nationwide Building Society said that during the preceding three months house prices had risen by 2 per cent in the East Midlands, but were static in Yorkshire, the South East, Wales, the West Midlands, the North and Scotland. Prices were falling in East Anglia, the South West, the North West and Northern Ireland.

In the year to November 1981, price rises were only 1 per cent. The evidence to indicate the unthinkable is now happening is overwhelming.

There is more money tied up in residential property than in any other single physical asset. Accordingly, more vested interests dominate the residential property market than any other market. The information you are likely to receive and the views which are widely expressed will almost invariably favour those vested interests, not necessarily yours. The biggest vested interest of all is, of course, government. The 60 per cent of the British who now own their own homes are a very powerful political force. Any government ruling over a period when property prices collapse will not stand much chance at any subsequent general election.

If you were an investor in the stock market in 1974, you might have said, 'I bought Grand Met at 300, and it's now fallen to 60'. Can you imagine a dinner party where one of the guests proclaims, 'I paid seventy thousand for my house. Now it is worth fifteen thousand'? Or worse yet, 'I've owned this house for seven years, and the bank is coming to take it away on Monday'? If that came to pass, all the banks and building societies are likely to have been wiped out. Theoretically, that could happen.

The residential property bubble has burst, and we can and will have a crash in values; it's unthinkable, but possible, like a nuclear war. The political implications, however, may appear as a flaw in the thesis.

Essentially, my firm prediction of the collapse in residential property values relies on the hypothesis that the crash will not look like a crash. So, what are we going to have? To start with, we'll see the end of the idea that a home is a good hedge against inflation. For a time, house prices will continue to fluctuate. All along, the trend will be continually below the rate of inflation, even though it will look as if values are moving higher. Temporarily.

Once each month, The Times publishes an index of average house prices in conjunction with the Halifax Building Society. The degree to which this reflects the price of homes in general is suspect. In the past, there were severe pressures on homes selling at £50,000 and above,

Figure 14   The Times/*Halifax House Price Index*

The Times/Halifax house price index

Monthly index average of second-hand houses (seasonally adjusted)

| | Index | Average price | % change – over the preceding | | |
			1 year	6 months	3 months
1977 December	100.0	14,757			
1978 December	121.1	17,868	21.2	10.7	2.4
1979 December	151.0	22,291	24.8	9.6	3.8
1980 December	166.2	24,523	10.0	1.3	0.2
1981 January	167.7	24,752	8.9	2.4	0.8
April	170.5	25,164	7.5	1.5	1.7
July	167.9	24,779	2.5	0.1	-1.5
October	159.7	23,562	-4.1	-6.4	-4.9
1982 January	163.1	24,072	-3.7	-2.1	2.4
February	162.6	23,999	-5.6	-1.2	1.4
March	165.2	24,382	-4.1	1.7	-0.5
April	169.1	24,949	-1.6	+6.1	+3.6

Average regional price of second-hand houses (not seasonally adjusted)

| | Average price £ | % change over preceding | |
		Year	3 months
North	19,075	-1.6	+6.9
Yorkshire/Humberside	18,631	+1.1	+14.9
North-west	20,597	-2.7	+0.8
East Midlands	19,890	-1.0	+5.7
West Midlands	22,226	-5.3	-2.5
East Anglia	24,614	+2.0	+8.5
Wales	20,161	+0.2	+3.7
South-west	26,403	-3.0	+4.2
South-east	34,490	+3.3	+4.3
Greater London	33,974	+0.2	+1.0
Northern Ireland	20,284	-7.6	+1.7
Scotland	22,999	+0.5	+9.5

while cheaper homes were rising strongly. It is therefore unlikely that the average person is going to have an idea of how the price of his house is performing from the indices that are available. At the earlier stages of the decline, most people will blithely assume this decline does not affect their particular home, and will not be unduly alarmed. As prices fall, many who had intended to sell investment properties will withdraw from the market, preferring to rent them out in anticipation of a more buoyant market later. A market for rented accommodation will appear. This will exert downward pressure on an already faltering residential property market. As the market for rented accommodation increases, there will be competition and downward pressure on rents. This will mean the gap between the interest on a mortgage and the rent on the capital value of a property will widen. It will become far cheaper to rent property than to rent money. This will further depress the values of residential property, adding to the self-feeding downward spiral.

As residential property continues its long slide, there will be many minor ripples. Prices will certainly not fall in a straight line until we approach the end of the property crash. After a speculative bubble bursts, there are many upward moves to trap the unwary.

Initially, many will see declining property values as a fleeting opportunity to buy at a slightly lower price. Estate agents will seize the opportunity, selling 'last chance' concepts . . . 'get in quick before property prices start soaring again'. Investors in commodities and the stock market often quote the adage, 'A rising market climbs a wall of worry. A falling market flows down a river of hope'. This means that after a market has had a long fall and begins to rise, investors mistrust the rise, remembering the many deceptive rises while the market was falling. After a time, the 'wall of worry' abates, and investors begin to think prices will rise forever. When the market suddenly falls, the psychology is reversed. Hope springs eternal at the early stages of a falling market, and each minor flip-up is considered to promise the next massive rise. Each dip in property prices will be classified as a 'healthy breathing spell' by most. Each rise will be hailed as beginning the next boom.

A complete liquidation of all property debt in Britain would wipe out consumer debt in its entirety, leaving enough spare change to cancel all of the national debt, in addition to funding the Public Sector Borrowing Requirement. Because of the enormous participation in the house buying boom over the past few decades, millions of Britons will be affected as they gradually become aware that property prices have been steadily falling. Eventually they will think that house prices may not start rising again for quite some time. Many will begin to doubt that property prices will 'always go up', and will become deeply concerned.

Lenders will place more restrictions on lending. House builders may try to hold their stocks of unsold houses, but most will be forced to sell at distressed prices to meet overdue construction loans. With professional property speculators adding to the supply of houses, and private individuals and lending institutions restricting demand, the fall in prices will increase in severity. The trend will not be easily reversed. Minor recoveries will become more brief, gains more modest. The declines will be sharper and longer.

The sense of urgency to buy a home will virtually vanish from residential property. As the secondary depression bites deeper, other necessities of life will take priority over owning a home. Rented accommodation will be plentiful by then. Investors in property will have no choice but to rent, since buyers will be a rare breed. There will be a steady increase in the supply of houses, but sales will be scarce. Losses on property will be making the headlines. Building and construction companies will be going bankrupt. Mortgage funds will have become virtually non-existent, so severe will be the struggle for survival among mortgage lenders heavily burdened by defaulters.

By 1987, there will be no real residential housing market in Britain for the owner-occupier. Some houses will be unsaleable at any price. This has been so during depressions in housing throughout history. In America, from 1931 to 1934, many people were abandoning their homes, unable to keep up the mortgage payments, crowding together in small ghettoes and slums. Although 75% of the working population in America was employed at the time, the 25% unemployed were sufficient to collapse the residential housing market. Those with jobs were certainly not prepared to risk their savings by purchasing a home or changing homes.

During the 1930s, the residential property market involved only sellers, no buyers.

The crash in house prices I envisage is all part of a scenario leading Britain into a 1930s style depression. As we enter the acute financial panic stage of the secondary depression, we are confronted with the forced sale and liquidation of financial assets, including houses. House buying has been the bubble of our recent prosperity. When a 'bubble' bursts, the average fall is 80 per cent from the peak.

In the period immediately ahead, property prices will continue to fluctuate and the severity of the decline will go unnoticed. For six or seven months, prices may decline. They may then rise for a few months. People will jump to the conclusion that the decline is over. They will buy. Then prices will begin falling again for another six or seven months, taking the index to a new low. Suddenly, there will be a revival, and prices will rise for three or four months. Once again people will rush in to buy. Prices will then begin to fall once more. This could well continue for 5 to 10 years. At the terminal stage of the decline, perhaps after values have fallen by 30 to 40 per cent, there will be an almighty flush-out, with values falling as much as, or more than, in the first 10 years. It is my forecast that house prices could decline by as much as 80 per cent over the next 10 to 15 years. I expect half of that decline to take place over the next 5 to 10 years. The balance of the decline is likely to occur over a relatively brief period of 3 to 5 years, possibly as little as 12 to 18 months.

Chapter Eight

FACTORIES, FARMS, SHOPS AND OTHER TEARFUL TUNES

Oh, the farmer is the man, the farmer is the man
Lives on credit till the fall.
With the interest rate so high
It's a wonder he don't die
For the mortgage man's the one
That get's it all.

Populist song, 1896

An Englishman's home is his castle. The great American dream is personal home ownership. These are the popular clichés. Long ago it was said religion is the opiate of the masses. Today it is house prices. What price can be put on a dream? There is no limit. Those in the business of selling houses or encouraging people to take out a mortgage can always find justification for predicting that prices will rise in perpetuity. People in the home business very badly want to convince themselves that prices are going to rise. They do just that. They convince themselves very badly.

While an excursion into the wide-screen, vista-vision, technicolour fantasy of owning your home will mean many people will be prepared to pay a totally unrealistic price for the two up, two down, all mod. con. in Clapham, far more stringent criteria affect the value of commercial property. Ultimately the price of a factory, farm or shop is related to the potential profitability of the business using that property. This holds true for a greengrocer, farmer, widget manufacturer or porn merchant. The house price boom is relatively new in Britain. By contrast, crashes in commercial property have been going on for quite some time, and are well documented. Britain recently experienced one of these crashes in 1974 and 1975.

What causes a crash? What bursts the bubble? 'Prices got too high', sings the chorus, after the siren's song has been sung. The answer is correct, but tells you nothing. The most important aspect is, 'How high is too high?' It is extremely difficult to value a dream. That would be necessary with residential property. In commercial property, values are more readily quantifiable.

The Growth Assumption

As prices for commercial property rise, growth assumptions are established for the businesses which occupy the properties. Once that assumption has become the norm, a further assumption is made that the established growth pattern will continue into the future indefinitely. As an increasing number of investors accept this, prices will rise. Where there are growth assumptions, investors will buy because they anticipate price increases. The effect of this anticipation on prices is known as a premium. A premium is the increase in price caused by an assumed increase in growth. The greater the assumption of growth, the greater the price premium.

Here is how it works in real business. Suppose you have money to invest, and you want a 14% return. Further suppose that you believe in bricks and mortar. When you invest your money, the return will either come as immediate income, or growth in the value of your investment, or a combination of the two.

The estimate of potential growth will be a very large factor in the price for property. Thanks to successive governments who have taxed income into oblivion, while using inflation to penalise anyone investing for a fixed income, most investment considerations are now based on growth. In the market at large, even a modest growth assumption will produce a premium and amplify the price significantly.

Imagine you have the opportunity to invest in a franchise for McDonald's Hamburgers. Assume that the shop you intend to occupy was previously a Wimpy Bar, in a good location, on a busy street corner, and has made a reliable annual profit of £7,000 for quite some time. If we assume that there is unlikely to be any increase in the value of the property, given the current state of the hamburger business, we would pay no more than £50,000 for that site, because the income of £7,000 would represent the whole of the 14% return we are seeking. If you paid more than £50,000, you would earn less than 14%.

On the other hand, suppose the hamburger business is growing, and site values have been rising by 5% per annum. If we assumed a 5% growth in the value of the site, we can then pay as much as £80,000 for it. Although the £7,000 income from the hamburger business is going to be under 9%, the additional 5% growth will bring us back up to 14%. We also have a tax advantage, since tax will only be payable on the 9% profit. There will be no tax on the growth in the value of the site until it is sold.

The effects of such a small growth assumption should astound you. Assuming only a 5% growth, the value of the hamburger premises will have jumped by 60%. Consider the effect of 10% growth or 20%. The mathematics are staggering. The phenomenon is a product of inflation. During periods of rapidly rising prices, growth assumptions have been putting steady pressure on the property price accelerator.

However, the future is uncertain and an assumption is nothing more than an assumption. It is generally assumed that inflation will continue indefinitely. This is incorrect. As the long wave pattern of economic life demonstrates, inflation will continue for 20 to 30 years, sometimes longer, but then we have deflation, and assumptions change.

In the hamburger bar illustration, the assumption that business will grow has produced a premium in the price of the business. The £7,000 income would have justified a £50,000 price for the site. Growth of 5% per annum meant a premium of £30,000. If the assumption of 5% growth is correct, next year you can sell, take your £7,000 income and your 5% growth, realising a 14% return on the £80,000. If you can find a buyer who assumes 10% growth ahead you will make even more.

Naturally, there are two sides to every coin. Suppose that when you decide to sell, you cannot find a buyer who will assume 5% growth. Suppose growth in hamburgers has reached saturation, yet average returns on investment remain about 14%. Then you are only going to get what the income from the business justifies. The profit is £7,000 per annum. The expected return is 14%. All you will get for the hamburger business is £50,000, although it cost you £80,000. You will have written off that profit of £7,000 that you paid income tax on. You would have also lost a further £23,000. A pretty expensive exercise simply because there was a change in the growth projection. The hamburger business still churns out hamburgers, the profits are still £7,000 per annum. It is not unreasonable to expect to receive what you actually paid for the business. But if growth assumptions contract even slightly, changes in prices are dramatic.

Leave hypothetical assumption, and look at current facts and figures. Over the past decade we have seen growth projections based on an inflation rate as high as 26%, and as low as 8%. Currently, people think inflation will continue to fall, and so will growth assumptions. Commercial property in Britain today is faced with contracting growth assumptions. If investors expect commercial property prices to rise at a slightly slower rate than they have been, capital values will come tumbling down significantly. The effects on commercial property prices in that period of negative growth projections, characteristic of a secondary depression, will be catastrophic.

The Farmers' Dilemma

Dr. Raymond Wheeler of the University of Kansas invested 20 years and a staff of over two hundred to compile detailed charts covering 3,000 years of world weather, correlated with the exact dates of significant events in recorded history. With nearly 2,000,000 data entries, supplemented by maps and charts, Wheeler concluded that man behaves differently, but predictably, according to climatic shifts. The Earth's climate shifts from Warm-Wet phases to Warm-Dry phases, then from Cold-Wet to Cold-Dry phases, and back again in a continual circle. Significant economic events in history coincided with different climatic phases. The worst depressions appear during the Cold-Dry weather. The 'Drought Clock' indicates the world is entering a Cold-Dry phase. According to Wheeler, the drop in temperature will be accompanied by long, severe droughts, with a serious effect on world food production. Wheeler says that one third of the last 25 years of this century will involve severely cold and dry periods.

The growing season began to shorten in late 1974 in the U.S. An early September frost destroyed millions of dollars worth of maturing corn in the Mid-Western United States. Once the cold phase has stabilised in the coming years, frost in June and August can be expected in the world's corn belt. Early and late frosts will become a serious menace in southerly areas. Winters could become severe enough to cause serious problems for cattle and sheep raisers in the Northern Hemisphere. Blizzards will be much more common than for fifty years or more. Severe lengthy droughts and famines will strike worldwide.

According to Wheeler, the world should now be preparing for long shortages in water supplies and for shorter, not longer, growing seasons. Colder weather and longer droughts will bring a scarcity of food for the prosperous nations, famine and starvation for the less economically stable.

Along with the fall in temperature, there will be a serious decline in rainfall. This has happened consistently during the 100-year cycle on the 'Drought Clock', 26 times since the days of Ancient Greece. Each of those long term drops in temperature and rainfall can be seen in the sequoia tree-ring curves, the longest of which goes back to 350 B.C. In the fifth century, near the fall of the Roman Empire, world rainfall was so low that sequoias grew very slowly for decades. The Caspian Sea in Asia sank forty-five feet below its present level.

Wheeler contends that droughts and frost will influence the world economy, which he claims is linked to the weather cycle. The current climatic period is inevitably characterised by a succession of rapidly occurring and troublesome depressions.. Prosperity as we have known it is due to decline for an extended period. 'Times may have changed from the earlier terminations of 500-year cycles,' says Wheeler, 'but the laws of nature have not'. According to the weather cycle, the next era of prosperity is not expected to develop until around 1995.

Wheeler's findings seem to conform to the long wave pattern of economic life, even though his findings are the result of considerable non-economic data. There is little evidence in Wheeler's writing that he was aware of, or concerned with, the economic findings of Schumpeter, Kondratieff, Juglar, or Kitchin.

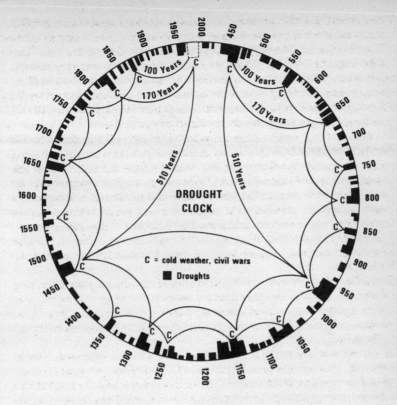

Figure 15   Dr. Raymond Wheeler's Drought Clock

The exact conditions Wheeler describes for the 1980s were experienced by American farmers in the 1930s in America's Mid-Western States. The great 'Dust Bowl of Oklahoma' gave farmers a double depression in that area.

> They were not farm men any more, but migrant men. And the thought, the planning, the long staring silence that had gone out to the fields, went now to the roads, to the distance, to the West. That man whose mind had been bound with acres lived with narrow concrete miles. And his thought and his worry were not any more with rainfall, with wind and dust, with the thirst of the crops.
>
> *The Grapes of Wrath, John Steinbeck, 1939*

Whether economic depressions bring steep contractions in farm production, or disastrous falls in farm output from adverse weather conditions lie at the root of cyclical depressions, is debatable. Obviously each affects the other. Like all commodities, agricultural land prices have been subject to widely swinging price trends, in sequence with our long term patterns of economic life.

Peter Aston, in his book, 'Farm Business Management and Land Ownership' (1979), notes the regular pattern of approximately 50 years up followed by 50 years down in what he defines as the 'Land Price: Money Value Ratio'.

Aston constructs a table of agricultural land prices back to 1770, in which can be seen the same rhythmic periodicity as the long wave pattern. In 1770, we find a low point in the price cycle, with agricultural land selling at £22.00 per acre. There is a high point in 1810 at £36.00 per acre, and another low, 55 years after the previous low, when prices fell back to £22.00 per acre again in 1825. The 'secondary depression' of the 1890s took land down to £20.00 an acre in 1900. In the depression of the 1930s, it was £23.00 an acre in 1933.

	Average land prices[1] (England and Wales)			Monetary[3] inflation scale		Land price: money value ratio		Trend duration (years)	Monetary inflation[3] as % of previous	
	£ p. acre	Scale	[2]		[2]		[2]		Low	High
1770	22	61	L	42	L	145	H			
1810	36	100	H	100	H	100			240	
1825	22	61	L	85		72	L	55		
1835	25	69		75	L	92				75
1875	52	144	H	88	H	164	H	50	116	
1900	20	56	L	66	L	85				75
1920	35	97	H	173	H	56	L	45	264	
1933	23	64	L	94	L	68				54
1946	47	131		230		57				
1972	800	2222		580		383	H	50		
1975	450	1250		935		134				
1978[4]	1000	2778		1275		218				
1979[4]	1425	3958	H[5]	1400	H[5]	283			1500	(still rising)

[1] abstracted from *The Value of Agricultural Land* by Colin Clark, and other sources
[2] H = high point   L = low point
[3] see also chapter 23
[4] January 1978 and January 1979
[5] *high* to date

Figure 16   Land Prices 1770–1979
Source: 'Farm Business Management and Land Ownership', Peter Aston 1979.

The analogy of our hamburger business can be seen in agricultural land values since the 1930s, when premiums for vacant possession on the basis of growth assumptions became significant.

Although Aston's book was published in 1979, his assumption was that inflation would peak in Britain in 1980 at 20%. Aston also assumes that the average agricultural land price will peak at either £1,800, £1,650 or £1,500 per acre. On the three separate price assumptions, Aston projects his table to the year 2022. Assuming agricultural land peaks at £1,800 per acre, Aston forecasts £514 per acre by 2022. If the peak is at £1,650 per acre, the projected low for 2022 is £537 per acre. From a peak of £1,500, the projected price is £302 by 2022.

	Average land prices (England and Wales)		Monetary inflation scale		Land price: money value ratio		Trend duration (years)	Monetary inflation as % of previous	
	£ p. acre	Scale						Low	High
(1)									
c. 1980	1800	5000	H	1680	H	298		1800	
19?	576	1600		1600	L	100			95
c. 2022	514	1428	L	1680	H	85	L 50	105	
(2)									
c. 1980	1650	4583	H	1680	H	273		1800	
19?	343	952	L	1120	L	85			67
c. 2022	537	1493		2240	H	67	L 50	200	
(3)									
c. 1980	1500	4167	H	1680	H	248		1800	
19?	227	630	L	840	L	75			50
c. 2022	302	840		1680	H	50	L 50	200	

Figure 17   Projected Land Prices 1980–2022

Source: 'Farm Business Management and Land Ownership', Peter Aston 1979.

Aston says: 'If these figures seem pessimistic, let it be remembered that very large price rises can be, and often have been, succeeded by very large price falls. For example, share prices on Wall Street rose by 1929 to ten times their 1922 value, and by 1933 they had fallen by 90%, right back to their 1922 level. Although it is unlikely, it is not impossible that average land prices could fall right back to about £150 per acre at some point. By comparison with this possibility, the above projections will appear relatively optimistic.'

In recent years, agricultural land prices have gone far beyond the level of farming profitability. As the 'secondary depression' deepens and the climate follows Wheeler's projections, both farming profitability and growth assumptions will fall sharply. This double-edged sword is likely to slash agricultural land prices more sharply than other land prices.

As the world moves into its 'secondary depression', the impact on prices of agricultural produce can be clearly seen. Since early 1980, it has been a desperate time for most agricultural produce. In mid-1982, world grain, cocoa and sugar values were at rock bottom, well below the cost of production. Many producers are comparing the current global decline in agricultural produce with the 1930s. 'Even three consecutive bad harvests in the Soviet Union have not been enough to prevent the worst conditions for U.S. farmers since the 1930s', says John Edwards, Commodities Editor of 'The Financial Times'.

In mid-1982, the All Commodities Index compiled by the International Monetary Fund, covering 34 prices from 30 producing countries, showed a fall to 127.5 (1975 = 100) from 155.0 in the first quarter of 1981. At the end of a secondary prosperity, commodity prices are the first to fall. Prices of other items such as residential property, land, and consumer goods follow. The existing trend of commodity prices offers further confirmation that a secondary depression is under way.

Current trends in commodity markets suggest that the secondary depression is only beginning. There is little doubt that disastrously low prices for agricultural produce have discouraged plantings, and the use of extra fertiliser to stimulate output. The adverse weather conditions envisaged by Wheeler will have an even greater impact than usual on agricultural land values and prices in general. Falling demand has meant a steady build-up of agricultural surpluses. It will take bad harvests over a considerable period to reduce supply sufficiently to meet current demand, and allow rising prices.

Factories for Sale, Rent and Demolition

Further evidence that a depression is upon us is clear from the state of Britain's industrial centres. Major industrial areas are littered with 'For Sale' and 'To Let' signs as thousands of redundant factories close. During 1982 bargain rents were being offered to encourage tenants. A free Mini Metro was being offered to any tenant willing to take up 9,500 square feet of factory space in one West Midlands example. Cash payments of up to £12,000 were offered with factory space in South East London. Rent-free periods of up to a year were being offered on brand new industrial estates in Solihull, near Birmingham.

Never in living memory have there been so many empty factories in Britain. At the beginning of 1982, King & Co., one of Britain's leading industrial estate agents, estimated that there was nearly 146m sq. ft. of vacant factory and warehouse space in England and Wales alone. This compares with just 54m sq. ft. in 1979. The fact that vacant warehouse and factory space has almost trebled in three years gives some indication of the speed at which the secondary depression is eroding values.

Since 1973, industrial property has been the weakest of all the commercial property markets. Between 1980 and 1982, the growth in rental values was declining at an average annual rate of approximately 7% according to the 'Investors Chronicle/Hillier Parker Rent Index'. This compares with an average decline in growth of 4.3% for office rentals and 3.7% for shops. Historically, industrial land has been amongst the most vulnerable areas of property investment in Britain, particularly during a depression. The median price for industrialised land during the secondary depression of the 1890s was £1,000 per acre. It more than doubled to £2,600 an acre by 1905. By 1916, industrial land was £400 an acre in most of Britain.

It took more than 40 years for the price to return to the 1905 level. In the late 1940s, industrial land was £2,700 an acre, and the rise continued to 1969, when prices reached £12,700. Over 69 years from 1900, the value of industrial land increased in money terms by 1,256%. However, after adjusting for inflation, using 1900 prices as a constant,

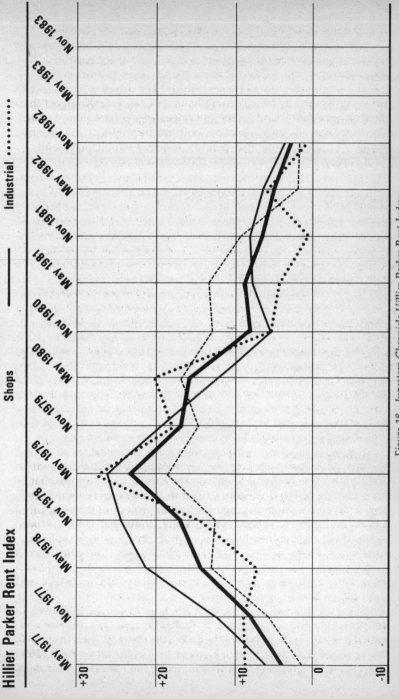

Figure 18   Investors Chronicle Hillier Parker Rent Index

the increase was 62%, or less than 1% per annum.

If we include the price of buildings, there is little to encourage prospective investors in industrial property. The median recorded price per square foot between 1892 and 1909 was about 50p, falling to 22p in 1910–1916, then rising gradually and reaching 50p once again in the 1930s. By 1967–1969 the price was 390p per square foot, an increase of 650%. However, adjusting for 1900 constant prices, the increase was a mere 9.4%. The combination of industrial buildings and land still leaves a growth rate of under 1% per annum for this century. During the depression of the 1890s, the fall in industrial property prices was greater than either shop properties or office properties. The same holds true for the depression of the 1930s. As an investment, industrial buildings have a poor record at the best of times compared to other classes of property. During periods of depression, industrial property has a horrifying record. Current trends confirm the long term historical records.

The Commercial Property Bubble

The greatest percentage of owner-occupiers are in residential property. Next are those who hold farm properties; then comes industrial property, where the factory or warehouse is owned by the business which uses it. The smallest percentage of owner-occupiers are in shops and offices. This is relevant to the price of the various classes of property. An owner-occupier will often place a much higher utility value on the premises he occupies, than a mere investor. Accordingly, assumptions of growth, combined with current rates of return, play a greater role in office and shop property prices than in other property. Historically, prices for commercial property, have been far more volatile than for other property.

The median price for commercial land in 1892–1895 was £5,000 per acre. It had risen sharply during the boom following the 1890s depression. The median for 1905–1916 was five times the 1892–1905 level. Following World War I, commercial land prices began to fall, reaching a low in 1922 at £18,500 per acre. Commercial land prices appeared relatively stable during the depression years of the 1930s, actually rising slightly to reach £22,000 for the period 1936–1938. However, while the price in commercial land was rising, the overall unit price per building was falling, due to the decline in building prices.

The median price for buildings for 1892–1900 was approximately 200p per sq. ft. While land prices increased five-fold by 1916, building prices only advanced to 280p per sq. ft. After World War I, while land prices showed a modest rise, building prices fell.

There was a thundering collapse in commercial land prices prior to World War II. The price per acre fell below the 1890s level of £5,000 to £2,500 per acre for the period 1940–1946. Building prices were under

100p per square foot by 1944, well below the 1892–1900 level. The collapse in commercial land prices was followed by the biggest commercial land boom in history. By 1967–1969 prices reached £233,000 per acre, an increase of 4,506% since 1900. The increase was far greater if measured from the low point of £2,400 in 1944. The gain over 25 years approached 10,000%. Building prices also soared. There was a slight rise during the late 1940s and 1950s, followed by an exceptionally rapid rise in the 1960s. The 1967–1969 figure was 1,200p per square foot.

The growth in commercial property values during the post-World War II period was truly tremendous. The gains in property in other areas paled in significance. Commercial property became the 'speculative bubble' of the last upwave. Every manner of investor was attempting to jump on the bandwagon. British insurance companies increased the amount allocated to property investment by 900% from 1927 to 1965. From 1939 to 1962, the number of publicly quoted property companies increased from 35 to 183. In 1939, the total market value of all public property companies stood at £30 million. By 1962, the figure was £800 million.

The starting gun for the most intense commercial property boom in British history was fired on the afternoon of November 2nd 1954, when Nigel Birch, Minister of Works in the first post-War Conservative Administration, announced to the House of Commons that building licences were to be dropped entirely. 'Licences are now issued freely in nearly all areas and neither the cost nor the inconvenience caused to architects and contractors can any longer be justified . . .'

In Oliver Marriott's book, 'The Property Boom', he tells the story of Gabriel Harrison. Just a week before the government's announcement, he clinched a deal in Grafton Street, off Piccadilly. Unable to get a building licence from the Ministry of Works, Harrison sold a bomb-damaged site next door to the Medici Galleries for £59,000 to a twenty-six year old estate agent, Harry Hyams. As soon as Harrison discovered that licences were abolished, he cursed his luck and contacted Hyams on the off-chance that he might be able to repurchase the site. Hyams replied that he would sell it back. The price would be £100,000. At the stroke of a pen, the government's edict had changed values.

That was just the beginning. Between 1945 and 1965 more millionaires were made in property than in any other industry in history. Marriott cites 108 men and 2 women he believes accumulated at least £1 million in profits during the golden age of the commercial property boom. Few of them started with more than the odd hundred pounds.

The boom in commercial property continued throughout the 1950s and 1960s, and was given a further boost during the 'Barber Boom' when the Chancellor opened the floodgates of monetary expansion. The credit explosion was inaugurated in May 1971 by the introduction of a new framework for monetary policy called 'Competition and

Credit Control'. The idea was that the banks would be freed from direct restriction on the volume of loans made, a device which the governments of the 1960s had increasingly relied upon. In return for this new freedom, it was intended by the Bank of England that the practice of non-competition over interest rates would be abandoned. The Bank of England was to control the volume of credit in the economy through increased intervention in the gilt-edged market. If the Bank of England wanted to restrict credit growth, it would increase the sale of government securities, reducing the amount of cash in the economy. The result would also cause interest rates to rise, since money would be more scarce. This, in turn, was supposed to deter lending to the private sector. That was theory. We are warned, never underestimate the imbecility potential of men in high places. The theory did not work.

In practice, during the early part of the 1970s the Bank of England made no serious attempt to maintain credit controls. By the second quarter of 1972, growth in the U.K. money supply was 31%. It is assumed the government strategy of encouraging profligate credit creation was meant to stimulate industry and capitalism. It stimulated capitalism, but failed to stimulate industry. For several years prior to the 'Barber Boom', there had been a distinct decline in the profitability of British manufacturing industry. Entrepreneurs are much more skilled than government in determining where potential profit lies. The newly created supply of paper money quickly found its way into property, which had been booming, and whose potential return left little encouragement for investment in manufacturing industry.

In retrospect, the bursting of the commercial property bubble in 1973 was the culmination of a fifteen-year process, fuelled by government miscalculation. Restrictive legislation on commercial property was eased, and then credit controls were eased. Official control over raising finance had ceased. Those who wanted to borrow for speculation no longer had to satisfy bankers that their projects were in the national interest.

By comparison with the early 1970s, the commercial property boom from the 1950s until the later 1960s was relatively orderly. There was a slight lull in growth from 1969 to 1970, but by late 1971 the property market was in a buoyant mood again. The Conservative Government, on its return to office in June 1970, had abolished the Land Commission and system of betterment levy brought in by the previous Labour Government. Planning procedures had been relaxed. From 1971 to 1973, commercial property entered that period of explosive growth which always precedes the coup de grace which bursts the bubble.

Property activity during 1971–1973 included development on a wide scale. Large numbers of new commercial blocks were built. There was considerable investment in existing commercial buildings on the basis of revised growth projections. Many found buying reversionary leases attractive on the assumption that rents would rise significantly at the end of the leases. The 'break-up' specialists moved in, buying large residential buildings, and selling individual flats in those buildings. All of these projects required massive amounts of cash.

Margaret Reid in 'The Secondary Banking Crisis 1973–1975' says: 'The optimism of developers was the greater in 1971–1973 because of the usual British method of valuing properties which, in simple terms, involves applying to rent income a multiple of a number of years' purchase which is the obverse of a given yield'.

Thus with a going yield of 5% and income of £100,000, the value would be £100,000 × 100/5 = £2m. Low prevailing yields and rising rent levels therefore boost asset values, and in the buoyant atmosphere of much of 1971–1973, yields were low (along with interest rates) and rents rising. The increase in prime shop, office and industrial rents in 1972 was 13.4 per cent (the average annual rate since 1969) and in 1973 as much as 41.6 per cent. Capital values thus swung sharply upwards and, on average, the yearly increase in property prices accelerated from 11 per cent in 1971, to 24 per cent in 1972, and 26 per cent in 1973.

With such growth, property operators were willing to pay far more for money than the rest of British industry could possibly afford. A string of second-line banks emerged to provide a greater percentage of finance than the more conservative clearers. Cut-throat competition broke out. Bankers were lending from 75 to 80 per cent of the value of property projects. Some were lending as much as 100 per cent, sharing in the profits. Lending on such small margins was imprudent, but only if it was considered that property values could fall. Borrowers and lenders generally agreed property values could only go up, never down. They saw very little risk.

In December 1973, following a steady decline in economic activity and an unacceptable rise in the rate of inflation, the government decided to put on the brakes. The Bank of England began to exercise effective control over credit expansion. It did so by returning to quantitative controls over bank lending, implicitly admitting that the Competition and Credit Control system was unworkable. The rug was pulled out from under the property speculators.

If you recall the analogy about our hamburger concession, yield plus expected returns make the premium which establishes the price of a property. If a property yields 4 per cent and expected returns are 15 per cent, then the additional 11 per cent growth makes up for the premium which would have to be paid for the property. If growth expectations are reduced, then the premium disappears, and the 4% yield is no longer justifiable. The income yield must rise to compensate for the fall in the expected growth. That means a decline in the capital value.

That is exactly what happened in 1973. Yields on office properties reached a low of 3½ per cent in early 1973. Yields on shop properties dropped to 4 per cent. Industrial properties were yielding 7 per cent at their low point. Then came calamity. Property prices plunged as previous growth assumptions lost credibility. Yields on shops and offices rose to over 8¼ per cent, which effectively meant that values had halved. In the industrial sector, yields rose from 7 per cent to just under 10 per cent. The decline in values was not so great, since the previous growth assumptions had not been so great as for offices and shops.

Banks who were lending 100 per cent of the value of properties collapsed, or had to join the Bank of England lifeboat. In many cases, more than half the value of the security against outstanding loans had evaporated while the property developers had gone bankrupt.

The peak in property values is, of course, matched by the peak in the growth of inflation, and other factors confirming the terminal stage of the upwave circa 1973–1974. The collapse in property values, commodities, the stock market, and other capital markets, and the bursting of the commercial property bubble, are normal for the first major recession in the downwave. During the period of secondary prosperity that follows the first major recession in the downwave, it looks as if things get back to normal. The mistakes of the upwave are repeated all over again. This is clearly what happened in commercial property.

The secondary prosperity began in late 1974, and so did the rebirth of the commercial property game. Lenders began lending again. Speculators began speculating again. By 1979, the yields on shops were back to 4 per cent, yields on offices were 4½ per cent, and industrial premises were down to 6½ per cent. Growth assumptions were justifying big rises in capital values once more, as if the property world was the same as it used to be. The more things seem to change, the more they stay the same.

Since 1979, storm clouds have been gathering over the economy and over property. The growth in rental values has slowed appreciably since 1979. Industrial property rental growth was the first to suffer. In 1978, industrial rents had been growing at an annual rate of 11.8 per cent against 12.6 per cent for shops, and 13.7 per cent for offices. By November 1982, the growth rate had fallen to 3.1 per cent for industrial properties. In May 1980, office rental growth was still fairly high at 9.8 per cent. But between May 1980 and May 1982, it had fallen to 3.7 per cent. At May 1982, shops remained the last bastion of reasonable rental growth at 7.1 per cent, half the 1977 peak of 14.6 per cent. Growth assumptions are declining, indicating that a plunge in commercial property values is imminent.

The property market is governed by supply and demand, like any other. The myriad of offers for sale shows there is no shortage of supply. As demand contracts, and the number of properties for sale increases, prices will plummet. The supply will be raised by deepening depression as more and more businesses go bankrupt, and others cut back and seek smaller premises. Demand for property in Britain is primarily determined by insurance companies, pension funds, superannuation funds, managed funds, property unit trusts and property bonds. Here lies the major weakness.

New money accruing to institutional investors in 1980 amounted to £20,342 million, an increase of 13 per cent on the previous year. Property remained the largest single outlet for institutional investment. Direct and indirect involvement in property accounted for 38 per cent of institutional cash flow. The three basic institutional investment categories are insurance companies, pension funds and property unit trusts. Of the three, the largest is the insurance companies, the smallest is unit trusts. Other financial institutions comprise a relatively small portion of institutional property investors. Institutional investment in property is concentrated almost entirely in the commercial and agricultural sector.

While institutional investors continue to pour funds into property, they are not doing so with the same fervour as prior to the collapse in commercial property in 1973–1974. As a percentage of cash flow, institutional investment into property peaked in 1973. There has been a mild recovery since 1974, but the 1973 peak is yet to be surpassed. While investment in property by insurance companies and pension funds remains close to the peak of 1973, investment by property unit trusts and other financial institutions is at a ten-year low according to 'Money into Property 1970–1980' (August 1981) by Debenham Tewson & Chinnocks, Chartered Surveyors.

The somewhat static growth in institutional investment in property since 1973 is not too difficult to explain. Except for shops, property investment has been less rewarding. The average increase in capital values for all property during 1981, according to the Economist Intelligence Unit, was 10.1 per cent. Income returns on all three categories of property were below the 1980 levels. Since 1978, there has been a steady decline in the total return on property investment. The average capital growth has fallen from 13.8 per cent to 10.0 per cent. The average income has fallen from 7.0 per cent to 5 per cent. In 1981, of the 15.1 per cent return realised by property investors, 10.1 per cent was based on anticipated growth assumptions, which could be highly suspect. Income on shops was at the lowest ever in mid-1982, at $3\frac{1}{2}$ per cent compared to 4 per cent before the property debacle of 1973–1974. The income yield on office properties was only marginally higher than in 1973 at 4.5 per cent. Income on industrial premises was marginally over 6 per cent, against 7 per cent in 1973. While the British economy is embarking on the worst depression since the 1930s, growth projections are at their highest levels ever. It is abundantly clear that a state of unreality exists in property markets, and it cannot persist for long.

The love affair institutional investors have been having with property can be short-lived. The introduction of index-linked government securities, index-linked bonds, deep discount bonds, zero coupon bonds and other investment vehicles with a more certain rate of return than growth projections leaves very little justification for further investment in property. It is much more viable for the pension fund manager to lock in a known rate of return for decades, than to be subjected to fluctuating capital values. The more responsible trustees among institutional investors have, in recent months, been increasing the fixed interest content of their portfolios.

Financial institutions have, in recent years, been among the largest net purchasers of property for investment. They have helped to support the market, and push prices to levels which bear no relationship to the potential profitability of the businesses on the sites they have been buying. Competition from alternative investments which promise equal, or higher returns with lower risk, will bring a fall in institutional property purchases. Institutional investors will no longer prop an overvalued market. As long as property is providing inadequate returns from a risk-evaluated standpoint, premises will continue to be vacated and not taken up by purchasers. Even after the secondary depression has run its course, I do not see how commercial property values can possibly return to the lofty levels of recent years.

The current state of the commercial property market and its likely future is put quite succinctly in an article of 20th May 1975:

> The great weakness of commercial property is that it depends on the level of domestic business activity; empty offices, as in Manhattan, mean cheap rents. On the other hand the harvested value of a field of barley will always be based on its world market value; if the pound falls against the dollar, the value of a field of barley, or a field capable of growing barley, will rise. In effect commercial buildings gain their value from the domestic economy, residential property from the level of domestic wages, and farm land from the world price of farm products.
>
> *The Times*

Look around you, and the prospects for commercial property values can readily be seen. As for farm land, one commodity market after the other is collapsing. In offices, the last defence in the economy, the service sector, is beginning to decline as the amount of office space available is swelling. Britain's manufacturing base is steadily shrinking, and the need for industrial premises is continually diminishing. Retail sales are in the early stages of a renewed decline as the secondary depression bites deeper into the consumer sector, and an increasing number of investors enter bankruptcies and sell up.

The current commercial property market is behaving precisely as expected in the early stages of a secondary depression. The latter stages of a second depression bring a collapse in values. This is likely to be evident early in 1983 and 1984.

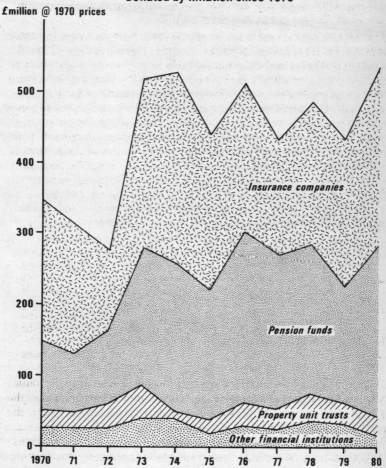

Annual Institutional Investment in Property
Deflated by Inflation since 1970

£million @ 1970 prices

500

400

300

Insurance companies

200

Pension funds

100

Property unit trusts

Other financial institutions

0

1970 71 72 73 74 75 76 77 78 79 80

Figure 19   Annual Institutional Investment in Property, Debenham Tewson
& Chinnocks

Chapter Nine

GLOBAL BANKRUPTCY . . . THE COUP DE GRACE

Banking establishments are more dangerous than standing armies.
President Thomas Jefferson

The 'coup de grace' is the final blow that ends all of the suffering.

The secondary depression of the 1980s will bring excruciatingly high unemployment, massive bankruptcies through industry, a collapse in capital markets, a sustained decline in property values and a great deal of hardship for many people. International tensions will heighten. This will lead to trade wars on an unprecedented scale. The 'coup de grace' will be global bankruptcy at the nadir of the depression.

During the depression of the 1930s, the world broke itself up into trade blocs. Each country was attempting to gain a trade advantage over the other by depreciating its currency, so that exports could be increased and each country could provide employment for its people. The game was called beggar-thy-neighbour. Everyone lost, no one won. World trade was brought to a standstill. The collapse of financial institutions ricocheted from one country to the other. Bank moratoriums were declared, and the U.S. experienced a 'bank holiday', when all of the banks were closed.

In 1944, the finance ministers of forty-four countries met at the mountain summer resort of Bretton Woods, New Hampshire. They did so to avoid currency and trade wars for the future, and to arrive at a system of greater international co-operation and stabilisation of world trade. Out of the Bretton Woods Agreement came the International Monetary Fund, to govern international monetary relations; the International Bank for Reconstruction and Development, to reconstruct a world that was in industrial shambles; and the General Agreement on Tariffs and Trade (GATT). The GATT rules against discriminatory tariffs were intended to prevent the misuse of devices to beggar your neighbour. The GATT was incorporated into international law, rendering various methods which might restrict foreign trade 'illegal'. Among such barriers to trade were multiple exchange rates and discriminatory tariffs.

Before the Bretton Woods agreements could operate, massive currency depreciations against the U.S. dollar were required. With the exception of France, these were completed by 1949. By 1958, it appeared that Bretton Woods was a huge success. International trade was booming. Some countries were doing better than others, and ingenious administrators found little difficulty in devising new methods which, while outwardly respectable, would allow a competitive edge.

In the United States, there were 'voluntary' restraints on the import of foreign textiles and on the export of U.S. portfolio capital and direct investments, the interest 'equalisation' tax, the reduction of duty free import allowances for tourists, the order to government agencies to buy foreign products only if they were priced 60% below the U.S. substitutes, and the strict enforcement of sanitary rules and other rules on quality, and labelling, which discriminated against foreign imports.

In the U.K. we have seen 'temporary' surcharges on foreign imports, and imposed wage and price freezes. In France, we have seen similar moves. Western European countries where value added tax and taxes on turnover are important revenue sources, currently manipulate funds to exporters and provide other subsidies such as those offered through ECGD and other insurance schemes. The lesser developed countries have constructed a complex system of tariffs, direct controls on imports, and subsidies to exporters and producers.

In other words, the Bretton Woods Agreement is now in shambles. A fully fledged trade war appears ready to start. Exactly the same type of trade barriers which fuelled the last depression and the resulting world-wide unemployment face us today. The Europeans are blaming the United States for delaying global recovery by maintaining high interest rates. The British have accused the Japanese of undermining the auto industry through unfair competition. U.S. efforts to limit European steel exports are claimed to have wrecked the recovery at the British Steel Corporation. They also threaten the Davignon scheme to restructure the EEC steel industries, which had already lost 218,000 jobs at the end of 1981. The ban on high technology exports to the Soviet Union by the U.S. is placing at risk thousands of jobs throughout Europe as a result of delays on the construction of the Siberian gas pipeline. The United States accuses Europe of being anti-competitive, citing the controversial swap arrangements between ICI and BP last year. The U.S. also accuses the Europeans of subsidising their interest rates through credit schemes, and charges that Europeans are effectively exporting high unemployment to them.

In a report by Manufacturers Hanover Trust, international trade friction is claimed to be increasing at a frightening level, particularly over accusations of unfair subsidisation and dumping. The number of trade disputes brought before the GATT arbitration panel in 1981 reached a record level, and is likely to be exceeded in the years ahead. Various summit meetings over the past few years reflect basic differences in national policies and priorities, and none of these basic differences have been resolved. The fundamental problem continues to be the inability of nations with widely differing social, political and economic characteristics to co-ordinate economic policies.

The global economic structure is interrelated now as never before through international trade. Yet, there is no international will to promote interdependent free trade adequately. Throughout the 1970s and early 1980s, we have seen a direct return to beggar-thy-neighbour policies. Nations have ceased to seek free trade along the original intentions of the Bretton Woods Agreement. As various economies have weakened, or been threatened by imports from other nations, political leaders have resorted to measures to protect their own self-interest by protective tariffs, embargoes and trade restrictions.

Early in 1977 the Japanese Prime Minister, Takeo Fukuda, warned that protectionism could take us back to the 1930s.

> The world economic situation following the 1973 oil crisis was quite similar to the developments of that particular time. In the 1930s major countries, one after another, abandoned the open economic system of free trade, switching to the closed system of protectionism. I am not suggesting that we are once again on the road to World War. Yet, I feel deep anxiety about the social and political consequences with the world if we slide once again into protectionism or a breakup of the world economy into trade blocs.

An international trade war of horrifying dimensions looms. Everyone will suffer. The trade war will be the direct result of the underlying monetary crisis within the international system. A secondary depression of ostentatiously obvious dimensions will be needed before measures similar to Bretton Woods are once again instigated. Government usually reacts to crisis, rather than taking measures to prevent crisis. Accordingly, an international trade war, a collapse of the banking system and global bankruptcy, are virtually inevitable.

The International Debt Mountain

Following the global bankruptcy on the 1930s, a 'new deal' was inaugurated. There were stricter controls over government spending; banking regulations were tightened and new regulatory bodies were set up to make certain that a calamity of such proportions would never happen again, and that so many seeds of debt would never be sown again.

For about a decade, the new regulations worked fairly well. Shortly after World War II and Bretton Woods, the seeds of the process that brought the international banking collapse of the 1930s were being sprinkled across the credit-thirsty field all over again, but on a much larger scale.

Following World War II, governments wished to rebuild their economies. They borrowed to do so. Debt was piled upon debt. War recovery debt was followed by expansionary debt. Expansionary debt was expanded by anti-contractionary debt. Debt spread throughout the developed world, and finally through to the Third World of lesser developed countries. When consumers were creditworthy, they were urged to borrow well beyond their earning capacities. When saturation was reached in consumer borrowings, corporate borrowings were encouraged. When both consumers and corporations had reached the limit of their debt servicing capacities, further borrowing was encouraged to 'remain afloat' until the next economic recovery. The monetary explosion of the past three decades involving the most tremendous expansion of credit in history transcended territorial borders.

Shortly before the oil crisis, there was a boom in commodity prices. Third World producers became eminently creditworthy. There was a mad scramble from international bankers to provide credit so that lesser developed countries could expand their productive capacities. Steel plants, hydro-electric power dams, and all forms of capital projects were financed. Unfortunately, the commodity boom has now come and gone. Many of the plans which were intended to raise productive capacity for Third World borrowers have turned out to be white elephants, leaving lesser developed countries with massive debt they are unable to service.

During the pre-OPEC period, world trade increased by nearly 9% per annum, and trade in manufactured goods by 11% per annum. After the price of oil was increased five-fold, both figures were cut in half. Following the oil crisis, an aggressive lobby from several lesser developed countries demanded a larger share of the profits from global economic activity to finance their burdens. What they received was a deepening global catastrophe and credit. The five-fold increase in oil prices was expected to impel the industrialised West to run up massive balance of trade deficits. It did not work that way. The recycling of petro-dollars from west to east and back to the west again worked to the advantage of the more advanced countries, leaving the major trade burden on those countries least able to afford it, the poor lesser developed countries.

At the beginning of 1979, the lesser developed countries had external debt burdens of some $230 billion, mostly from private banks and the International Monetary Fund. This was more than a quarter of their total output, and three times the level of their debt at the end of 1973. The gap between the combined imports, including oil, and the combined exports of all lesser developed countries has been estimated at over $50 billion a year. These countries face a $25 billion rise in their annual debt service payments since 1977. About half of that rise is due to higher interest alone. In recent years that has been higher still.

The International Monetary Fund receives secret data from the governments of the lesser developed countries on their individual total debt and economic posture. Estimates of total lesser developed countries' debt vary enormously from the official figures. It has been suggested that about $500 billion would not be far off. Of this, the disbursed foreign debt of Latin America stands in the region of $125 billion. Gross medium term euro-borrowing for 1980 was estimated to be about $26 billion, rising to $50 billion for 1981. The effects of current OECD growth projections will be a substantial reduction in the non-oil producing lesser developed countries' holdings of international reserves by about $12 billion for 1982.

Even before the global recession began in 1979, several countries had severe strain servicing their debt. North Korea defaulted in 1977. The Philippines and Peru, among others, had been forced to 'roll-over' and reschedule their debts as early as late 1977. Officially, Turkey was not in default in 1977, when its debt to foreign banks reached $4 billion, but it has built up substantial 'overdrafts' at major New York banks. During 1982, a domestic banking crisis was narrowly averted in Turkey.

The most serious international debt problems have emanated from the Comecon countries. Over the past few years, the Soviet Union and the European members of the Comecon trading group . . . Poland, Czechoslovakia, East Germany, Hungary, Rumania and Bulgaria . . . have amassed combined debt of over $60 billion. The problems of Poland are the most severe. Public foreign debt there has climbed to over $15 billion, with debt repayments reaching $4 billion a year. In 1977, debt repayments were equal to Poland's total hard currency exports. It is now believed that debt servicing costs are far in excess of their total hard currency exports.

During early 1982, the Polish situation seemed more fragile than ever, with the Warsaw Government failing to fulfill a promise to clear back interest payments of $75 million from the previous year. At the same time, Poland owed Western bankers a further $400 million of overdue interest which had accrued in January and February of 1982. By the end of March 1982, the overhang of 'new' interest had reached $600 million on top of uncleared old interest. In addition to back interest payments, the Poles will still owe Western banks a further $2 billion in capital repayments for 1982 alone. Similar sums, in addition to interest, will continue to fall due every year to 1985.

The banks agree that if Poland does not keep its interest payments up to date, the country's overall indebtedness to Western banks will have doubled to around $30 billion by 1987. If the game is played according to the rules, Poland is in default, and lending bankers should be required to treat all Polish debt as bad debts, making adequate provisions in their balance sheets, and closing credit markets to Poland. The fact that Poland has been in effective, but undeclared, default for so long gives a stark indication of the make-believe world of international banking.

The judgment of bankers who had deluded themselves into assuming that Poland would ultimately be able to repay its obligations is now deeply in question. Many commentators imply that the Polish crisis can be confined to Poland, without considering the wider issue of Eastern Bloc debt. There is little doubt that the entire Eastern Bloc debt structure is about to collapse. Even those who are aware of the problem are yet to bring themselves to consider the implications for lesser developed country debt. All the indications are that a chain-reaction collective default is not only possible, but probable.

The net hard currency debt burden of the Eastern Bloc alone, including Yugoslavia, involves estimates ranging from $80 to $97 billion. The United Nations Economic Commission for Europe estimates $90 billion plus. The Vienna Institute for Comparative Economic Studies says $80 billion plus. The Bank for International Settlements believes it is in the vicinity of $84 billion. A recent study by the Wharton Centrally Planned Economics Service claims around $97 billion. These figures refer to net obligations from which deposits in Western banks have been deducted. Since, prior to a default, it is likely the debtor countries would run down deposits with Western banks, a further $15 billion should be added to the aforementioned figures. The problem is immense if one bank or country defaults, and the effects ricochet around the world.

The combined current account deficit of these Comecon countries in hard currency trade (including gold sales) is estimated to have risen from $9.5 billion in 1980 to $14.5 billion in 1981. The final figure for 1982 is likely to be even more horrifying. There has been a sharp deterioration in the terms of trade between the Eastern Bloc and the West, resulting from the deepening global recession, falls in commodity prices, and falls in gold and energy prices, all of which are likely to continue. The Eastern Bloc's ability to service its debt obligations is being continually curtailed, while the problems are made worse by the steady reduction in the availability of credit.

What banker can possibly justify further loans to Poland or any other potential defaulter? Yugoslavia had been forced to withdraw from a syndicated loan market because of reported 'lack of interest' from prospective lenders. Rumania's credit standing disappeared some time ago. While the decision by the United States to return gold held as a lien on assets seized by the Communists will provide temporary relief for Czechoslovakia, the country is still in no position to raise hard currency funds. Dr. Janos Fekete, Deputy President of the National Bank of Hungary, commented in early March that his country was no longer able to raise loans from euromarket sources. Supplies of credit to Eastern European countries are not being renewed, a development which amounts to an effective withdrawal of short term capital on a truly gigantic scale.

The problems are rapidly spreading beyond the Comecon countries to the lenders to Comecon countries. The economic difficulties of the Eastern Bloc have hit Austria twice over. Markets are virtually closed to Austria, a country which is looking to exports as the boost to a near-stagnant economy. Austria has been burdened with a share of the West's problematical claims out of all proportion to its size. The total gross debt to Austria from Comecon countries at the end of March 1982 came to $5.4 billion. The largest single item was a Polish obligation of $1.8 billion. That makes Austria the largest creditor per capita of any country. As the Polish crisis has been deepening, Austrian credit institutions have become increasingly more reluctant to extend any further credit to Poland, except where the credit was strictly export related. Simultaneously, Comecon countries ceased to expand their purchases of Austrian goods as part of a general drive to retain scarce resources exacerbating the problems for Austria. Memories of Creditanstaalt linger.

The picture is bleak indeed. Poland is a bankrupt nation, and can expect little help from its bankrupt Comecon trading partners. Rumania has declared a moratorium on all of its debt, including supplier credits. Hungary is making the round of international money markets, cap in hand, without success. Credit markets are closed to Czechoslovakia. Austria, previously a source of credit, can no longer extend credit to the Eastern Bloc. East Germany's special 820 million Deutschemark credit facility with West Germany is expected to be cut. Many bankers cling to the hope that the Soviet Union will come to the aid of the Eastern Bloc, but this appears no more than wishful thinking. The Soviet Union has been an active seller of gold, diamonds and oil in order to finance a rapidly deteriorating food supply.

The unity that enabled large banking consortia to reschedule and refinance debt, thus averting the crisis, is now beginning to split. Severe cracks are beginning to appear in the solid front that Western governments and banks presented to Warsaw in 1981. Rather than acting in consort with the rest of the banking group, Brazil jumped the gun last year, and rescheduled the 1982 Polish debt independently. Austria, also independently, announced its willingness to reschedule Polish debt in early 1982. Bankers fear that despite an agreement by NATO members not to negotiate with Warsaw, France, Germany and Italy might also break ranks and reschedule Polish debt independently. This would leave the U.S. and Britain high and dry.

Bankers believe that certain members of the banking consortia that have been lenders to the Eastern Bloc will be unwilling to forego interest payments and increase their reserves. As a consequence, tardy debtors would be threatened with default unless other major creditors assumed their loans. Business Week reports that two U.S. banks did just that in 1981. And Bank Handlowy decided to pay off $35 million in floating rate notes held by Banque Nationale de Paris as agent for private investors following similar pressure.

The consortia of Eastern Bloc lenders involves about 500 commercial banks. As the situation intensifies, individual banks will desperately attempt to protect their own interests and many will attempt to act independently. Under these strains, the entire delicate Eastern Bloc debt situation could suddenly come to a climax and collapse bringing financial holocaust and chain-reaction bankruptcy around the world.

Even if it does not happen this year, one U.S. banker explained in 1982, 'What about 1983, 1984, 1985 . . . how long will this thing go on?'

At the height of the Iranian crisis in 1980, World Business Weekly asked: 'How much more debt can be heaped on the international system before the entire house of cards collapses into default? A minority of euromarket bankers, and many critics of international lending practices, suggest that the straw-that-broke-the-camel's-back-stage has been reached, while others point to the LDCs high overall liquidity . . . the product of better debt management and prudent euromarket borrowing . . . in arguing that the day of reckoning is way off, if it ever comes. Since 1976, the international reserves of LDCs . . . the amount they have locked away in their treasuries to pay off loans and other foreign debt . . . had risen a healthy 43 per cent to upwards of $128 billion, more than enough in theory to service the debt. The spectacular rise in the price of golds adds to this safety valve.'

The weakness of those optimistic arguments is now apparent. The gold 'safety valve' has collapsed. Since 1980, gold has fallen by nearly 60 per cent from its peak, and looks likely to continue to fall. Some analysts forecast a gold price of $100 before the end of 1985. The suggestion that there are sufficient international reserves to service existing debt appears to border on the absurd. Debt is escalating at an accelerating pace, while reserves are likely to have been run down at an even faster rate. This shows from the number of countries unable to service outstanding debt.

In their 1977 annual report, the Bank of International Settlements, a major authority on the development of euromarkets, was more outspoken than usual on the subject of capital market developments and the problems of international deficits. A major point was the concern over the possibility of a chain reaction default in the international banking system which could result from a country suspending interest payments on its debt, even temporarily, or the serious result of a formal debt moratorium. The BIS devoted considerable coverage to the growth of commercial bank lending to sovereign risk borrowers, in particular, the question of whether the risks borne have been excessive.

Not surprisingly, the commercial banks reply that, in view of the volatile state of capital markets and the somewhat lethargic state of the global economy, the shift in lending from commercial risk to sovereign risk has been intended as an upgrading of debt lendings. The commercial banks also argue that 'while private firms are liquidated in the event of bankruptcy, a country will hardly cease to exist as a result of external insolvency'.

On the surface, this argument may appear to have some merit, because a nation will not sink beneath the sea because it repudiates its obligations. This does not mean that lenders to those nations will survive. The worthless debt certificates of China, Russia, Hungary, Rumania, Latvia, Dresden, Saxony, Bulgaria, Costa Rica and U.S. Confederate borrowings, several of which decorate my office walls, suggest that bankers might be too optimistic considering the sad history of what has been described as 'certificates of guaranteed confiscation' by international monetary analyst, Franz Pick.

Many of the loans to these sovereign borrowers appear as Triple A investments on the balance sheets of most major commercial banks. Yet it is difficult to see how these loans will ever be repaid, while the number of potential defaulters and the size of these obligations is rapidly increasing. It is astonishing that the international banking system has held together as long as it has. The problems began to surface as early as 1968, when it was declared that Peru was $5 billion in debt to both the commercial banking system and the central banking system. There was little possibility of interest payment on those loans, much less capital repayment. Peru had threatened the international banking system with a debt moratorium on a previous occasion. It then took a consortium of 145 banks in the United States, Canada, Europe and Japan to roll-over and reschedule debt repayments. During the early 1970s, a new consortium was formed to refinance Peru's obligations over a longer term. The conditions were that the consortium would take over the financial management of the country.

Peru is merely one of many bankrupt countries now being confronted with economic management by foreign bankers. Politically, it would not be feasible for the Peruvian people to be subject to any further austerity as the depression deepens. But, unless further aid is now extended to Peru, once again the international banking system will be threatened with the possibility of writing off massive debts, exposing a severe illiquidity situation.

In 1978, severe difficulties began to surface in Zaire. Even before the Shaba invasion, Zaire was unable to honour previous obligations, due to the fall in the price of copper. One major banking institution assumed the task of refinancing a U.S. $250 million loan for Zaire, a relatively small amount in sovereign borrower circles. That bank had considerable difficulty. The only course of action was to approach the original lenders, asking them to refinance the Zaire loan or be faced with a default which would endanger all previous credits to Zaire. If Zaire was allowed to default, several commercial bankers would be forced to write-off previous loans. That could threaten the solvency of some smaller lenders. Since then, the price of copper has fallen further, and the Zaire debt obligations have increased.

Since 1978, the list of countries requiring refinancing and rescheduling for outstanding obligations has been increasing at a horrifying rate, along with the scale of such refinancing requirements. Indonesia is on the rescheduling list. In 1978, Indonesia rescheduled its outstanding obligations and borrowed a further $2.5 billion, raising the total foreign debt to $13 billion at the time. Only the IMF knows what the total outstanding obligations are now. They will soon require refinancing. Given the current economic conditions in Indonesia, and the prospects over the next few years, it is difficult to see how these obligations will be met.

In late 1978, Pakistan received massive lending. The loans were basically grants disguised as loans. But they had to be financed by someone. Following Indonesia and Pakistan, along came North Korea, needing a financial rescue operation. North Korea spends 16 per cent of its GNP on the armed forces. Iran, once considered an eminently creditworthy sovereign borrower due to oil exports, has since become one of the world's high risk debtors, with obligations to the commercial banks totalling some $7.2 billion.

In just two years, the economic forecast for the South and Central American nations has turned from bright to bleak as the deepening world depression has cut into exports, and political unrest has been escalating. There are several Latin American countries whose short term debt exposure is causing grave concern to the World Bank and the International Monetary Fund.

Mexico, for example, was riding high on oil revenues, and was considered a safe sovereign borrower. Last year, Mexico attempted to refinance a $6 billion short term obligation, extending it on a longer term basis. All they were able to raise from commercial banking sources was $350 million of the $6 billion required. Essentially, Mexico has been cut off by the major banks, who are now worried about short term debt in Mexico, and are unwilling to make any further loans.

Argentina's shaky financial position has been well publicised during the Falklands crisis. Industry in Argentina has been operating at 55 per cent of capacity, and private economists believe that under-employment may be as high as 40 per cent, against the claimed level of 13 per cent. To keep pesos deposited in Argentina, bankers raised call money rates to 400 per cent, and annual rates on fixed deposits to 200 per cent. Banks increased interest rates on 30-day loans to 196 per cent on an annualised basis for their best customers. Other borrowers had to pay 275 per cent. $7.2 billion was due to repay the interest and principal due on foreign debt in 1982. That will swallow nearly all of the export earnings, which were expected to reach $9 billion.

Brazil's massive external debt, much of it due for repayment during 1982 and 1983, is also a major cause of consternation. Venezuela, another oil-rich country, is facing grave problems as a result of the world energy glut, and has had difficulty extending short term obligations in longer term credit markets. Chile, with raging imports and declining exports, is on the 'high risk' list.

Figure 20

Debts of Latin American and Central American countries, June, 1981, in millions of dollars

Country	Total claims	Claims on:			Maturity of Claims		
		Banks	Public bo'wers	Other private	1 year or less	1 to 5	Over 5
Argentina	7483.3	2464.7	2106.9	2911.7	4961.5	1897.8	623.9
Bolivia	457.7	55.0	249.1	153.6	205.4	220.6	31.6
Brazil	15189.4	6989.5	4788.4	4411.3	6994.3	5214.8	2980.2
Chile	4701.3	2582.2	706.3	1412.8	2357.0	1506.4	837.8
Columbia	2594.6	1012.4	605.4	976.7	1769.6	470.5	354.4
Costa Rica	592.7	74.2	244.6	373.9	337.1	208.7	46.8
Dom'can Rep	489.9	122.3	271.0	96.4	286.1	183.0	19.9
Ecuador	1864.1	521.9	581.5	760.8	113.9	597.4	170.7
El Salvador	101.3	20.1	21.5	59.7	70.1	30.1	1.0
Guatemala	241.2	21.4	20.9	198.9	148.1	86.5	8.6
Honduras	274.9	24.5	80.9	169.5	173.6	86.1	15.2
Jamaica	190.4	13.0	157.1	20.3	72.0	100.9	7.5
Mexico	18101.2	3129.8	6345.6	9626.7	10697.0	4846.9	2557.2
Nicaragua	423.7	85.7	293.3	44.6	182.0	48.3	193.3
Paraguay	271.1	10.1	110.2	160.7	141.5	92.6	36.9
Peru	1783.6	702.5	811.7	269.4	1263.4	42.3	92.8
Tr'dad/Tobago	115.9	4.4	101.0	10.4	28.9	76.0	11.0
Uruguay	1188.7	1068.1	30.5	89.9	1156.1	30.4	2.2
Venezuela	20776.0	5325.2	7921.8	7529.0	14059.0	5313.5	103.3

The situation for some of the smaller countries of Central America is even worse. The United States Export-Import Bank has stopped making loans to Costa Rica altogether, and the U.S. government has asked private and government investors to reschedule Costa Rican debt. The economic problems and debt burdens of war-torn countries such as El Salvador and Nicaragua are well known.

Economic conditions in Latin and Central America are even more dismal than the debt schedule of June 1981 actually suggests. A Latin American specialist with the United States commerce department says that the debt figures are worsening each day. Yet, the international banking system continues to hold many of these loans to Latin America, Central America, the Eastern Bloc, and elsewhere, on its books as 'assets', completely disguising the true state of illiquidity in the international banking system. If these debts were written off in the same manner as for a commercial company, the conditions would be terrifying. Lending is a matter of judgment, claim the polyglot bankers. As long as a country can avert default by borrowing more, and having its debt rescheduled, the dangers of not lending are as great as those of lending too much.

The emerging debt crisis is now actually more serious than that which led to the series of bank moratoriums and 'bank holiday' in the 1930s. The international financial problems of the 1920s and 1930s represented intergovernmental funding problems, and a rash of foreign debt failures, leading to losses mainly, by individual bond holders. Historically, sovereign debt defaults did not necessarily undermine the international banking system. But such potential defaults are now threatening the solvency of all international lenders, rather than just governments and individual foreign bond holders.

The problems facing the international banking system are magnified by the level of indirect investment in potential defaulters. Whereas investors have not been prepared to purchase the debt instruments of Third World countries such as Argentina, Poland, Venezuela, they have placed deposits with commercial banks which have loaned out more than 100 per cent of their capital resources to defunct borrowers.

In the U.S.A., $200 billion has been placed in money funds. The assets of many of these money funds include certificates of deposits from bankers who have been exceptionally heavy lenders to the Eastern bloc, South and Central America. Accordingly, potential losses are not limited merely to bond holders, but extend to those whose savings have been invested in these banks. Recently, many of these money funds have been reducing the bank paper in their portfolios, while bond rating organisations have down-graded most of the major banks from AAA to AA. There is a clear danger that depositors will begin to withdraw funds from those heavily exposed institutions once the scale of these debt problems becomes clearer to ordinary depositors, rather than just an open secret among informed members of the international banking community.

At this stage, international monetary policy can only take one of two directions, both of which lead to the same end. The system can continue to act in consort, rescheduling debts, rolling-over credits, extending time limits for payment with printed fiat money. That would ultimately lead to global hyperinflation, and would merely postpone the inevitable. The price which would have to be paid would involve a far longer period of reconstruction than if the escalation of the debt pyramid was halted now. The deepening depression of the 1980s has meant that we have growing deflationary pressures built into the economic system in the form of steadily deteriorating liquidity and too much debt. Attempts have been made to offset these pressures by creating more inflationary credit. From 1974 to 1978, over-borrowing on a vast scale was encouraged, and insolvent borrowers were supplied with a continual flow of credit. This climate has now disappeared, and the global economic environment is faced with a depression which questions the sense of either extending or accepting further credit.

The second direction monetary policy could take would be to keep a tight prudent rein on lending. If defunct sovereign borrowers find their debts are written off as bad debts and they are no longer able to obtain credit, a major default will be precipitated either in Latin America or Eastern Europe. This would lead to a chain-reaction of bank failures and a credit crisis, and a collapse in the international banking system which would make the 1930s look like an era of prosperity.

It is likely that bankers will attempt to pursue a policy of debt rescheduling and roll-overs for as long as possible, thus blunting the deflationary pressures. There was evidence during the early part of 1982 that many central bankers were preparing for a liquidity crisis, shifting deposits between banks. There was little to suggest that major moves were being considered to avert an actual solvency crisis which would affect the viability of the international banking system.

The only remedy which has been suggested in stemming an actual solvency crisis has been the nationalisation of the institutions concerned, and the large scale injection of public funds. It is also likely that the international monetary system would have to consider extending loans by a special procedure to countries unable to service their debt in order to prevent the chain-reaction default from gaining momentum and running out of control. We have the mechanism available to the international banking system. The initiatives which have been suggested would require considerable co-ordination in the event of a major default, and probably could not be introduced in time to head off a multiple credit collapse. That would force a moratorium on international payments between banks, a temporary freeze on all bank deposits in major financial centres in order to avoid a 'run on the banks', and possibly an interim nationalisation of the banks.

The Perils of the Domestic Banking System

Beneath the veil of complacency, the underlying structure of the domestic banking system in Britain is no less precarious than the international banking syndicate. Bankruptcies in Britain have been soaring, by number and by size. Dun & Bradstreet, the credit rating organisation, reports that 200 companies a week were declaring voluntary liquidations and bankruptcy during the first quarter of 1982. The 'lifeboat' floated in the secondary banking crisis during the first half of the 1970s has been well publicised. Surprisingly, little attention has been paid to the second 'lifeboat' now floating alongside as British bankers, encouraged by the Bank of England, have been persuaded to support ailing members of British industry who are technically bankrupt.

While the British government has laid claim to a tight monetary policy, the U.K. economy has sustained an extraordinarily vigorous monetary explosion since Mrs. Thatcher came to power in 1979. The government steadfastly refused to allow lame duck companies to go to the wall, continually pouring in good money after bad. In January 1981, Sir Keith Joseph revealed that a further £990 million of public money would be made available to British Leyland. In early February 1981, the British government announced it would be injecting some £880 million into the British Steel Corporation. This was in addition to the £1.1 billion 'lent' in 1980, after £3.5 billion had been written off as bad debt. Both of these companies continue to lose money at a rapid rate and, if allowed to continue, will require increasing amounts of cash which will act as a non-productive drain on the system and weaken the government position as 'lender of last resort' in a domestic banking crisis.

Massive debts had to be written off in the commercial banking system with the collapse of Laker Airways in early 1982. An increasing level of bad debts is being written off by bankers as new bankruptcies reach record levels each month.

The collapse of the secondary banking sector in 1974 was triggered by a run on London & County by depositors who became suspicious about the solvency of the bank. That led to a run on other similar banks, and the total demise of the second line banking complex which ultimately required the support of the Bank of England. We now have problems on a far larger scale, involving banking institutions of far greater significance.

In June 1982, the Isle of Man Government was forced to put together a rescue operation for one of the Island's banks after a substantial drain on the company's funds. The government withdrew the banking licence of Savings and Investment Bank on the 25th June 1982, to protect the depositors and creditors. This was followed by the usual bail-out. The banking system is held together by confidence. If depositors lose confidence and withdraw their funds, the banking system collapses. No bank in the world could possibly cope if, suddenly, all depositors turned up at once and demanded their money.

Those who had deposited funds with the Savings and Investment Bank in the Isle of Man will no longer be willing to deposit money with this sort of bank. People who have funds with banks of this sort are likely to withdraw them, and place them with larger banks. In turn, this will lead to a collapse in the Savings and Investment Bank type of bank. If, by chance, one of the larger banks had been a heavy supporter of these smaller banks, then the solvency of the larger banks would come into question. If one of the major clearing banks has to write off a large debt on loans to a medium size bank, which had suffered problems from a smaller bank, then even the major bank would come under question. That is the formula for a chain-reaction banking crisis which, once begun, becomes extremely difficult to contain.

The immensity of the problem and the extent of the potential disaster can be seen from the recent U.K. banking statistics. During the period 1977–1982, bank lending to the private sector in Britain rose by £40 billion. This took place during a period when corporate profits as expressed by the real rate of return on corporate assets were at their lowest level ever. The real rate of return on trading assets was estimated to be less than 2.75 per cent for 1981, an abysmally low return. This makes it fairly clear that very little of the additional loanable funds absorbed by industry has gone into investment and increasing productive capacity. Look at the actual level of corporate investment in the U.K. Like borrowers in the lesser developed countries, corporate borrowers in the U.K. have been using the banking system merely in an attempt to stave off insolvency. Given high interest rates, and low profits, companies forced to borrow from Peter to pay Paul are likely to be sinking deeper and deeper into debt.

British banks no longer make any secret of the fact that they have been 'carrying' many corporate customers by 'bending' their normal controls, when prudent policy would send the receivers in to wind-up or sell off a company's assets. Some very large 'household' names should have long since been declared bankrupt, but their bankers are keeping them in business. They are hoping economic recovery will save the day, an illusion perpetuated by the irresponsible mouthings of politicians. Ultimately, the companies themselves will recognise the futility of further borrowing, and will voluntarily call in the liquidator, as they did during the 1930s. When this occurs on a large scale, a chain-reaction corporate default is likely to lead to a chain-reaction banking default.

The problems in banking are certainly not limited to the corporate sector. In recent years, there has been a massive drive to intensify lending to private individuals, spearheaded by plastic money and, most recently, amplified by mortgage lending by the banks. The commercial bankers, recognising the size of problem loans to business customers, did not take long to discover how the risk could be spread by wooing the private individual, who is not interest-rate sensitive. If someone wants a washing machine, they really are not too concerned by the rate of interest. All they really think about is the weekly or monthly repayments. If someone wants a house, the reasoning is similar. They would be willing to pay 10, 20 or even 30 per cent on the loan, whereas a prudent businessman could not consider such a price, since there would be little chance of his business making a profit. Furthermore, by attracting new customers, bankers in Britain can earn a high return on current account balances of private customers to whom they pay no interest.

Compared to their international competitors, British bankers have been slow to attract the savings of the ordinary working man. In 1980, less than 60 per cent of Englishmen had bank accounts, and most factory workers would not even consider one. Sir Anthony Tuke of Barclays Bank said in 1980. 'The real challenge to us over the next few years, will be our ability to create the necessary modern banking system and facilities to attract profitably the eleven million wage and salary earners who today have no active clearing bank accounts.'

The banks have gone about attracting those eleven million wage and salary earners by stuffing credit down their throats. They have been issuing credit cards to customers, and customers of customers, like confetti. Then there are bank cards which allow cash withdrawals at any hour, and overdrafts without prior approval. Some bank customers use their credit cards to make payments on other credit cards in a never-ending chain. The latest innovation has been mortgage lending, with some banks offering 100 per cent mortgages in a floundering property market. The greater the fall in property prices, the more of that amount of mortgage will be unsecured lending.

All of this has brought a staggering accumulation of personal debt. All sorts of consumer lending, ranging from building society lending to overdraft lending, to credit card lending to instalment debt lending, are at record levels. Unemployment and personal bankruptcies are also at record levels, and an army of potential defaulters is forming up. Over-indulgent lending has left millions of Britons in trouble. People believed that inflation would continue to guarantee big annual salary increases, and the prospect of repaying loans with cheaper money. Now many face very unpleasant consequences. Not just the poor, who have always lived on the brink, but the prospering and hopeful middle classes who have been lulled into a false sense of security by promises of better things to come, and which show absolutely no sign of coming.

The deepening depression has shattered all of the illusions. The vast majority of personal debtors never declare bankruptcy. They just go on borrowing, scrimping, stalling off payments and trying to survive until, somehow or other, their prospects improve. Sometimes, of course, they do. During a deepening depression like now, entering the 'panic' stage, prospects get worse rather than better.

Understanding the Banking Mechanism

History tells us that sudden shocks leading to financial panic in the past have often come like a bolt from the blue. Who would have thought a piggy bank like London & County could have brought a large portion of the banking system in Britain to its knees, requiring support from the Bank of England? Who would have dreamed that the collapse of the Hatry Organisation could have led to one of the worst stock market crashes in history?

A collapse in the international and domestic banking system could occur at any time, without warning. It is my firm belief than an international banking crisis similar to that in the 1930s is not a matter of 'if', but simply a matter of 'when'. To understand how and why, a brief acquaintance with the way the system works would be useful.

At the root of banking is the 'fractional reserve' system where money can be created by the banks. Banks in Britain (along with those in most other countries, supposedly under the watchful eye of the Bank of England, the Federal Reserve, or some other central bank) may not only lend the money they have on deposit, but may also lend several times that amount. How many times depends on the existing fractional reserve requirements. For example, suppose the reserve requirement is 33 per cent. That means a bank can lend £2.00 for every £1.00 on deposit. If the reserve requirement is 25 per cent, then the bank can create £3.00 for every £1.00 on deposit. If the reserve requirement is 10 per cent, the banks can lend £900 for every £100 on deposit. You can now begin to see how the system may have some built-in perils. But the fault is not with the system, but the way it is operated.

The prospects and stability of the banks revolve around 'solvency' and 'liquidity'. When the system is solvent and liquid, it is considered sound and stable. When the system becomes illiquid, soundness and stability are threatened. When the system becomes illiquid and insolvent, the consequences are usually disastrous.

Solvency involves matching the total of banking assets against the total of banking liabilities. As long as the assets of a bank are as great as its liabilities, the bank is solvent. Liquidity involves current assets, as opposed to aggregate assets. A bank is considered liquid if its cash on hand equals current liabilities. If, suddenly, all of the bank's depositors showed up at once and wanted their money back, if the bank could meet all of those withdrawals, it would be liquid. If it could not, it would be illiquid. As a result of the fractional reserve banking system, all banks are illiquid.

Banking involves confidence. As long as depositors believe the bank is solvent, only a few of them are likely to want their money at a given point. The bank, although illiquid, will continue, and remain solvent. However, if it is suspected that the bank may become insolvent, a sudden rush of depositors could force it to sell investments at a loss, or suddenly write-off bad debt, in which case illiquidity can lead to insolvency. When a financial institution becomes insolvent in Britain, its banking licence is withdrawn and it must close.

This is an over-simplification. While most banks are illiquid, most are also solvent (at least on paper) as we move into the panic stage of the depression of the 1980s. Unfortunately, this is unlikely to continue as the depression and insolvency of borrowers intensifies. The banker's current predicament can be better understood by considering the things likely to affect the difference between solvency and insolvency, the difference between a situation where assets exceed liabilities or liabilities suddenly exceed assets, leaving the bank defunct.

Banks essentially have four major assets. These assets are capital, cash, investment and loans. The capital is the money put at risk by the owners or the shareholders. Cash refers to the currency at hand, along with deposits held by other banks. The investments are usually interest-bearing government securities, such as Treasury Bills, longer term government paper, and loans to local government. The loans are loans outstanding to customers of the bank.

The assets of a bank can deteriorate quite quickly, leading to insolvency. Looking at capital first, the banker will try to obtain the highest possible return on the capital of the bank. His profit is the difference between what he pays for money, and what he lends it out at. Investments should perhaps also be taken into profits. However, quite often, the return on investments is barely sufficient to meet operating costs.

The more a bank can take in deposits, the more it can lend out. The more it lends out, the greater the return on initial capital, providing nothing goes wrong. Unfortunately, an increasing level of deposits often leaves less of a cushion to protect existing depositors in the bank against loss in the event of a major default.

Suppose you decide to go into the banking business with £1,000,000. After a few months, you take in £10,000,000 in deposits. Your deposits would be ten times your original capital. Deposits are a liability to be repaid at some future date, giving you a liability to capital ratio of 10 to 1. Now, if you are going to be prudent, you may leave £2,000,000 of that £10,000,00 on deposit in cash. You might also decide to be equally prudent with your investments, placing a further £3,000,000 in short term Treasury Bills. The most profitable side of your business is going to be lending money, so you lend the remaining £6,000,000 to the bank's customers. Of your original £1,000,000 and your deposits of £10,000,000, you have only £6,000,000 at risk. In this instance, 17 per cent of your loans would have to go bad before your capital was wiped out and the depositors' funds endangered.

Placing £6,000,000 out of £11,000,000 at risk would be relatively prudent banking. But suppose you decide you want to get rich quick? Suppose you really want to be a high flier? Then you will want to attract as many deposits as you can, as fast as you can, and lend out at the highest return you can. The first thing you will have to do is pay over the odds for your deposits to attract greedy investors. If you are going to maintain your profit, you will probably have to charge higher rates to borrowers and accept some loans that other banks turned down. You will also want to lend a far greater percentage of your deposits to maximise your profit. Assume you managed to take in £18,000,000 in deposits, and lend out £14,000,000. With your original capital of £1,000,000, you will have loaned out £14,000,000 of your £19,000,000. That means that if only 8% of your loans went bad, the entire capital of the bank would evaporate.

Any serious deterioration in the ratio of investment-type assets to loans places a bank in a progressively more vulnerable position. The most secure asset a bank can have is supposedly the investment portfolio of loans to sovereign borrowers (countries), national government securities and loans to local authorities. These assets are supposed to be highly liquid, and convertible into cash at any time. The only problem is that they normally act as a drag on profits.

Loans to customers, although higher risk, offer a much better return than funds held in cash deposit with other banks, or funds invested in government securities and Treasury Bills. In the constant quest for higher and higher returns on capital employed, banks have consistently run down the ratio of investment assets to loans. This not only increases the danger of a bank becoming insolvent as the number of defaulters required to wipe out the bank's capital becomes smaller, but also places the bank in an increasingly illiquid position, since funds which are loaned out are not as rapidly turned into cash as those held in investment-type assets.

Because the ratio of investment-type assets to loans of progressively higher risk has steadily weakened international confidence in banking, we are closer to a situation where depositors become anxious and begin to withdraw their funds in greater numbers. This factor has been one of the causes of high interest rates. Illiquid banks in need of immediate cash to meet withdrawals, with a relatively small portion of investment-type assets to liquidate, have been forced to pay steep interest rates to get immediate cash from money markets.

Loans, which make up the large majority of bank assets, can be divided into three categories: mortgage loans, business loans and consumer loans. Virtually every quarter, the number of new bankruptcies in Britain increases, and the number of bad debt write-offs also increases. Personal bankruptcies have also been reaching new all-time highs each quarter, and the number of consumer bad debt write-offs has been increasing.

British banks have now entered the mortgage lending market, the most dangerous form of lending there is. This began just as the residential property boom was nearing the final stages. Most mortgage payments will be applied to interest only until well into the late 1990s. If a bank forecloses on a mortgage, it may lose a significant part of the principal should the price of the property be unduly depressed. It is no coincidence that property prices have been most depressed when mortgage defaulters and foreclosures were at a peak. I have already described how a crash in residential property will come as the depression deepens. Without a doubt, the potential vulnerability of the banks has been aggravated by their rush into mortgage lending.

Mortgage lending also poses a severe threat because it involves the very dangerous practice of borrowing 'short' to 'lend long'. Mortgage lending involves commitments of 20 years or more. Yet, there is no long term market for banking debt which can be matched against long term mortgages. Like building societies, bankers will have to fund their mortgages through short term deposits. A withdrawal of depositors' funds, coupled with a collapse in property values, and a surge in mortgage defaulters, could trigger insolvency, without considering the other problem areas in banking.

Finally, look at the quality of the investment portfolio of the international banking system. A large number of foreign loans are not actually listed as foreign loans, but appear under the investment-type assets of a bank's investment portfolio. Now, remember, these investment-type assets are supposed to be assets readily convertible into cash. Instead, many have turned out to be riskier than some of the higher risk loans. Many represent loans to foreign governments which will never be repaid, yet they are still on the balance sheets of many banks as accounts receivable.

As interest rates have been moving up, the value of fixed interest investment-type assets of a longer term nature has been moving down. The number of defaulters on foreign lending has caused a reduction in the ratio between investment-type assets and high risk loans. The fall in value of long term fixed interest securities has aggravated this situation. Recently, interest rates reached their highest ever levels. Long term fixed interest investment-type assets have fallen to their lowest levels, seriously prejudicing the solvency of the banks. The extent to which solvency has been prejudiced by foreign defaulters who have not yet been declared in default, and the fall in the value of fixed interest investment is difficult to determine. In the U.S.A., and elsewhere, these fixed interest loan obligations are on the balance sheets at cost, rather than current market value. In a frightening number of instances, that is either a fraction of original cost, or nil.

The seemingly impervious asset of a bank would therefore be cash on deposit, and cash held with other banks. Maybe it was at one time, but not now! If the entire banking system is in a precarious state, then cash with other banks is cash at risk. If a major borrower of the Hypothetical Investment Bank Ltd. goes into default, the Hypothetical Investment Bank Ltd. may also go into default. If the Imaginary Investment Bank Ltd. is a depositor with the Hypothetical Investment Bank, the Imaginary Investment Bank would lose its deposit. If the deposits were large enough, this could also mean a default for the Imaginary Investment Bank. Should the Grabbit and Runn Bank Ltd. have been a depositor with both the Hypothetical Investment Bank and the Imaginary Investment Bank, then the default of both banks could lead to a default of the Grabbit and Runn Bank. And, if the Happy Mousing Cat Food Company Ltd., a customer of the Consuming Credit Bank Ltd., was a depositor with the Grabbit and Runn Bank, it could lose all of its money, defaulting on its obligations to the Consuming Credit Bank Ltd., who may also have had funds on deposit with the Imaginary Investment Bank Ltd., the Hypothetical Investment Bank Ltd., and the Grabbit and Runn Bank Ltd . . . ad infinitum, ad nauseam. That is what the 'domino effect' is all about.

The problems in the banking system are like a cancer spreading unmercifully through every cell of banking activity. The hiatus . . .?

Chapter Ten

BEATING THE DOWNWAVE BY USING IT . . . A STRATEGY FOR SURVIVAL

Evaluate the past, understand the present, think in the future.
Donald B. Decker

According to ancient mythology, the nymph Echo fell madly and hopelessly in love with the handsome youth Narcissus. She gave her love freely and willingly, but, in time, discovered her love was unrequited. Echo wept and pined at first, but her sorrow soon turned to a desire for vengeance. Accepting that her love for Narcissus was in vain, she demanded of the Gods that Narcissus be punished for not loving her as she had hoped. Her wish was granted. Narcissus was made to fall in love with his own image reflected in a pool. He became mesmerised by it. Narcissus gradually wasted away, and perished, while gazing at his own reflection.

The Gods of Greek mythology were a tricky sort. Although they sympathised with Echo's grief, they had little sympathy for her desire to inflict vengeance on the poor Narcissus, whose only crime was a lack of desire for her. Echo's vindictive behaviour certainly did not escape the action of the Gods who condemned her to solitude, wandering through the hills, unseen but not unnoticed, fated to repeat continually 'the last sounds which fell upon her ears'.

There may be a corollary to Echo's fate in what has been happening in the world over the past few years. Large numbers of people seem to have been echoing the words of politicians, who spew forth optimism in an effort to placate the electorate. It seems that very little effort is being made to determine the validity of hopes for economic recovery and other excursions into wishful thinking.

Professional propagandists are fully aware that the public is always prone to believe what is palatable, and what it prefers to believe to start with. It is easy to be optimistic when almost everyone else is; it is also easier to echo optimistic sentiments than to seek out a scenario which may be pessimistically different to the official line. Politicians and others with a vested interest take full advantage of this tendency. As a result, very few people are prepared for the inexorable difficulties which occur with unfailing repetition. Since the early part of 1980, politicians have been promising improving conditions the world over. Others have echoed their sentiments. But the global economy has steadily deteriorated, and continues to do so. Many people have allowed themselves to be sheltered from reality by merely an echo.

Falling in love with your own image or opinions can be no less dangerous than the fate of Narcissus when it comes to planning your future. Successful planning involves the evaluation of circumstances as they exist rather than the way we would like them to be, or the way we have perceived them in the past. The only certainty we really have is the certainty of change. Narcissus and Echo could have avoided disaster had they been a little more open-minded and a good many people are likely to do far better for themselves in the period ahead if they avoid the temptation to echo what they have heard.

I have often been reproached for what seems to be a knack of making myself unpopular by telling people the things they don't like to hear. I could win a lot more friends and influence a greater number of people by telling people what they love to hear, even if it is a lie. But I will not.

Most of my life I have spent enjoying the fruits of the upwave, the long prosperity which allowed me to borrow, speculate and steadily increase my standard of living. But all good things must end. As an investment adviser, it is my responsibility to determine when that end might come.

In 1972, the upwave ended. The recession at the end of the upwave was classic. The system experienced a severe shock, with the world economy contracting far deeper and for far longer than anyone had anticipated. I recognised this as the post-peak-inflation-recession which has meant the terminal stage of prosperity for the past 200 years. This was only the initial warning sign. Writing for subscribers to Investors Bulletin in 1974, I told them to expect a share boom and a strong economic recovery. Both the U.S. and the U.K. stock markets met my forecasts of a secondary prosperity.

But the secondary prosperity is now over. We have entered the period of a gradually declining plateau, which will soon become a secondary depression, leaving us on the brink of a monetary collapse, faced with the prospect of the worst depression of this century, possibly the worst since the beginning of the Industrial Revolution. What that means in simple language is . . . breadlines, applestands, bankruptcies, panic, riots in the streets, anxiety, business foreclosures, depletion of capital, bank failures, ruin, worry, joblessness, hunger . . . for 50 per cent of the population, possibly more.

The symbol for crisis in Chinese is composed of two symbols which represent two separate words. The words are 'risk' and 'opportunity'. It is just conceivable that the crisis on the horizon could be a period of opportunity for many people.

The Brighter Side of the Great Depression

The traditional view of the depression of the 1930s is of massive dole queues and 'hunger marches'. A closer study shows that hardships were certainly not suffered by everyone. It is true that 25% of the workforce was unemployed. But 75% was employed, and those with steady jobs enjoyed a rapid increase in their standard of living throughout the depression. A study of the 1930s and previous depressions is by no means a study in black. It is one of contrasts. We see England impoverished and unemployed, but also England embracing the bustling home counties, by-passes and housing estates, and suburban villas and cocktail bars gleaming with chromium trim. The 1930s also saw the widespread introduction of motorcars, electric cookers, radios, rayon underwear, and talking films. It was a depression for many, but certainly not for all.

High unemployment during the depression resulted in a redistribution of income from the unemployed to the employed. The man with a steady job fared well. The demise of the old staple industries brought businessmen face to face with economic reality, and gave a new sense of urgency and action to innovation. Businessmen who took advantage of the emerging industries of the 1930s built fortunes which lasted for decades. Labour productivity during the depression rose faster than at any time this century. Most of the growth in productivity was in the 'new' industries, including chemicals, electric engineering, vehicles, artificial fibres, precision instruments, paper and printing and utilities. Often 'new' industries grew out of old industries, the tangible results of modernisation.

Rayon production, for example, advanced sharply during the 1920s, and continued to increase during the 1930s. In 1930, Britain overtook France as the largest producer of passenger and motor vehicles in Europe. Higher production brought a marked fall in prices. The average price of a popular family car fell by nearly 50 per cent between 1924 and 1937. The average factory price of all cars dropped from £259 in 1924, to £130 in 1935.

The number of cookers sold rose from 75,000 in 1930 to 250,000 in 1935. The number of radio receivers increased from around 500,000 in 1930 to nearly 2 million by 1937. An evening ritual in millions of homes across Britain was dispensing with dinner as quickly as possible to gather the family around the 'wireless'.

A chumminess was in the air, epitomised in the songs of Gracie Fields, like 'Sally', where she sang of a Lancashire remote from its depressed 1930s state. People around radios were soothed by a sweeter and more sentimental kind of popular music broadcast by the BBC. Henry Hall's band, with 'Teddy Bear's Picnic', was the most popular of all. Vocalists with the big bands developed a soft upper-class crooning style, perfectly elocuted. The national nightingale was Jessie Matthews, who sang just that way. Her voice delighted millions. Radio had a phenomenal growth during the depression, particularly in the U.S.A., where it was commercialised in 1922. During the 1930s, radio was considered to be on the threshold of a 'Golden Age'. It attracted top stars from the entertainment world, famous orchestras and concert artists, who were among the highest paid in the land, such was the demand for 'escapism' in any form.

Professional workers rapidly increased in numbers and relative importance. This was the necessary offshoot of the rise of new science-based industries like chemicals, rayon, electrical equipment and aircraft, as well as large-scale administration. Professional workers remained a small proportion of the working population, but their absolute numbers increased by more than 50 per cent from 1931 to 1951. In Britain, those in the professions expanded from 968,000 to 1,493,000. The biggest growth was in professionally trained employees of industrial firms and in local or government authorities. Technicians, draughtsmen, supervisors, progress chasers, professional engineers and scientists were in great demand, and commanded exceptionally high relative wages.

During boom times and during hard times, there are always those who possess and accumulate wealth. The crisis of the great depression hit the wealthier classes very little. During the 1930s, it has been estimated that 5 per cent of the adult population of Britain owned 79 per cent of the wealth, and the richest 1 per cent owned 56 per cent of it. Although corporate profits fell 30 per cent at their lowest point during the thirties, shareholders' dividends fell much less. Income from rent and fixed interest investments remained stable, in spite of the sharp fall in prices. On the whole, consumption was maintained by the wealthy, even if some of it had to come from reducing investment or temporarily spending capital. There was little sign of austerity for the rich.

The deep contrasts during the 1930s were divided by class and locality. In many areas of Britain, conditions were horrifying. In some areas, the effects of the depression were minimal.

London entered the 1930s with all the outward signs of opulent prosperity, and continued so in many areas. Throughout the thirties, the London season remained in full glory, including the ritual of the debutante's presentation at Court in white dress and ostrich feathers. A society or county family with a daughter of marriageable age was still expected to provide the 'coming-out' dance. Each dance cost several hundred pounds, without the cost of the dinner parties which the average deb was required to attend during the May to July season. The fashionable world of the socialites, with their clubs, parties, and chic luxury flats, so well depicted in the early novels of Evelyn Waugh,

Changes in Occupational Class (Percentages)			
	1921	*1931*	*1951*
Professional	4.53	4.60	6.63
Employers and managers	10.46	10.36	10.50
Clerical	6.72	6.97	10.68
Foremen and manual	78.29	78.07	72.19

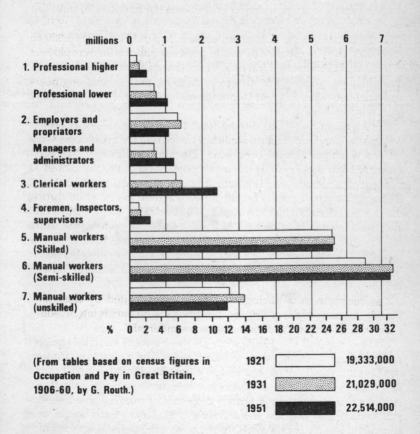

Figure 21   Changes in Occupational Class

continued to stamp a brittle smartness on Mayfair and the West End. Those catering for the rich prospered.

In many areas of Britain, and in prosperous London in particular, it seemed as if the mass of people refused to face the very existence of the depression. A little car such as an Austin Seven or a Ford was within easy reach of many Londoners at £100. There was a new emphasis on popular, democratic enjoyment among the lower and middle classes who had jobs. The general surroundings were more decorous than in the twenties, while a far more gentle, corporate spirit prevailed. The bright young things of the twenties had become young couples with families ensconced in their suburban semi. The wild open-air parties, reached by gleaming sports cars in the twenties, were replaced by 'road houses', and by wholesome entertainment for all the family.

During the 1930s, the cult of the body suddenly emerged. Lidos were opened in London. There was a craze for physical fitness without rhyme or reason. Some sociologists believe the craze for fitness and elegant dress came from a desire to present a better appearance, to be more suitable for employment.

Hemlines lengthened after 1930. Hats became floppy, and the ubiquitous cloche appeared. Charmeuse and crepe de chine became the fabrics of fashion, and synthetics like rayon gained popularity for their practical features. The effect aimed at was for 'sheerness' and 'delicacy', particularly in women's stockings of 'artificial silk'. Long legs were definitely 'in'. From 1933 onwards, there was a revival of the softer line. A great deal of muslin was used in women's clothing, and the 'body line' of the previous era was reintroduced. There was a distinct period quality about women's clothes through the 1930s. This was helped a great deal by the popular films, like 'Gone With the Wind'. Regency period and 18th Century fashions became exceptionally popular. Crinolined dolls made into telephone covers graced the bedrooms of the ladies of the richer suburbs. 'Old Vienna' was also in vogue, and popularised in film and a popular operetta. Princess Marina was considered the best-dressed woman of 1934. Her wedding to the Duke of Kent was the fashion event of the year.

Social conduct involved a new morality. More entertaining was done at home. Married women were discouraged from working. There was greater emphasis on human relationships. For most people, divorce carried a heavy social and moral stigma, as King Edward's supporters found to their surprise in the abdication crisis.

Life went on during the depression for most people. We have been brainwashed into believing the depression of the 1930s represents an evil of the capitalist system under which we must all suffer. Suffering was widespread, but it was certainly not universal, in Britain or elsewhere. A large number of businesses failed, but many also prospered. A large number of banking and financial institutions closed their doors, but most remained open.

Millions were made in various industries in a way which would not have been possible without the Great Depression. The same will hold true during the Great Depression of the 1980s, which is now on our doorstep.

For those who are able to adjust, the coming depression can be a period of profit, opportunity, increased purchasing power, maintenance of real capital, better living standards, relaxation and a vastly improved quality of life. Believe it or not, each and every one can choose how to approach the current depression, and how to prepare for it.

I firmly believe that the chances of averting the natural course of the long term economic pattern are no better than infinitesimal. There is absolutely no way the boom and bust, upwave and downwave, pattern of economic behaviour, which has been repeated for centuries, is suddenly going to change.

I run the risk of attack from critics who may think it illegal or immoral to show people how to profit from a calamity which is likely to cause hardship to millions. Is it immoral to buy your investments when they are cheap, and sell them when they are too high? Is it immoral to buy assets at a fraction of their future value? Is it immoral to postpone buying a house so that you can pick it up at half the price later on? Is it immoral to purchase an undervalued business or underpriced stocks when money is scarce, and you have the money? Is it immoral to save your money and live within your means? In short, is it immoral, illegal, or unpatriotic to try and protect yourself, your family and your life savings, the results of a lifetime of toil and effort? These are the things I advocate.

If you believe that wishing will make things so. Or you believe in luck, or that some mystical power, some 'regulations', some government edict, will spare you from the secondary depression, what I have to say will have little meaning for you. If you believe that over the past 50 years, politicians have suddenly discovered something which eluded them in the preceding 300 years, preparing for what I believe is in store will appear to serve little purpose. If you are firmly convinced that, no matter what, government should take care of you, or will take care of you, nothing I have to say is likely to change your attitude.

But, if you believe that the only help you are going to get is what you provide for yourself; that your personal destiny will be guided by you and no one else; that no one is going to be more concerned with your personal savings and ambitions than you are, then the strategies I recommend for the next five to ten years could be of inestimable benefit. You may not see the benefits immediately. It could take a year, maybe longer. But the potential rewards are near enough for you to begin making your preparations now.

The Nature of Business During the Downwave

In order to plan your personal and financial strategies during the coming years, it is important to understand the drastic changes likely to take place. We are entering a long period of deflation. Deflation means falling prices. The effects of deflation on business are likely to be dramatic. We have lived through the period of inflation, and many assume that deflation, or falling prices, will be a boon to business. This is a misconception.

Coping with deflation is likely to be as difficult as living with constantly rising prices. As the prices of various goods and services level off and start to decline, more and more companies will discover that profits are squeezed, balance sheets weakened and capital spending plans are thrown awry.

Price deflation is likely to occur far sooner than wage deflation. The benefits from lower labour costs will diminish as companies will have difficulty maintaining prices and profit margins. Since prices will be falling faster than labour costs, the unit cost of production will rise as the volume of trade drops. The fall in general prices, and the decrease in volume, will mean that cost increases cannot be passed along to customers.

Deflation will mean that prices will be falling across an extremely broad front, from raw materials to services. The fall in raw material prices will mean that many companies will lose the paper stock profits which helped buoy balance sheets, and were of great assistance in obtaining credit. The fall in asset values will make it more difficult to borrow.

Some industries will be more vulnerable than others over the next two to three years. Industries where costs rise faster than prices, or fall more slowly than prices, will have the most difficulty. Primary industries like mining, steel, copper, and metal fabricating will be worst hit. Wage levels have been the most stubborn in these industries, while markets are likely to be among the weakest. Prices for basic products have come down faster than the cost of items used in making these products.

Food retailers will have problems during the early stages of deflation, as rapid stock turnover quickly translates falling wholesale prices into lower shelf prices. The biggest problem for business is that the last in the chain of costs to weaken during a deflationary spiral is wages.

Generally, when inflation is high, companies can expand profits by holding stocks and gradually increasing them. As inflation declines, so do stock profits. When inflation becomes deflation, these stock profits turn into stock losses. Many companies will find themselves with stock they bought at a higher price than they can sell their goods. This in turn will add to the squeeze on profits.

Deflation will also aggravate the debt burdens of many companies. When inflation was roaring at the end of the recent secondary prosperity, many companies borrowed at high rates to make long term investments. Assuming inflation would remain around 18 per cent or more, it made sense to borrow at 14 per cent, expecting a normal profit of 4 per cent plus inflation. With inflation at 5 per cent in the U.S.A., and 9 per cent in Britain, the cash flow generated by investments at 14 per cent is not sufficient to set off the borrowing costs.

During most recessions, companies cut stocks, and reduce short term borrowings. Since 1980, businesses have been slashing stocks but short term borrowings have continued to rise. This is because high interest rates have made long term borrowing prohibitive for all except government. Many companies have been unable to raise long term debt, and have had to service the increase in the long term borrowings by continually rolling over short term debt. The result has been a steady increase in stock liquidation, and a steady increase in short term borrowings.

The overall effect is self-feeding. Cuts in expenditure, and planned lay-offs will mean the depression must deepen. This in turn will mean that the pace of deflation will quicken, eroding corporate cash flows so that more firms in more industries will be forced to cut prices drastically, even though they will not be able to offset cuts by cost cuts. Decreasing demand will mean that companies will be unable to absorb price cuts through increased sales. Many companies will be forced to make further cuts in investment, and slash payrolls as the economy keeps sliding. The deflationary spiral will ultimately resemble the inflationary spiral to which we have become accustomed, but up-side down.

The strategy for businessmen during the downwave is opposite to that for the upwave. Borrowing must be steadily reduced, wherever possible. Borrowing today because rates will be higher tomorrow will be most imprudent. Borrowing must be cut to the bare bones. Cash is king during the downwave.

Many companies have been anxious to increase stocks during the upwave, allowing inflation to maximise both real profits and stock profits. Deflation will be the problem in the months ahead. The wise businessman will keep stocks at rock bottom, just sufficient to meet existing demand. Demand forecasts should be steadily revised, and downgraded periodically if necessary.

The Implications for New Businesses

Many businesses began life during the secondary prosperity, when it looked as if the world was returning to normal. In some areas, business opportunities looked marvellous during 1979 and 1980, despite inflation. Say our businessman decided to build a plant capable of producing a fixed amount of chromium-plated Coca-Cola bottles, which were in great demand in 1979. Many believed they would become art treasures, and would be a good hedge against inflation.

Any businessman setting up to make goods can be expected to use the traditional capital structure, with some equity and some debt, to build a plant capable of producing a fixed amount of goods based on existing demand projections. The National Enterprise Board in Britain is thoroughly familiar with this formula and provided funds for many lame duck companies at just about the last inflationary peak in Britain.

Say our prospective manufacturer of chromium-plated Coca-Cola bottles borrows £5m., and has to pay 16 per cent interest on a 25-year bond. In other words, he has taken out a 25-year mortgage on his business, and will pay 16 per cent until he repays the capital. There is a small possibility that our man may actually survive the next decade. If he does, then his problems will really start. In a decade or so, it is likely that anyone else starting up in the same business will be able to do so at a far lower cost. Given the prospects of a severe decline in property values, it is likely that a competitor would be able to erect the same plant and equipment at a much lower cost. In addition, the competitor will be able to finance the plant at a much lower rate of interest since falling interest rates are a product of deflation. The competitor will be able to purchase far more modern equipment capable of greater productivity. The net result will be that the entrepreneur who goes into business ten years later than the man who went into business at the inflationary peak will have a better plant, and lower overheads. He can operate at a higher profit margin, producing goods at lower costs.

During the latter stages of inflation, price sensitivity barely exists. During the early stages of deflation, price sensitivity intensifies. In a price sensitive environment when demand is falling, the first major move a manufacturer usually takes is to cut prices to maintain trade and compete with others who are cutting prices. Internationally, deflation means trade wars. Domestically, it means price wars. If manufacturing overheads are lower than those of his competitors, he can cut prices and still survive. If he cuts prices below the cost of production, he will go bankrupt. Many firms will be driven out of business, but a nucleus of highly profitable, well managed firms will be left as a base for a sustainable general recovery.

The Winners of the Downwave

The method most widely adopted to combat price competition and falling prices during the previous downwave was to form monopolies and cartels. Firms would combine into increasingly larger companies, fixing prices amongst themselves once the number of competitors had been reduced. This was particularly widespread during the 1870s and 1880s in the U.S.A., the era of the magnate, the railroad baron, and monopolist. Only the downwave made these activities possible. They never occurred during the upwave, since they were unnecessary with rising prices. Most activity of this type was aimed at limiting the steady erosion in prices by reducing competition.

In the great depressions of the past, industrialists joined with some competitors, and sought to destroy others. Many were destroyed. Markets were divided amongst cartel members, both geographically and on a percentage basis. John D. Rockefeller set out to create a monopoly in oil. Those who did not join him had to fight, and usually lost. The downwave, with its pressure on prices, provided exactly the right climate for business to seek relief through monopolistic combination, and this can be expected to happen again during the years to come.

In the end, most cartels are doomed to failure. No matter how large the combine, no matter how great the force on the market place, economic forces are greater. The one entrepreneur who demonstrated the weakness of cartels and managed to master the nature of the downward spiral better than any other was Andrew Carnegie. Playing the downward price spiral was far from the sole reason for Carnegie's fantastic success, but it was a significant factor, a perfect long range strategy in which he demonstrated far more diligence and foresight than his contemporaries.

Carnegie's plan was basically very simple. It required tremendous nerve and self-discipline to succeed. The downwave involves long periods of contraction and short periods of recovery. During the brief prosperity that followed the U.S. Civil War, Carnegie began selling his assets and steadily accumulating cash, building his liquidity as quickly as he could. During the next depression, Carnegie held the cash generated during the early part of the depression. As the depressionary trough neared, he began to expand as quickly as he could. Carnegie's core of operations was in steel, and he purchased as much plant and equipment as he could afford to expand his manufacturing capacity. This was roughly opposite to most other entrepreneurs, who were suffering the contraction in demand in what they considered the worst depression in history. The steel industry has habitually suffered worse than most in a depression.

Most businessmen are trend followers. They expand capacity and production while demand is increasing. They cut back when demand decreases. At the trough of the depression in the latter part of the 19th Century, steel stocks were being slashed. Plant and equipment were being sold for a song. No matter how desperately the steel cartel tried to maintain prices, many broke away and ran in different directions for survival. It must have taken great discipline and enormous courage and self-confidence for Carnegie to have spent huge sums, adding to his steel production capacity while his steel works were idle. Yet, he perceived and accumulated while his contemporaries were distributing.

There were many offsetting factors in Carnegie's grand design. The materials and goods he needed for production came at bargain prices during the depression. Because he had planned ahead he was highly liquid, with strong assets, and represented a good credit risk. He found it easy to borrow at low interest rates, while many of his contemporaries were poor credit risks and could not borrow at any price.

It was customary for America's steel magnates to meet at least once a year. Then they would set the price of steel to ward off competition, and to ensure that they themselves made an adequate profit. Carnegie boldly announced that he could deliver finished steel to any user at a price far below that which any member of the cartel could afford. As a consequence, he demanded the largest stake of the distribution. Carnegie had single-handedly broken the steel cartel. Before long, he dominated the entire steel industry.

Andrew Carnegie emigrated to America from Scotland intent on building a fortune. By the age of 34, he had amassed several million dollars, and owned an iron company, locomotive works, railroads, a bridge-building company and, of course, Carnegie Steel. These were the rewards for acting contrary to those who were failing. These were the rewards for anticipating events, and adopting the appropriate strategy at a time of desperation.

Expectations During the Downwave

Not everyone can be an Andrew Carnegie. But even the wage earner and small proprietor can improve his lot by being able to anticipate changes coming with the downwave.

As part of the survival kit for businessmen, I have prepared a list of expectations during the downwave, in contrast to the upwave of the previous decade. Top priority is to build liquidity and reduce debt to the bare minimum. Many people feel that if they abide by these old-fashioned rules, they will be missing out on something. This may have been true during the upwave, but it is no longer so. Profitable borrowing comes only in an inflationary environment. The world of the borrower has been turned upside down. Over the past few years those who have raised liquidity, and kept commitments low, have generally done far better than those struggling with accumulated debt costing more and more as the days pass.

Some of the greatest fortunes have been made during panics, collapses, and depressions, when businessmen with cash bought whatever they wanted at 5p to 10p in the pound. Wherever possible, everyone should now prepare to do the same. Study the downwave expectations which follow, to take advantage of the changed environment, and survive the downwave which will last 10 to 15 years.

Normal Activity During the Upwave

Normal Activity During the Downwave

1. Commodity prices soar until it appears that an explosive curve has developed.

Commodity prices enter a long cyclical downtrend.

2. Debts are easy to pay and the rate of debt repayment is low.

Lenders have difficult in obtaining repayments. Slow payers and defaulters increase.

3. New bankruptcies fall.

New bankruptcies rise.

4. Holders of debt issue do badly, but can get capital repayments.

Holders of debt issue profit handsomely, so long as borrowers are stable.

5. Earnings in life insurance companies rise.

Earnings in life insurance companies fall sharply.

6. The buying power of charities decreases, but new funds come in.

Charities suffer, because new funds fall off, and income declines by more than the likely increase in purchasing power.

7. Buying on credit is very popular and is strongly encouraged.

The creation of debt is abhorrent.

8. Government revenue is brisk, and taxes are easy to pay.

Government has difficulty in collecting taxes.

9. Public service and local government spending increases.

There is a sharp decline in the standard of public services. Rate payers will form protest groups, but little will be accomplished.

10. The derelict element of the community virtually disappears. 'Soup kitchens' are empty.

Many self-respecting people suddenly need to be fed at public expense.

11. An era of 'nouveau riche' develops.

The 'nouveau pauvre' arrive.

12. There is a sharp increase in trade union membership. Trade unions wield extraordinary powers.

Labour union membership falls. Labour unions steadily lose ground.

13. Wages steadily lag behind the rise in prices, but there is plenty of work.

Wages rise faster than prices, but jobs disappear.

14. Workers find easier promotion.	Promotions are slow. Demotions and lay-offs are common.
15. Farmers prosper steadily.	Farmers are amongst the worst hit, and face a long and severe depression.
16. The standard of living in the Midlands and North improves sharply.	The standard of living in the Midlands and the North shows the most severe declines.
17. Construction in urban centres is checked.	Construction in urban centres is overdone, and then stopped.
18. Fire insurance losses fall.	Fire insurance losses escalate.
19. Goods are hoarded.	Cash is hoarded.
20. Services like laundries, TV repairs, dry cleaning, auto repairs, and home improvements prosper.	There is a sharp decrease in the demand for labour intensive services, and do-it-yourself movements appear.
21. Doctors fees lag behind price increases, but business increases, and outstanding bills are easy to collect.	Doctors fees continue to lag. Business decreases, outstanding bills are difficult to collect.
22. Suicides decrease.	Suicides increase.
23. Interest rates rise.	Interest rates fall.
24. There is a decrease in crime against property, but an increase in violent crime.	There is a decrease in violent crime, but more crime against property, fraud and deception.
25. The size of life insurance and commercial insurance cover increases.	There is a sharp decline in the amount of insurance cover applied for.
26. Property prices steadily advance.	Property prices steadily fall.
27. Rents steadily increase, but are easy to collect. There is a shortage of commercial property.	Rents fall more slowly than most prices, and are difficult to collect. There is an over-abundance of commercial property.

Many businessmen extend credit to keep their clients. This could be disastrous, particularly for the small businessman who is likely to suffer from delayed payment. It would be wise to employ one of the credit rating organisations, such as Trade Indemnity or Dun & Bradstreet, and to give credit only to customers with an outstanding rating, even if it means losing business. You lose a lot more than your profit margin if your customer suddenly finds he cannot pay you. Profit margins can also be eaten up by the financing costs of other people's debts to you.

If you are in a business where transport is essential, place additional emphasis on independent road transport. You may find you can deliver goods while your competitors cannot, improving your business prospects.

If possible, concentrate your business in areas likely to be the least affected by the contraction in business. Study the unemployment levels. Areas with the highest levels are likely to continue to suffer inordinately as the depression bites deeper.

Due to the expected increase in crime, it is vital that your business is adequately insured. While a decrease in violent crime is expected, there will be more crime against property, fraud and deception.

If you own your business premises, it would be wise to arrange a 'sale and leaseback' of the premises, or sell them in favour of rented accommodation. The cost of renting is likely to be far less than the return on the capital you will free from the business. Your long leasehold or freehold business premises will represent a depreciating asset, which will detract from credit worthiness and liquidity.

There are special considerations in property. Before the collapse in commercial property values in 1973, I designed a list of strategies for subscribers to my Investors Bulletin. All who implemented some or all of them profited by them. We are again approaching a rapid fall in property values.

* If you are in residential construction, discontinue all unsold projects and expansions, everywhere, whether or not foundations have been laid or poured.
* Wherever possible, shorten the maturities of your debt to the absolute practicable minimum.
* If you are an investor in property, sell all of your low income-producing property, regardless of what looks like the reversionary value. The perceived reversionary value could change drastically.
* While reducing longer term debt and shortening maturities, it would be wise to increase liquidity and to restructure the debt which carries personal guarantees. Personal endorsements should be minimised.
* Creative financing should play an important role in your property dealings. To improve liquidity, many dealers have been issuing long term non-recourse obligations secured against their low income or non-income producing properties.
* Offer sale terms which are as attractive as possible . . . *now*. Cut profit margins to the bone, if necessary. Issue a mortgage or a top-up mortgage if necessary, providing you are dealing with a private buyer. If you issue a first mortgage, even if your borrower defaults, you will have had the initial deposit, several repayments of capital and interest, and keep the property if the mortgage deed is drafted properly.

* A little known device to help in financing is a 'rent charge'. Investigate the possibilities.
* If you are a residential property owner depending on income from lettings, raise rents to the maximum on any property where a fair rent has not been fixed. Take advantage of providing furnished lettings to companies, upgrading the rental value with a minimum of expenditure. A good interior designer can be of immense value. Residential property owners who concentrate on the top end of the market will do far better than those who attempt to struggle through in the medium and lower end of the market.
* Owners of commercial properties should raise rents to the maximum the traffic will bear. Rents are still cheap compared with the cost of ownership.
* In general, it would be wise to dispose of as many of your property interests as possible. In times of trouble, mass hysteria seeks scapegoats. One of the first has always been the 'blood sucking landlord'. Do not forget, one of the first acts of Prime Minister Harold Wilson was to allow wages to rise unchecked, while freezing rents. As the depression deepens and as troubles surface, property will again become the favourite political football of the do-gooders. They will use property men as scapegoats to draw attention away from other areas of bureaucratic ineptitude.
* If you want to sell larger properties with a poor pre-tax cash flow, sell them through estate agents who are active in the institutional investment market. Most institutional investors will cling to the illusion of property forever. The structure of the institutional investment market and the sums involved will often encourage over-payment and a poor assessment of risk. Lending and investing officers rarely have great talent for reading balance sheets as well as they are able to read proforma cash flow. They are unlikely to be able to assess operational problems any better than they read balance sheets.
* Top of the league in terms of potential buyers for the larger properties are the pension funds. There remains widespread demand for property by pension fund managers, all of whom have suffered in the fixed-income market as a result of high inflation while there has been little real growth in the stock market. Most pension fund managers are not genuine investors. They think like the private investor who purchases his shares after a long market rise, and then panics out after a sharp fall. They work for a salary. The major difference between the pension fund manager and the small investor is that the managers are investing other people's money, not their own. The incompetence that normally weeds out loss-making amateur investors does not operate among pension fund, unit trust and institutional investors.

Pension fund managers are human. Like all of us their first priority is protecting themselves. Attempting to achieve superior performance has little to do with keeping their jobs. Pension fund managers protect themselves by doing subconsciously (and/or unconsciously) what they believe everybody else is doing. No pension fund manager is going to get the sack for losing 90 per cent of the value of a portfolio by investing in agricultural land or prime shop property if all of the other pension fund managers are doing the same.

On the other hand, he could very well get the sack for losing money investing in fixed interest markets while his peers were investing in property. A pension fund manager might also get the sack by being liquid when all of his associates were fully invested, and the market went up. The pension fund manager, and institutional fund managers in general, have nothing to gain, but everything to lose, by attempting to achieve superior performance by leaving the herd. The herd is likely to remain mesmerised by property until the very end of the collapse, when the decline in values becomes ostentatiously obvious. Pension fund managers will continue to follow the trend of mass opinion, and provide a relatively constant market for larger properties. 'Property is safe', they will say. 'Property isn't volatile like other markets, property is a basic necessity. They're not making land any more.'

Chapter Eleven

PERSONAL PLANNING DURING THE DOWNWAVE

Sauve qui peut
(Let he who can, save himself)

French Proverb

There are two ways of becoming poorer: your income goes down, or your income goes up, but buys less. There are also two ways of becoming richer: your income increases, or your income falls, but buys more.

I believe that Britain and the rest of the industrialised West will soon be in a deep depression. I also believe that a majority of the people in Britain and other industrialised countries will remain employed. Even during the worst years of the coming depression, most people will be better off than during the latter part of the 1970s.

There may be an improvement in some incomes, but the main benefits will come from a dramatic fall in the cost of living. The price of food and manufactured goods will fall most, bringing a real improvement in the standard of comfort for many people, especially the middle classes. In most industries and in government service, wage rises are likely to be difficult to come by. Families are likely to be smaller, with a higher disposable income, and greater affluence than in the 1970s, when many prices rose beyond the reach of many households. Many of the old staple industries are likely to decline to their lowest ever levels, yet within the next four years, 'new' industries will be forging ahead at an unprecedented rate.

Everyone must decide whether or not the world economic, political, financial, sociological and technological climate will actually change along the lines I have been suggesting. If you feel that I am probably right you may have to decide whether to continue working at your current job, remain in your existing business, learn a new trade, perhaps even move out of Britain to another country where the economic climate may be better over the short run. Many of the early developments I have projected are unpalatable, while those who will benefit in the longer term will need drastic revision of life-styles and expectations.

Many people may feel they do not have sufficient knowledge to decide whether or not what I expect to happen is likely. So important are the decisions ahead that I implore you to take time and effort enough to enable you to decide. Read the reference sources listed in the bibliography. Compare the conclusions I have drawn, and the reasons for them with opposing views. Ignorance usually carries the worst possible penalties. The material and knowledge to help you make a decision is available, providing you are not blinded by the masses, and the vested interests who govern the decision-making process of the masses. Think for yourself, objectively, without preconception or prejudice. No one is likely to care as much about your future as you are. After all, you are going to spend the rest of your life there!

The Social, Cultural and Political Environment

As the downwave progresses, fashions will change to reflect the shift in people's psychology. Dress will generally become more conservative, and be of a higher standard. Skirts will be longer. Designers will fashion clothes for a slim, youthful, feminine form. Cotton will be used more. Natural fibres like linen, wool and silk will be treasured. Female fashions will range from the severely tailored look for day wear, to the ultra-feminine look for the evening, with taffeta petticoats and crinolines, emphasising the female form although covering it.

Men's fashion will become far more stable. There will be little of the extremely narrow men's lapels from the late 1970s, or the enormously wide lapels of the 1960s. The same will hold true for trouser widths, and the width of ties. Men's clothing will be less colourful and more sombre, and veer toward the more elegant. The object will be to be conspicuously inconspicuous. Jeans will lose their popularity completely. It will be unheard of for a gentleman to dine at more fashionable restaurants without a jacket and a tie. Less fashionable restaurants will join the trend. In general, there will be a return to sobriety and conservatism.

The frantic popular music of the 1970s and early 1980s will disappear. Initially, we can expect a revival of nostalgia. Recordings of the music of the 1940s and 1950s will be reissued. This is now happening in America. Reflecting the change in attitudes will be the popular dances and dance rhythms. The music will be slower and more romantic. Couples will once again hold each other on the dance floor, discarding the narcissistic gyrations that were part of the frenetic discotheque mania of the 1970s. People will begin listening to the words of songs again, associating the lyrics with the subdued, idealistic romanticism of their life.

The changes in dress and music, and a desire to escape from the prevailing realities, will be reflected in the literature of the next few years. The current boom in women's literature is likely to continue. Publishers will take an increasing interest in minority groups. There will be a boom in self-help books, particularly those geared to physical self-improvement. Do-it-yourself and money-saving books will top the list of best selling non-fiction. Romantic novels and science fiction fantasy will be the best selling fiction.

Puritanism is likely to return. Sex shops will be closed. Censorship will be tightened. New laws will lead a return to more prudent moral standards. Church attendance will rise, and alternative religions will lose their followers. There will be fewer working wives, but more working youngsters. All of this will strengthen the family unit. A deterioration in human relationships is characteristic of the upwave. Morality is low. Divorce is high. Cohabitation is the norm. During the upwave it has been said that married people live like single people, and single people live like married people. This trend is reversed during the downwave. During the upwave, the emphasis is on materialism, and people become progressively more insular in their human relationships. Empathy is a forgotten word. During the downwave, brotherly love is rediscovered. People become aware of far greater fulfilment in the family than in a second car; that a good friend is a far greater asset than a mini-computer; that a woman's love and undivided loyalty is a far more meaningful symbol of a man's success than a Rolls Royce.

During the downwave, there is a distinct tendency toward right wing politics and strong political leadership. The government elected during the middle of the 1980s is likely to have a strong leader, and remain in power for quite some time. Generally, the middle 1980s to the middle 1990s will be a period of relative stability, unlike anything in the past two decades. While the affluence of the 'swinging sixties' will not be repeated for quite some time, the recurring crises of the 'sobering seventies' and 'agonising eighties' will also not be repeatable. In general, the decade that lies ahead will be one of sobriety, peace and tranquility.

The depression will leave its mark for quite some time, and will take considerable steam out of the industrial society, slowing it down, making it less intimidating to people even after the downwave is over. People will move closer to the resources, to land, water and woods. There will be all sorts of new opportunities for small-scale economic activities. The big corporations will find themselves in bitter trade wars, with contracting markets, and will find it progressively more difficult to sell everything they produce. As the vast scale of society contracts, the need for a 'big brother' government providing all will also contract. It will be more of a face-to-face world.

The period immediately ahead will be one of rampaging unemployment and considerable economic disruption. Most people will feel threatened by the changes, but those who are willing to adapt efficiently and quickly will actually enhance their position.

Those who hold on to a declining way of life, to a job in a declining industry, to a business with little future, merely because they are unwilling to accept change, will find the next few years extremely difficult.

Those who are probably best prepared for the years ahead are those who have never been wealthy, but have engaged in physical labour, have skills, and are prepared to get by on reduced material goals. The repairman, the car mechanic, the artisan, the craftsman, the handyman, will all be able to channel their skills into areas which will be resilient to the changes in society.

The individual likely to suffer more than most, unable to adjust to a short frugal period, is today's vociferous, greedy investor in property, the stock exchange and other business enterprises which are a product of a bygone era. This type of individual, who is probably carrying an enormous debt burden, will be wiped out by any prolonged set-back, and will find his life-style rested on quicksand. Suddenly he will be faced with poverty. He has probably never worked with his hands for £1.00 an hour, and knows very little beyond exploiting the angles.

Over the next three to four years, there is likely to be less of everything in material terms. Less clothing, fewer cars, fewer possessions. But there will be more spare time, more time to enjoy friends and family, more individual opportunities, more physical work, more community, more contact with nature, generally a more challenging life-style. One of the more beneficial aspects of the period we are entering is that we are likely to experience a far more sustainable life-style. People will have more time to enjoy what there is to enjoy. People are likely to become more alive to opportunities and ideas. People will be able to afford to take themselves less seriously. The frowns will become smiles, and people may once again be able to laugh at themselves. Those who adapt will find more pleasure from simple things, with a new set of standards geared to the quality of life.

Warren Johnson, in his book 'Muddling Toward Frugality' (1978), offers suggestions on the best way of preparing for the changes over the next few years, changes which will bring smaller cars, bankruptcies, high unemployment, and all the symptoms of a society which has been living beyond its means.

DON'T	DO
1. Don't get involved with status symbols.	Savour the simple pleasures of life. Learn to appreciate them.
2. Don't be too acquisitive, and wrap yourself up in your private successes.	Build your life around family, friends and work.

3. Don't become so involved in debt that your freedom is restricted.

   Always be willing to adapt to change and be aware of change.

4. Don't become too special-ised. The need for your skill could disappear.

   Save your money to allow you the flexibility change may warrant.

5. Avoid positions in industry which depend on non-renewable energy.

   Find work which will expand should existing resources become scarce.

6. Don't become addicted to affluence.

   Learn as many skills as you possibly can.

7. Don't live in areas which depend on transport for basic necessities.

   Try to live in an area where there are renewable resources . . . good water, wood, and so on.

8. Don't buy land in remote inaccessible places.

   The best place to live is in or near a small town.

9. Don't be greedy, and get caught holding a speculative bubble when it bursts.

   Repay the mortgage on your home before undertaking any investment, or assuming any other debt.

10. Do not keep yourself too much to yourself, and risk isolation and hostility.

    Develop loyalties with neighbours in your community.

Career Opportunities During the Downwave

As the world emerges from the depression, there will be a shift in careers and job opportunities. Industries where jobs are at risk fall into two categories: the energy intensive, and the makers of inessential luxuries. Some industries are vulnerable on both counts. Tourism is one of them. It involves transport and high energy usage. Many people will find that a holiday is one of the first items they cut back on. People will spend their holidays at home. Others will work to earn extra money during their holidays.

The car industry is declining because of energy costs. A car is a luxury item for city dwellers. Energy costs are likely to fall, but never back to the levels of the 1940s and 1950s in real terms. Car sales are now declining sharply, and are likely to decline for the next few years. A sharp contraction in the motor industry will hit industries like steel, rubber, and electronics. The construction industry will also be one of the major sufferers in the period ahead. There will be a protracted slow-down in building roads, shopping complexes and manufacturing plant. Service industries, like marketing, finance and banking, will suffer indirectly, influenced by the general contraction in the 'smoke-stack' industries. During a depression, retail sales suffer, and most other services contract.

Industries associated with the affluent society are also at risk. Makers of recreational equipment, holiday homes, second homes, food processing, electronic games, electrical appliances, jewellery, furniture, carpets, and retailers of 'big ticket' items offer very poor job prospects.

Jobs in service industries linked to the affluent society are also vulnerable. These include banking, advertising, public relations, accounting, investment services, property, insurance, and marketing. Enterprises where customers must come by car are also highly vulnerable, and include motorway restaurants, suburban shopping centres and tourist companies. Essentially, jobs in urban areas are among the most vulnerable of all. There is likely to be a drain of funds out of urban economies as manufacturing industry continues to decline and populations decentralise.

There will not be as many textile, motor or steel workers. The enormous advances in robotics, coupled with the high cost of labour will see to that. There will not be so many clerks, nor sales assistants and stock assistants.

All industries will attempt to cut labour costs to the bone during the depression. Computers, robots and machines to do the work of people will be employed readily. During a depression, a large number of stock brokers and stock jobbers go broke. Some people feel that this in itself is sufficient justification for a depression. They feel the same toward solicitors, barristers, and other members of the legal profession. There will always be solicitors, but there will not be as many of them ten years from now, because the demand will not be as great. There will not be as many doctors, accountants and surveyors for the same reason.

Most job opportunities in the years ahead will be in science and engineering. The next generation of robots will be able to see, touch, hear, smell and even talk to you. But robots are not human. They are mechanical devices, subject to periodic mechanical failure. Industry will require highly skilled technicians to look after these robots. They will need extra loving care. It has been forecast that there will be 1.5 million jobs for robot technicians by 1990. And career opportunities for robot engineers will be bright.

The drive to become independent of fossil fuels is likely to continue indefinitely. This will mean new job opportunities as new energy sources become available. Demand will greatly exceed manpower in nuclear power stations; in the processing and distribution of solar system manufacturing, installation and maintenance; in synfuels production; in biomass facilities operations and industries involving coal, shale and tar sands extraction. 'O' levels and two years training at a technical college will be required for energy technician jobs.

The world population is expected to double in the next 35 years. The need for low cost housing will intensify as the downwave deepens.

This will lead to the mass production of modular housing, employing radically new constructions, techniques, and materials. Modular housing will be fabricated with heating, electric waste disposal and recycling, and communications systems already installed. People who learn skills of this sort will be in steady demand.

In 1948, the transistor was launched. At the time, it was difficult to determine what would emerge from the development of the transistor. Initially it appeared to be nothing more than a replacement for the vacuum tube. The transistor led to the development of the silicon chip, upon which massive industries have been built. No less dramatic than the transistor is the laser. The laser is likely to replace machine and foundry tools in every tool and die making shop in the world. The machine tool makers of the future will be the laser technicians. It has been estimated that 2.5 million laser technicians will be required by the end of this decade. The wages of laser technicians will equal those of robot technicians.

No new industry will make more of an impact on society than gene splicing. Demand for PhD. biologists and chemists for genetic engineering firms will explode. Gene splicing will be hailed as one of man's most awesome accomplishments. Through the work of genetic engineers we already have the laboratory synthesis of insulin, interferon, human growth hormones, new antibiotics to treat bacterial infections, and new anti-coagulants to break up blood clots in the arteries. The years ahead involve amazing feats, like the genetic alteration of corn and wheat to suck nitrogen out of the air and eliminate the need for ammonia fertilisers. The genetic engineers believe they will be able to produce fuel from wastes; plastics from sugar; sweeteners from cheese; leach metals from ores and clean-up oil spills . . . if we actually continue to use oil.

A B.Sc. in chemistry, biology or medicine is likely to be the minimum educational qualification for the initial industrial production work. As the field widens, a great deal of the production operations will be accomplished by process technicians with lesser qualifications, and perhaps two years training in a technical college.

No skill will be in greater demand over the next decade than that of a computer programmer. In America, Harvard University now insists that all undergraduates be able to write a simple, two-step computer programme before graduating, regardless of their chosen career. Some already suggest that demand outstrips supply for computer programmers.

In the years ahead, certain established trades will flourish while new trades will appear. There will be work for operating engineers, men who are experienced at running cranes and bulldozers; motor mechanics; heating, cooling and refrigeration mechanics; skilled craftsmen and appliance service men.

Alternative energy industries will require solar technicians for sunny areas, and conservation technicians for colder climates. There will still be energy companies attempting to produce as much fossil fuel as possible at the lowest cost. Improved technology on-shore will increase drilling, and there will be a rising demand for oil field technicians in the U.K. and elsewhere. People will be needed to service the next generation of fuel cells and batteries to power the cars and homes of the future.

In the years to come, there will be no genuine shortage of jobs. The major shortage will be in adaptable, creative, imaginative people needed to fill these jobs. The 'help wanted' columns are unlikely to be barren, even during the depths of the depression.

Business Opportunities During the Downwave

The downwave will last from ten to fifteen years. First, we will have a 1930s type depression, followed by short periods of expansion, but longer periods of recession. When the downwave is complete, there will be a change as significant as when the world shifted from an agricultural society to an industrialised society. By the year 2,000, post-industrialised society is likely to be in full swing. Individuals who have adapted to the downwave, preserving their capital and energies, will reap the greatest benefits. The initial problem will be to make certain that the changes in the coming years do not set you back too far to share in the rewards of the next upwave, which will certainly come.

The man with a steady job in an established company attuned to the needs of the future will fare much better than the entrepreneur over the next few years. Business opportunities for the remainder of the 1980s and early 1990s are going to be limited. The small businessman will do far better than the big businessman. The entrepreneur who can sell his personal specialist skills will do far better than the man who has nothing to offer but a dash of accountancy skills and the ability to buy and sell things.

Over the past few years the British Government has encouraged many people to go into business with various business loan schemes, with the co-operation of the banking system. The programme has been a dismal failure. Unemployed workers have lost part, or all, of their 'golden handshakes'. People lacking skills and business accumen have lost their homes and savings. Business opportunities during a depression and the period that follows are limited. But there are some.

As budgets tighten, and more people are thrown out of work, the demand for cash will increase. Watch for the appearance of pawnbrokers again. A pawnbroker will lend money at what is usually an exceptionally high rate of interest. He will take your goods and hold them until you repay the loan, or continue to pay the interest on the loan. If you do not repay the loan, he sells your goods. This type of lending is exceptionally secure since most will only lend a small portion of the resale value of the goods they hold. When there is no one to turn to for immediate borrowing, the pawnbroker can help. It is likely to be very profitable in the years ahead.

Up and down the country there are small firms, often employing no more than three or four people, who call themselves 'Public Loss Assessors'. These assist in preparing claims for people who suffer insurance losses. Their function is important in the current environment. Crime is likely to increase, and will bring a dramatic jump in insurance claims. Insurance companies will be caught between falling premium income and heavier claims. There will be increasing pressure on loss adjusters to cut claims wherever possible. When someone makes an insurance claim, the insurance company will appoint a loss adjuster. The loss adjuster is supposed to be impartial, but is employed by the insurance company.

The 'loss assessor' acts for the insured to achieve the highest pay-out on the claim. Public loss assessors have no standard qualifications, and either gain experience as loss adjusters or by working for an insurance company. The loss assessor usually works on a percentage of the claim (10% is the norm). This could be boom business in the years ahead.

Remember Charles Atlas and the 7-stone weakling? This summer, as the sand-kicking season comes up, the tiny coupons will come pouring in asking for the 32-page booklet 'showing how dynamic tension can make a new man'. Ectomorphic adolescents, hungering for the great triangular chest Charles Atlas sports in the advertisements, find their salvation in body-building.

Charles Atlas, born Angelo Sciciliano in Brooklyn, New York, the Horatio Alger of the human body, died about a decade ago, but the business continues under the direction of Charles P. Roman. Every month, he sends out thousands of Charles Atlas lessons. The package costs $25,00, the same price as when Angelo Sciciliano and Charles Roman began in 1929. As a fledgling advertising man, Roman was given the Charles Atlas account, and decided that the best endorsement for the body-building plan called 'dynamic tension', was Charles Atlas in swimming trunks. The two men incorporated their efforts in 1929, a year when most men had nothing more than their bodies to bank on. The Charles Atlas technique was an immediate success. It is easy to imagine how profitable it must have been. The price of the course has been able to withstand inflation over fifty years. During the depression, people become more concerned with their appearance and wish to look more attractive, possibly to enhance job prospects. Businesses designed to exploit this could prove profitable.

As an increasing number of firms are squeezed for cash during the depression, there is a normal tendency to delay payments. In some cases payments are not made at all. Debt collectors do a brisk trade, along with companies who specialise in credit investigations and credit ratings.

As the depression deepens, more companies will be declaring voluntary liquidation and involuntary liquidation. There will be a booming trade in buying and re-selling bankrupt stock. Receivers and auctioneers will also find businesses booming.

An increasing number of unemployed will have a considerable amount of time on their hands. Do-it-yourself businesses and businesses leasing tools and equipment for the do-it-yourselfer will benefit.

Fast food chains usually thrive in a depression. The demand for cheap food increases as people seek to fill their stomachs cheaply. During the 1930s, the Horn & Hardart chain was born. These 'automats' employed a minimal labour, and dispensed hot food from coin-operated units. Throughout the 1930s, 1940s and 1950s the Horn & Hardart chain was among the most profitable American catering businesses.

Businesses which help people save money are good propositions. High quality, slightly used secondhand clothing shops should prosper. Appliance repairs, tailoring alterations, car repair and maintenance, and general repair work should do well. So will businesses involving salvage work, recycling old cars and other equipment and reclaimed building materials. It would also be worthwhile pursuing handyman skills such as carpentry, plumbing, welding, electrical repair work.

Currently there is considerable growth in centres for small manufacturing units serving regional needs. As the downwave goes on, people will try to avoid buying expensive items which are produced elsewhere. This will create opportunities for local producers and manufacturers. The town tradesman could find his business is recession-proof. The shopkeeper, the baker, the butcher, cafe operator, second-hand shop proprietor, tool sharpener, and the general repairman may well find his small town business prospering. Until recently, small towns were drying up, but now they are expanding again. No-one is getting rich, but there are opportunities for people moving into smaller towns. The small entrepreneurs are having a good life, and they are independent.

For the skilled craftsman, the idea should be to make things which are superior to machine-made ones. Leatherwork, pottery, musical instruments, quilts, knitwear, and exclusive made to measure clothing should all find a ready market, providing the price is right. Make it better, make it cheaper, and you will not have to worry too much about the depression.

A Consumer Stategy for the Downwave

At the early stages of the downwave, you can expect extremely wide price variations in routine items. At the time of writing, the price of a gallon of four star petrol varies from £1.39 to £1.84. Between the end of the secondary prosperity, and the beginning of the depression, this type of price variation is normal. Shoppers should constantly be making price comparisons on food, clothing and the necessities of life. On high priced goods, never pay the asking price, haggle. Do not be shy. Everybody does it. I do it all the time.

'January sales' . . . 'winter sales . . . 'summer sales' . . . 'autumn sales' . . . 'fire sales' . . . 'end of range sales' . . . 'beginning of range sales' . . . 'closing sales' . . . 'opening sales' . . . and all manner of sales will come with greater frequency as retailers attempt to unload stock. Postpone your purchases wherever possible, to take advantage of the retail price wars as depression bites into consumer industries.

As we move deeper into depression, price variations will disappear, and prices will decline in unison. Shoppers should only purchase sufficient for immediate needs. Buy daily, particularly with fresh produce like meat, fish, fruit and vegetables. Prices could fall day by day.

Second-hand 'big ticket' items are going to be available at enormous discounts in the months ahead. Stereos, videos, and other electrical items, prams, bicycles, gold, jewellery and such will be the most difficult to sell. The longer purchases are postponed, the cheaper they will be.

Your Home During the Downwave

Any form of property, commercial or residential, will be severely affected by the downwave for many years to come. Unfortunately, many home-owners who bought over the past year or so will also be exposed to great difficulties. People who took out a recent mortgage of 85–100% will be looking at very large losses if they sell, and fairly hefty paper losses if they do not. Often the deposit for a home represents the entire family savings. Already, many families have lost their entire savings, and do not realise it. I believe house prices will continue to fall, slowly but inexorably, for the next ten to fifteen years. Many people view their homes as a nest-egg, a source of money in the future, to be used for a second mortgage or security for bank borrowing.

When the day of reckoning comes, these people will be disappointed. They may find that their mortgage exceeds the value of their house, leaving their savings wiped out. Others are hoping to 'trade-up' to more expensive homes, assuming an increase in the value of their existing homes will let them make a larger deposit on a more expensive home. They, too, will be disappointed.

The mathematics are quite simple. Say you put down a deposit of £2,500, and bought an average priced house of £25,000. You would have £2,500 of equity, and would owe £22,500 on a first mortgage. Suppose the house falls in value by 15%, a conservative estimate given the likely conditions over the next year or two. A 15% fall would mean your house will only be worth £21,250. You will still owe £22,500 on your mortgage. That means your £2,500 savings have been wiped out. If you sell you will have to find £1,250 to repay the balance of your mortgage.

For those who recently took out a 100% mortgage, the mathematics get worse. Say you borrowed £20,000 on a £20,000 flat. If values fall by 15%, that £20,000 flat will be worth £17,000. If you want to move, you still have to pay back that £20,000 mortgage. Before thinking of moving, you would need £3,000. If the price of homes falls faster than your mortgage repayments, bearing in mind that during the first few years you are only paying back interest, it could be a long, long time before you build sufficient equity to repay the mortgage from the proceeds of sale. Your little castle could become your dungeon.

So far, I have only dealt with the possibility of a 15% fall in house prices, assuming that most people will be able to manage their mortgage payments. Say you have been 'trading-up', putting down larger deposits on more expensive homes, and taking out larger mortgages. Suppose you made a profit of £10,000 on your previous home, and put it all down on another home costing £50,000, with a mortgage of £40,000. With interest rates at 15%, that will involve a pretty hefty monthly outgoing. Higher priced properties have recently fallen in value much faster than lower priced ones. It is quite conceivable that cheaper properties could fall by 15%, and the prices at the upper end of the market could fall by 30%.

If you suddenly find difficulty in meeting your mortgage repayments, and find you must sell and move to a cheaper house, there are problems. Your £50,000 house would be worth £35,000. Your £10,000 deposit would have evaporated and you will still owe £40,000 on mortgage. Somehow you have to find £5,000 to make up the difference between the sale price of the house, and the amount you owe on mortgage. Technically you could be bankrupt, with liabilities greater than your assets. If you cannot keep up your mortgage repayments, you lose your home, and face Carey Street. That could be what home ownership means during the downwave. Bear in mind, this example involves a relatively small fall in house prices. My forecast is of a fall of as much as 80% over the next ten to fifteen years.

The home-owner must be fully aware that such a decline in property values will represent a *real* loss of spendable money. This may not be as clear to most home owners as it appears. Many bought their homes 10 to 15 years ago, perhaps even longer, at relatively modest prices, and rest happy that they are risking no more than their original investment, if that. Not so.

If the average man had put aside £20,000 in a bank 15 years ago, that £20,000 would have grown to £50,000, assuming a modest average gross return of 9% and after tax return of 6%. If, as a result of a bank failure or other catastrophe, you lost £15,000 of your accumulated capital, you would be very upset. The home-owner must accept that his loss from the coming collapse in house prices will be the same type of loss. Money you thought was yours will no longer be yours; the same type of spendable money that could be used to pay medical expenses, send a child through school, or buy a new car.

There is a thing called 'opportunity cost' in leaving your money in a depreciating asset. If you took £50,000, and put it into a long term fixed interest investment such as British government securities yielding 13.5%, in three years time you would have £64,000, a rise of £14,000 as opposed to a £15,000 loss which would come if your house fell in value by 30%.

Without a doubt, if practicable, the immediate sale of property, given the current high return on safe investments, is the most positive course of action any home-owner could take. If you have a home worth £50,000, with equity of £35,000, and an outstanding mortgage of £15,000, you can take your tax free capital gain and achieve an additional gross income of £4,725 on your equity before that £35,000 disappears into the property mêlée. You will have no further mortgage instalments to pay and no more insurance premiums or repairs. Depending on your area, you should be able to rent accommodation as good as you sell, given the increase in income which the investment return and savings on home ownership will allow. You will also be able to freeze that £35,000 equity. The mathematics speak for themselves.

My recommended strategy for the downwave is that, if you are thinking of buying a house, do not if you can possibly avoid it. Wait! If you own a home with substantial equity, sell if possible, and rent.

The best deals in rented accommodation are in short leases, and the unexpired portion of longer leases. Estate agents have been finding it difficult to sell these tail-end leases. Rents are well below market rents. Currently, most people are unwilling to pay a high premium for a short lease. Most people harbour the illusion of continued inflation and rising property values. It is therefore generally believed there will be an astronomical increase in rent when the short lease expires. This is incorrect, but explains why short leases can be had at bargain prices. A two to six year lease on residential property offers excellent value. It is now a buyer's market for short leases, and this should continue for quite some time, though newly created leases should be viewed with suspicion.

If you do not, or cannot, become a renter, and are unable or unwil-

ling to part with your existing home, there are other alternatives. These
are not so satisfactory, but they will offer some additional protection,
and are better than taking no action at all.

It would be wise to investigate refinancing your home, and investing
the proceeds. The object will be to achieve an after tax return on the
additional borrowed funds in excess of the interest payments after tax.
In some cases this may be possible, and could increase your income.

There are also companies offering what is, in essence, a sale and
leaseback on your home, guaranteeing you a life-tenancy. This is
known as selling a reversionary interest, and allows the original owner
to stay on as a tenant at a peppercorn rental for life. The discounted
price you receive for your home will depend on your age and the value
of the property. Many larger estate agents can help with a quote for
selling a reversionary interest in your home.

Several useful plans are offered by insurance companies. Hambro
Life offer the Home Income Plan, basically designed for those aged 65
or over. A 75 year old person with a house worth more than £32,000
could take out a loan from the company of £25,000. This loan would be
used to purchase an annuity. If the individual were paying 55% tax
(40% plus 15% investment income surcharge), a net income of £1,750
per year would be receivable after interest on the loan. In this way, the
equity in the property is used to provide additional income. Like the
annuity, the loan is fixed for life. When the individual dies, the loan is
automatically repaid and the house reverts to the estate of the original
home owner. Several other companies offer similar schemes, which
are worth investigating.

If you have absolutely no alternative and *must* buy a house, do it with
the maximum possible mortgage. I would also recommend that your
mortgage be with a bank rather than a building society. Recommend-
ing a maximum possible mortgage may appear as a direct contradiction
to my previous recommendations. Bear in mind, this is only directed to
those who are forced to buy a home, or be homeless. I hope you are not
in that position. If you are, here is why I recommend the maximum
possible mortgage:

a. Mortgage funds are subsidised. They are the cheapest funds you
can borrow. Rather than put your savings into a home, it is far better to
put them in a bank or other safe investment and earn the difference
between what you have to pay as interest on a mortgage and the
interest you will receive on your investment. Take as much as you can
at the subsidised rate, and invest your money at prevailing rates.

b. The home you buy is likely to be a depreciating asset. The smaller
the amount of your own money in the house, the lesser the chance of
your savings losing value. Your savings should go into low risk, high
income producing assets which will enable your funds to grow. Property is a high-risk non-income producing asset, which is over-valued

and which will virtually assure the decline of your savings.

c. The financial environment now carries an ever increasing risk. Personal liquidity during such times is paramount. Funds tied up in property are illiquid, and may not be available when you need them most. Liquidity will give you the flexibility which is mandatory for the financial climate of the next few years.

d. If the worst of all things happens, and you are unable to make your mortgage repayments, the greater the negative margin between the value of your house and the outstanding mortgage, the further back you will be in the queue when the lender considers calling in your mortgage. Say you take out a 95% mortgage on a £50,000 property. You will owe the lender £47,500. If the bank is forced to foreclose on the mortgage, the bank will have to write off £2,500 on a 10% decline in property values. (£50,000 minus 10% equals £45,000 minus £47,500 mortgage equals deficit £2,500). Given the same decline in property values, another borrower in trouble with a 90% mortgage instead of a 95% mortgage, would leave the bank with nothing to write off. It would be far more tempting to the bank to foreclose where they did not have to take write-offs, than where a bad debt will arise.

e. I recommend a mortgage with a bank, as opposed to a building society. My discussions with bankers and building society managers leave the distinct impression that a banker will take a more lenient line when it comes to calling in a mortgage than a building society which may soon be experiencing severe strains from mortgage defaulters and withdrawals by depositors. In addition, lending rates are likely to fall more quickly than building society rates, due to problems which may be peculiar to building societies rather than banks.

Your Holiday Home

While buying a home is unlikely to be a good investment in the years ahead, holiday homes are likely to be an even worse investment. Holiday villas in less industrialised nations are likely to fall steeply in value, with many countries being forced to impose exchange controls. The weaker countries will get weaker. Unfortunately, many of the sun-drenched villas are in areas with exceptionally weak economies, like Italy, Malta, Spain, and France. These areas are also becoming more politically unstable.

A recent study by Forecasting International, using a technique which predicted upheavals in Iran, Poland and Afghanistan several years before they occurred, shows turbulent times ahead for Italy and Spain. The Forecasting International model devises a set of 'vital signs' for each nation. These include general welfare figures, the number of fertile females and their offspring, the trade balance and energy dependence, the number of guest workers, the treatment of dissidents, arms sales, and the rate of increase of military salaries (if military pay doubles in two years, someone is attempting to buy loyalty). Also considered are the income gap between the top and bottom tenths, racial and ethnic tensions, and the number of educated males between 18 and 28 living in cities and unemployed (a prime source of political dissidents). These are all related to potential world events in energy, non-renewable resources, capital formation, inflation, deflation, population and food.

In the years ahead, some of the most dramatic changes in outlook will affect nations now in the mid-range of economic and political stability. Italy is expected to fall to 20th place, putting it on par with a country like Nigeria. Italy's decline in stability corresponds with the end of the brief co-operation between the Italian Communist Party and the ruling Coalition that followed the dramatic Moro kidnapping in 1978. Continuing terrorist activities could ultimately lead to the collapse of Italy's constitutional government. Italy is also vulnerable to many political, social and economic weaknesses which will be exacerbated by global trends over the next few years. The worst Italian problems will be related to food, population, energy and raw materials.

Spain is another country likely to suffer a dramatic decline in political and economic stability. In 1980, Spain ranked 15th in terms of stability. It is forecast that Spain will fall to 25th place, making it one of the world's most unstable countries. Spain is troubled by economic stagnation, and burdened with one of the heaviest external debt problems in recent history, at $5 billion. The deteriorating world trends over the next few years will have a greater destabilising effect on Spain than on other nations. Over the near term, Spain faces serious problems which include a lack of energy resources, dependence on foreign capital and technology, and internal strife caused by the separatist activities of the Basque and Catalan parties.

Israel is expected to fall from 14th in terms of political and economic stability, to 23rd, placing it among the five least stable countries. The decline can be attributed to increasing violence between Arabs and Jews in the occupied territories; the increasing influence of the West on Israel's Arab neighbours, and the continued lack of ideological unity among the Israelis. Inflation in Israel is an incredible 130%. The birthrate for Israel's Arabs is more than six times greater than that of Israel's Jews, and will aggravate internal tensions. The admission of Spain and Portugal to the EEC will mean an Israeli loss of citrus and flour exports, adding to the weakness of the economy.

While the value of holiday homes inside the U.K. will fall dramatically as people build liquidity, it may be difficult to get money out of holiday homes outside the U.K. And in areas of growing instability you may also find difficulties in getting yourself out.

Chapter Twelve

INVESTMENT DURING THE DOWNWAVE

Much has been written about panics and manias, much more than with
the most out-stretched intellect we are able to follow or conceive; but one
thing is certain, that at particular times a great deal of stupid people have
a great deal of stupid money . . . At intervals, from causes which are not
to the present purpose, the money of these people – the blind capital, as
we call it, of the country – is particularly large and craving; it seeks for
someone to devour it, and there is a 'plethora'; it finds someone, and
there is 'speculation'; it is devoured, and there is 'panic'.

Walter Bagehot
'Essay on Edward Gibbon'

The final stages of the upwave produce explosive growth in 'collectibles' like works of art, antiques, diamonds, gem stones, stamps,
coins, gold and silver. During the downwave, there is likely to be a
total collapse in the value of these collectibles. Many of them will fall by
as much as 90% from their peak. During the latter part of 1980, super-
cyclical downtrends began in many of them. Diamonds, gem stones,
wines, coins, and stamps had lost as much as 50% of their previous
values by mid-1982. These downtrends are likely to continue for the
next 10 to 15 years. Many people will still harbour the belief that they
will ultimately return to their peak prices. This may take place, but it
could take 40 to 50 years.

When we reach the 'panic' phase of the downwave, which is now
rapidly approaching, there will be a collapse in equity markets across
the board. On the other hand, there is likely to be a complete rejuven-
ation of fixed interest markets. During the early stages of the 'panic',
individuals who take advantage of the high yields in high quality fixed
interest investments will be able to enjoy the capital gains falling
interest rates provide, along with high income. As the downwave
progresses, the yield gap between equity investment and fixed interest
investment will disappear. Ultimately, equities will yield more than
fixed interest investments to compensate for what is likely to be perceived as higher risk. First and foremost, investors must make every
effort possible to protect their capital during the downwave. This
means avoiding speculative endeavours like poison, and discarding

any investment where there is a risk to nominal capital. If you are merely able to emerge from the 'panic' phase of the downwave with your capital base intact, you will have done far better than a great many investors. You must exercise extreme caution.

Frauds, Swindles and Deceptions in the Downwave

As businesses become over-extended during the upwave, there is an increasing tendency toward financial mismanagement. Commercial and financial crises are intimately linked with transactions which overstep the confines of law and morality, shadowy though these confines may be. The propensity to swindle and be swindled runs parallel to the propensity to speculate during a boom. Crash and panic, with their motto 'sauve qui peut', prompt still more people to cheat to save themselves.

Greed not only creates suckers to be swindled by professionals, but also pushes some of the amateurs over the line into fraud, embezzlement, defalcation, and such. The forms of financial felony are legion. In addition to outright stealing, misrepresentation, and simple lying, there are many other practices close to the line of morality and legality: diversion of funds from the stated use to an alternative use; paying dividends out of capital; dealing in shares on insider knowledge; taking orders but not executing them; borrowing against shares owned by another; selling securities without full disclosure of prior knowledge; using company funds to benefit insiders; mixing clients' funds with personal funds; using discretionary powers for matters of self-interest; altering a company's book; falsifying confirmations and contract notes; dealing to the disadvantage of individual clients. The list of tricks the trickster can get up to to feather his nest at your expense is virtually endless.

It would be comforting to believe that illicit financial practices have declined over the past 250 years or so. Yet, recent evidence suggests that the terminal phase of each economic cycle brings a vast array of swindles and the collapse of an uncomfortable number of financial institutions. The last cycle brought the saga of Investors Overseas Services. The securities sold by IOS were not sold in the United States because the Securities and Exchange Commission stopped it. Many U.K. financial institutions refused to handle IOS securities long before the scandal broke. Yet, many greedy investors saw IOS as a safe haven for European money seeking to escape withholding taxes and wanting action in the world's stock markets. The plungers at IOS also proved to be losers. When Bernie Cornfeld went to prison for his role in the operation, Robert Vesco took over. It is rumoured that Vesco looted $200 million.

In addition to IOS, there was the usual sprinkling of bank frauds and banking failures. There was a scandal at the Chiasso branch of Credit Suisse. The bank suffered large losses from speculation through a Liechtenstein subsidiary which was believed to be illegally exporting Italian capital.

During the last cycle, there was also the failure of a small private bank in Geneva called Le Clerc. The Franklin National Bank in New York failed, and so did the Herstatt Bank of Cologne. Both failures were deemed to be aided and abetted by unauthorised foreign exchange speculation by employees of the banks. As the shock waves of these financial difficulties travelled around the world, many other banks were brought to the brink of failure. The First National City Bank in Brussels, Banque de Bruxelles, also in Brussels, Lloyds Bank in Trentino, were brought to their knees. And, how can we ever forget the infamous London & County in Britain? Their failure sparked a chain reaction which took many other smaller banking institutions with it, and ultimately involved the joint stock clearing banks. When the situation got too hot for them to handle, in came the lender of last resort, the Bank of England.

What can of worms will we have as we approach the panic stage of the downwave? It takes little imagination to see that the can has already been opened. A financial panic does not occur all at once. It begins with a series of crises which build in size and frequency, until the straw which breaks the camel's back. This time around it seems the Hunt Brothers actually set the ball rolling. Their heavy losses in early 1980 as a result of the collapse in silver nearly brought a major crisis in some of the world's leading brokerage houses, a crisis only narrowly averted by the Federal Reserve Board in the U.S.

Since the Hunt Brothers affair, we have seen the collapse of an American Government Securities dealing firm, Drysdale & Co. in early 1982, and the fall of Penn Square, a bank which specialised in lending to the energy industry. In the summer of 1982, the Savings and Investment Bank in the Isle of Man hit trouble, while the Midland Bank and the National Westminster Bank declared Banco Ambrosiano Holdings of Luxembourg in default. Once again we see history repeating itself, with the sums in default becoming increasingly larger, and the defaults coming faster as we approach the panic phase of the downwave.

A depression brings bank failures and bankruptcies because the decline in business activity means that people will have to use money they have been holding as cash. When these funds are exhausted, people have to sell assets to survive. As the initial withdrawals increase, money becomes still tighter. Borrowers find it increasingly difficult to make repayments, and to refinance their debts. The result is a decline in the value of the assets which financial institutions are holding as security against loans, and in the liquidity of these financial institutions. The problems are compounded by inevitable loan defaulters. More and bigger companies go into liquidation. The financial institutions face soaring provisions for bad debts. During mid-1982, 226 companies a week were going bankrupt in Britain. There were 450 reported bankruptcies each week in the U.S.A.

How Safe Are Your Savings?

There are two other major threats to the international banking system as we enter the most serious and disruptive portion of the downwave. The first is the possibility of a major default amongst the lesser developed country borrowers, who are heavily indebted to the commercial banking system. The second is the threat of a major withdrawal of Arab money from both American and British banks, without notice. I am not alone in believing that the global banking system is in a very delicate condition, racing toward the most serious test it has had to face since the 1930s.

Banks can get into trouble from both sides of the balance sheet:
1. There could be a horrendous cumulative default by several of the lesser developed countries, hitting banks already troubled by failing companies. That threatens the bank's assets.
2. Savings accounts maintained by the banks, plus Certificates of Deposit, could be withdrawn or not renewed. That would affect liabilities. A rapid withdrawal of funds represents the classic 'run on the banks'. The result could be catastrophic. World-wide, it has been estimated that about 5% of bank assets represents cash on hand. The other 95% is lent or invested.
3. Banks operate under the assumption that conditions are always relatively normal, and nothing could happen to endanger their assets or liabilities enough to cause a 'run', or bring abnormal losses. Banks operate on a foundation of public confidence. As we have seen in the past, public confidence can suddenly turn to panic. The long list of failed financial institutions proves it. History shows many lost bank deposits.

Banks borrow short, and lend long. They honour cheques on other banks, and often allow depositors to draw on those cheques before they have cleared through the issuing house. A sudden and abrupt failure of a major bank could produce chaos at the clearing houses, and have a devastating affect on all of the clearing banks.

When one bank goes down, if it is big enough, it will take others with it. The banking panic of the 1930s began with the failure of a bank in Austria. The British banking panic of the 1970s began with the failure of London & County. Both of these were relatively modest outfits. This time around, the names are going to get bigger. The debts of the Austrian bank and London & County were miniscule compared to the combined sums in default at Drysdale, Penn Square, Banco Ambrosiano, and the money involved in the Nelson Bunker Hunt silver fiasco.

The real uncertainty comes when depositors become aware of bank problems, and begin to worry. In a real panic, people do not distinguish between good and bad, or between sound and unsound banks. They run to all of the banks to get their money out. All banks become suspect. The classic public reaction is to withdraw money while the bank is still solvent. This in itself leads to insolvency. The only thing that prevents people from running regularly to get their money out is their belief that the banks are not likely to fail. Once that changes, the banks will fail.

At the moment, the majority of financial institutions around the world, whether they be finance companies, banks, building societies, or other forms of lending institutions, are essentially illiquid. Any institutions predominantly in mortgages or consumer borrowing, or heavily into other long term lending could fail, regardless of how sound they appear now. It is time to take a very close look at where your liquid funds are tucked away, and to think very carefully about their safety.

How to Protect Yourself From a Banking Crisis

What would a banking crisis mean? At best it would mean great inconvenience. You might have to wait for your money until you found yourself in deep difficulties. At worst, it could mean the failure of the currency, with the near total loss of purchasing power of your funds. In between the 'best case' and the 'worst case', you are likely to lose whatever you have if it is invested in something which goes bankrupt.

That raises a very serious practical problem. What should you do? I cannot forecast just when the banks are going to hit severe trouble, or how badly the coming banking crisis will affect the average depositor. All I do know is that risks are astronomically high. If, on any given day, depositors representing a mere 5% of sums on deposit at the banks demanded their funds (Arab money alone could do it), even the strongest would fail. Obviously, conditions would have to deteriorate quite considerably before this kind of panic developed. But depressions breed this type of panic. We are now in a worldwide depression.

It should be obvious that you must exercise the utmost caution, especially if you are dealing with financial institutions outside the mainland of Great Britain. A branch of a bank outside the U.K. may not receive the support of the U.K. parent. As a general rule, avoid putting funds on deposit outside the U.K. if possible. If not, be certain those funds are being held (a) by a branch of one of the major clearing banks such as Barclays, Lloyds, Midland, NatWest, or a bank of similar stature; (b) by one of the issuing houses or accepting houses authorised by the Bank of England. If you go to a building society, it is vital to choose a member of the Building Societies Association. Recent changes have cut the degree of support the larger societies are prepared to give to non-members.

In America, banks which belong of the Federal Reserve System are likely to offer far greater security than those which are not. Under the Federal Reserve System, each account is insured for up to £40,000, by government guarantee. I would not recommend a deposit of more than £40,000 with any bank outside the U.S. top ten. Banks have been leaving the Federal Reserve System because that allows them to hold lower reserves against liabilities than if they were members. U.S. banks are more highly geared than any in major western countries. Be certain only to deposit funds with a member of the Federal Reserve System.

The liquidity policies of finance companies and banks differ widely. Deal only with those which invest mainly in short term government securities for their liquid funds. Always spread deposits between different institutions. If one of them experiences difficulties, only part of your assets will be hit. It would be very unwise to leave your funds with only one institution, regardless of how sound it may appear.

Most important of all . . . in fact . . . it's absolutely vital . . . do not . . . do not . . . do not . . . under any circumstances . . . deal with any financial institution offering a deposit rate appreciably higher than the major banks, no matter who. Each day 'The Financial Times' reports money market rates. Use these rates as your guidelines.

Any financial institution offering a higher-than-market return gives rise to serious suspicions. If they are going to pay you more than the average rate, it means that they find it difficult to attract funds at the market rate. There are likely to be good reasons for that. If they are to make a profit on the high rate, they must also receive a much higher-than-market return themselves on their investments. They can only do that if they entertain above average risk investments. The last thing you want, is to have your funds supposedly safely tucked away, and then find they are being used for above-average risk investment. In practically every case of financial failure, it happened because of high risk investment.

It is possible, but not probable, that we may have a banking crisis of such severity that it will make no difference which banks or building societies have your money. If the bank with your money is small, and among the first to go broke it will be rescued. If the building society is small, you will find that it merges with another building society, and you should be able to get your money without difficulty.

Should the entire system be threatened and shut down for a while, practically everyone with a deposit account will find themselves in difficulty. If there is a widespread banking moratorium like that of the 1930s, it will not make much difference which bank you were patronising. The banks most likely to re-open first after a crisis are the flagship banks, the big 'four' clearers in Britain, and the top ten in the U.S.A. The nation will have to restore a monetary system of some kind in crisis and it can only do it through the banking system. The banks which will receive the strongest support will be those with the highest safety for the greatest number, even though these may be the very banks exposed to the biggest defaulters.

There will be an escalating number of failures of financial institutions over the next two to three years. I have no way of knowing which companies are going under, and which will be the first of the British banks to suffer catastrophe. I have no idea to what extent the government might protect the interests of depositors, or whether the larger banks will be able to save the smaller banks, and thus protect the reputation of the British banking system. What I am absolutely sure of is that there will be failures, and that some financial institutions will be going into receivership. It is certainly not a matter of 'if', it is a matter of 'when'. There is certainly a possibility that you may now be dealing with a company which could end up in receivership. In many cases, it will mean a 100% loss of your savings. That chance is not worth the risk, when all that may be gained is an extra one or two per cent per annum in interest.

Seventy Years of Investment

Safety first must be the objective during the downwave. The rewards of such a policy may be far greater than you think. Money saved now and properly invested should yield many times its purchasing power in the years to come. We are entering the current phase of the downwave with exceptionally high yields which, if compounded, can produce staggering returns. Bernard Baruch was once asked if he knew of the seven wonders of the world. He replied: 'I'm not too sure about the seven wonders of the world, but I can tell you all about the eighth wonder . . . that's compound interest'.

There's a little calculation called 'The Rule of 72'. If you divide the number 72 by the yield on an investment, that is about how long it will take to double your money at a compound rate. At a yield of 12%, you double your money every six years. At 14%, you double it in just over five years. At 16%, you double it every $4\frac{1}{2}$ years. As we continue along the downwave, these rewards are available with fixed interest investments carrying the lowest possible risk.

There is an investment cycle related to the economic cycle. To maximise your investment returns and protect your capital, your investment strategy must be compatible with the economic environment. The investment cycle involves moving from cash or cash equivalents, to fixed interest, followed by equities, then inflation hedges like silver and gold, and finally back to cash again.

1910–1920

Taking real returns, the decade from 1910 to 1920 was the worst this century. Adjusted for inflation, real losses on preferred shares, fixed interest bonds and equities were quite heavy. Fixed interest issues fared worst, and equities best, but all three groups suffered losses in real terms. For a brief period, there was a commodity price explosion and investors able to spot the terminal stage of the upwave, and the way inflation hedges behave then, made fortunes. The profits were short-lived. The decade of 1910–1920 was similar to 1960–1970 in terms of investment performance.

1920–1930

The decade from 1920 to 1930 presented those once-in-a-lifetime years. All three major groups of stock exchange securities did well, with high real rates of return. Although the 1920–1930 decade was the first of the downwave, and included the Crash of '29, the decade ended with a satisfactory performance, except for those riding the commodity boom who failed to take their profits when the boom was over. There was a crash in commodity markets from 1920 to 1922, annihilating commodity speculators. Inflation hedges stopped working.

The 1920–1930 decade involved the 1922–1929 period of secondary prosperity. The crash in commodity prices sent a large flow of funds back into stock exchange investment.

During the decade, fixed interest investments fared best. The worst were preference shares. During this decade, fixed interest investment began to emerge as an excellent hedge against deflation, although, during the previous decade, fixed interest investment showed the worst negative real rate of return.

The decade 1920–1930 can be compared with 1970–1980. In Britain, a long term bull market began in government securities in late 1974, and was continuing in 1982. Although the government securities index had failed to reach the levels of the beginning of the decade, on a total return basis the performance was far better than other classes of U.K. Stock Exchange securities. The Financial Times 30 Share Index reached 545 in May 1972. By May 1982, there was relatively little change.

1930–1940

For investors who were able to hold fixed interest investments through the depression years, the 1930s provided some of the best real rates of return of the 20th Century. Preferred shares showed the second highest real return. Ordinary shares produced the lowest real return. In the early part of the 1930s, deflation was relatively severe. Initially, funds flowed into cash equivalents like Treasury Bills as the safety of the banks came into question.

As interest rates began falling quite clearly, investors wished to lock-in the high yields on longer term fixed interest issues. Funds began flowing out of cash into high quality fixed interest investments with high coupons providing an excellent hedge against inflation. The only trick was to spot the deflationary environment. Most investors missed it until much later in the decade. Ordinary shares were totally unsuitable as a hedge against inflation. The 1930s saw the end of the downwave. The decade of 1930–1940 could well offer revealing guidelines to what can be expected during the decade 1980–1990.

1940–1950

By the 1940s it was accepted that, after nearly 20 years of deflation, deflation was likely to be a permanent way of life. War brought the beginning of the long inflationary upwave. At the time, this inflationary trend was considered counter to the overriding deflation. The upwave had begun, but very few people were aware of it. Fixed interest investments continued to gain popularity during the 1940s. But over the decade, they failed to show a positive rate of return. Near the end of the decade, a long term decline began in fixed interest investments as inflation began to rear its ugly head. During the latter part of the decade, ordinary shares began to demonstrate their ability to cope with the gradually rising inflationary trend.

1950–1960

During the latter part of the 1950s, the 'cult of the equity' was born. Inflation was recognised as a serious problem, and it was thought that the best way to beat it was with ordinary shares. Inflation was growing moderately after World War II, and the cycle for fixed interest investment had turned decidedly down. For the next two decades, fixed interest investment was totally inadequate as a hedge against inflation. During the 1950s, only ordinary shares produced a positive real return. For the decade, fixed interest investment and preference shares produced negative real returns.

1960–1970

The 1960s, the third decade of the upwave, brought a replay of the previous decade. Ordinary shares were the best performers, preferred shares came next. Fixed interest investments were the worst performers. However, the real return in all securities was lower than during the previous decade. There was a marginal positive real return in preferred shares, and a more positive real return on ordinary shares.

Fixed interest holdings remained poor. But equity investment was beginning to lag behind inflation during the latter part of the decade.

1970–1980

No class of stock exchange investment could keep pace with inflation during the 1970–1980 decade. The decade was extremely similar to the 1920s. There was a boom in commodity prices. Gold and silver soared. The best performances were in the inflation hedges. In January 1969, the Financial Times 30 Share Index reached 520. Over the next ten years there had been very little progress. Fixed interest investments continued to decline in real terms, but the rate of decline was far lower than in the previous two decades. In 1974, British government securities began a long term bull market. In 1980, that long term bull market in fixed interest investment appeared to be continuing. Peak prices were achieved in most collectibles, which began downtrends. During the next two years, gold lost more than half of its value.

A closer study of investment in the seventy years from 1910 to 1980 is revealing. Before the peak inflation of 1920, the negative real return on fixed interest investment was at its highest for years. During the 1930s, what had previously been the highest negative return became the highest positive return in the fixed interest market. During the 1940s, fixed interest holdings continued to produce a positive return. But in the 1950s, 1960s and 1970s, fixed interest investment brought a negative return. By the latter part of the 1970s, the negative return in fixed interest was far lower than during the 1960s, suggesting that the long term trend was changing again.

In years of above average inflation, no class of stock exchange security proved an adequate inflation hedge. The only investments capable of producing a positive return against above average inflation were commodities and collectibles, but only for a short period during the final stages of the upwave. During periods of average inflation, the best returns were in the equity market. When deflation ruled, the best returns came from fixed interest investments.

The long term record shows that fixed interest securities, decade by decade, seem to be a better hedge against deflation than equity investment is against inflation. Since 1910, there were 35 years when the inflation rate was below average for the decade. For those 35 years, in only six years did fixed interest investments fail to produce a real return. Where there was a negative return, the performance was only marginally poor. Thus, on average, the return on fixed interest investment was positive.

The net positive real return for each decade proved particularly important during the 1920s and 1930s, the first two decades of the last downwave. In 12 of the 35 years when inflation was below the average of the decade, ordinary shares failed to produce a positive real return.

The performance of ordinary shares during the deflationary 1930s was disastrous.

This does not mean that fixed interest securities are a better long term investment than ordinary shares. On the contrary, although there were years in which ordinary shares generated a negative real return worse than that on fixed interest investment, overall returns for equities were greater than for fixed interest securities for most of the past 70 years.

Timing is of vital importance, more so with equities than fixed interest investments. The fluctuations in the equity cycle are far greater than in the fixed interest cycle. We are now entering the phase when fixed interest investments are likely to be abnormally strong, and equities abnormally weak. Over the next half of this decade, it is likely that fixed interest holdings will produce a positive real return against a negative return on equities. The gap between the two is likely to be greater than ever in the past seventy years.

Investment Recommendations During the Downwave

During the downwave, interest rates are likely to continue to fall, along with the rate of inflation. As they fall, the prospects for fixed interest holdings will improve. But there are certain dangers in fixed interest.

Treasury Bills

Government Treasury Bills are safest of all. They represent the first call on a government, and are safer than money in the bank. Their only disadvantage is that, because of their safety, their yield is lower than other fixed interest securities, and they have a short life. In Britain, the longest Treasury Bill is three months. Investors fearing the worst should have all of their money in Treasury Bills. As interest rates fall, so too will the yield on Treasury Bills. As the cycle progresses, those seeking the safety of Treasury Bills will have to accept a progressively lower return on capital, similar to a bank account. In view of the risks ahead, I feel that a minimum of 5% of all larger portfolios should be in Treasury Bills now.

Government Securities

The British Consols Price Index, an established measure of government security prices, touched 76 in 1922, and rose steadily to 151 by 1936. Conservative investors doubled their money during what were deemed the most disastrous investment years in history.

To determine the best investment for the decade of 1980–1990, simply study the best investments between 1930 and 1940. British Government Securities rank second for safety. They are the second call on the nation's assets after Treasury Bills. There are three classes of

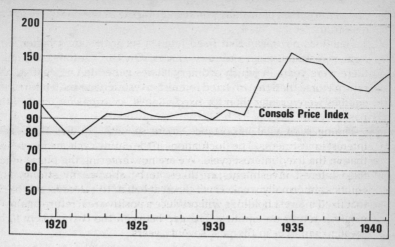

Figure 22   British Consols Price Index 1919–1941

Source: De Zoete & Bevan

Government Securities, short, medium and long dated. The longer the period, the greater will be the short term fluctuation and risk to capital. Investors who want the highest security are best advised to concentrate on short dated Government Securities. Those willing to speculate on the continued decline in interest rates may wish to concentrate on longer dated issues.

I have a relatively wide spread of Government Securities in the funds I manage. Until we reach the nadir of the crisis, I prefer short and medium dated securities. After the panic phase is over, I intend to move all of my sterling funds into long dated Government Securities.

Corporate Fixed Interest Securities

I do not recommend buying corporate fixed interest securities in Britain. The return on Government Securities is currently as good as the return on corporate fixed interest investments. For the average investor, there are far greater tax advantages in British Government Securities than British corporate fixed interest stocks.

There is one exception, however. The prospects for U.S. fixed interest corporate securities in companies with a Triple A rating are outstanding. For the next five to ten years, the U.S. dollar will be the world's strongest currency. The advantages of buying U.S. corporate fixed interest securities in Triple A rated companies outweigh the tax advantages of British Government Securities.

Fixed Interest Eurobond Investment

The Eurobond market offers several advantages to the investor seeking high income. Eurobond yields for issues traded in sterling usually have been higher than on British Government Securities with corresponding maturity dates. Many government issues are now available on the Eurobond market, as are high quality corporate issues. One of the advantages of Eurobonds is that tax is not deducted from the interest payments which are made once each year, giving the investor the full return on his investment. Once again I must emphasise, stick to quality in corporate bonds, the higher the quality the better. Do not sacrifice quality for that extra bit of income.

With government fixed interest stocks, stick to the strongest countries. Denmark, Sweden and Norway are among the strongest. Fixed interest issues from the European Investment Bank, the World Bank and other government guaranteed fixed interest bonds are recommended. I am not suggesting that other countries with Euromarket bonds are likely to go bankrupt. But countries engaged in profligate spending, such as France, may have an unquenchable thirst for funds, and may pay a far higher rate than others. If the internal interest rates of a country are rising while interest rates in other countries are falling, this will affect the value of your bonds.

Deep Discount Bonds

When a fixed interest investment is first issued, it is priced in accordance with prevailing interest rates. Say prevailing interest rates are 7%. Then a bond will carry a coupon of 7%, and be issued at par (100). If interest rates rise to 14%, this bond, issued at 100, will fall to 50 to compete with other bonds with a 14% coupon, selling at par. There are many government securities and corporate bonds selling at a deep discount to their original issue prices, since they were issued when interest rates were far lower. For those interested in capital growth, for every percentage fall in interest rates, a deep discount bond will show a greater percentage gain in capital value than a bond with a coupon at or near current interest rates. Likewise, for any percentage rise in interest rates, deep discount bonds will suffer greater falls than bonds with a current coupon trading at or near par value. While deep discount bonds offer greater capital gain potential, they also offer greater risks.

Zero Coupon Bonds

The zero coupon bond is the ultimate in terms of a deep discount bond. The bond itself pays no interest, but trades with accrued amortisation. What is deemed to be interest is paid in full at the end of the maturity period. The major advantage of zero coupon bonds is that you have the chance to compound your return. Most who purchase a bond will receive their annual or semi-annual interest payments, and subsequently spend these modest payments, never benefitting from the marvels of compound interest. Zero coupon bonds are priced at their fully discounted level. For example, a compound interest rate of 12% will double your money in six years. A zero coupon bond maturing in six years at par (100) would thus be priced at 50 to yield 12%. Zero coupon bonds vary in their maturities. During 1982, when prevailing interest rates were around 13%, the General Electric Zero Coupon of 1995 was priced at 20. If you purchase this zero coupon at 20, you would make five times your money by maturity in 1995, backed by the guarantee of General Electric.

There has been considerable controversy over the tax treatment of zero coupon bonds. Make your profit first, then think about paying the tax. It is very easy to avoid tax, if you have no profits.

National Savings Certificates

The lure of vast stock exchange profits has been the downfall of many an investor. While the yield on British National Saving Certificates may appear derisory compared to what might be made on the stock market, in the real world the majority of people are likely to do better in National Savings Certificates, freeing themselves of the capital risk of stock exchange investment. The famous American comedian, Eddie Cantor, tells an amusing story in his hilarious book, 'Caught Short'. He says, 'I decided to go to a stockbroker so he could provide me with a portfolio of investments for my old age. After watching the rise and fall of my savings in this portfolio, I was an old man in six weeks.'

National Savings Certificates are an excellent investment during the downwave, since inflation is unlikely to be a threat to your savings any longer.

Index-Linked Government Securities

As the inflation spiral exploded during the 1970s and once again during the early 1980s, many people found negative returns were the only reward for prudent investment. As the rate of inflation passed its second peak in Britain, the Government decided to begin issuing "Index-Linked" Government Securities. Initially, these Index-Linked issues were only available to pension fund investors. During the Budget of 1982 the Government allowed all private investors to purchase Index-Linked Government Securities and a further tranche of these securities was issued. Essentially, the Index-Linked Government Security gives the investor a return equivalent to the rate of inflation plus a yield ranging from 2 to $2\frac{1}{2}$% per annum across a range of maturities spanning 1988 through 2011.

Between 1980 and late 1982 the rate of inflation in Britain has fallen from over 22% to under 7%. It seems as if the British Government has waited until inflation had become a diminishing problem before issuing these Index-Linked Government Securities designed to protect the investor from the ravages of inflation. If inflation begins climbing into the double digit range again these investments will be indeed attractive. However, it is my view that inflation will continue to fall, in which case the yields and capital value of index-linked investments will also fall. Should inflation be replaced by deflation or falling prices, we are yet to see how the yield will be calculated. Currently, the yield on the index-linked securities represents the rate of inflation reflected in the Retail Price Index plus the coupon stated on the stock. Theoretically, if the Retail Price Index is falling at, say 6% per annum, and the investor receives 2% above the rate of inflation, which would be minus 6%, you would have to pay the Government 4% per annum. Of course, this is unlikely to happen, but the concept is worth considering.

Index-Linked Government Securities, or other index-linked investments, designed to protect the investor against inflation, are not recommended during the remainder of the current investment cycle since their function is likely to be totally incompatible with the type of investment environment the future holds.

Insurance Policies

At one time, the bulk of the average person's estate could be found in his insurance policies. Whole of life policies and endowment policies were often sold as savings plans. Before the inflation explosion, most of them adequately served their purpose. Over the past 15 years, inflation has wrecked insurance policy investment. Whereas £1,000 was a considerable amount of money 20 years ago, that £1,000 now looks a pittance in terms of purchasing power. People who purchased endowment policies 10 or 20 years ago paid their premiums with dear money, and are now receiving their endowments in cheap money. I believe that will all soon change. The purchasing power of your endowment in 10 to 15 years time is likely to be greater than the purchasing power of premium payments made today and over the next few years.

When considering insurance as a forced savings plan, you must avoid a policy linked to equity investment, or any other type of investment with a risk to capital. The plain old simple 'With Profits Whole of Life' or 'With Profits Endowment' is your best bet.

I feel I must add a word of caution on the subject of life insurance policies. Many insurance companies will be suffering heavy claims experiences and will be highly vulnerable. It would therefore be prudent to confine consideration of a life insurance policy only to those companies which are pure life offices rather than those which are involved in underwriting general insurance.

A further factor to be considered is the heavy exposure of many insurance companies to property investment. The fall in values in property prices which I envisage could lead to bankruptcies amongst several insurance companies. Utmost caution should therefore be taken when choosing your life insurance company. Stick to the well-known companies. Do not consider smaller companies even though they may pay higher bonuses. It might also be a good idea to spread your insurance savings plans amongst a few different companies.

Building Society Deposit Accounts

I am somewhat suspicious about the stability of the building society movement. The possibility that you may not be able to get all your money back in the event of difficulties is worrying. The Building Societies Association prides itself on the fact that no one has ever lost money on a deposit with a building society. This does not mean, however, that depositors have not experienced problems when smaller building societies have had to be bailed-out by larger building societies.

During 1982, a scheme was devised by the Building Societies Association under which members of the Association would no longer be responsible for a 100% payout if a society had to be rescued. Depositors with a member building society requiring a rescue would still be entitled to a 100% payout, but those with share accounts would only be entitled to a 90% payout. Shareholders in building societies who do not participate in the scheme or do not belong to the Building Societies Association may only be entitled to a 75% payout. It is likely that the Building Societies Association would only give a 75% payout to non-members if the worst comes to the worst. In my view, we are heading for the worst.

You should also remember that building societies pay interest net of tax. Tax is deducted at the standard rate. If you pay tax at less than standard rate, or no tax at all, you cannot reclaim the tax deducted from your interest. Since tax is deducted at source, you do not receive the full benefit of compound interest over a year. The final rate of return you actually receive is therefore less than you would receive from an equivalent amount paid by a bank which does not deduct tax from source.

The future stability of building societies will be linked to the future stability of the housing market. According to my projections, the building society movement could find itself in severe difficulties, and many smaller societies will be forced to close. I can see little benefit in placing funds on deposit with a building society, instead of putting your savings on deposit with one of the major banks.

It is certainly not suggested that a debacle in the housing market will bring the entire building society movement to its knees and building societies will evaporate in total. There will always be a place for building societies in Britain. The period ahead is likely to involved the closure of many smaller societies, and possibly one major society, in addition to a multitude of 'rescue operations' such as we've seen in the U.S. savings and loan institutions which are the equivalent of building societies in Britain. Since it is not possible to determine at this stage which of the building societies will be the most vulnerable and which of the major societies may suffer, nor the degree of the problems that may exist, I feel the prudent course of action is to avoid building society investment completely in view of the much more attractive alternatives in the period that lies ahead. Essentially, building society investment may not be as riskless as it appears. Small savers are likely to be better off with their savings elsewhere.

Epilogue

First and foremost, your investment strategy for the period ahead should be designed to preserve your capital. I have tried to assemble some ideas, strategies, concepts and tactics which will help you meet the problems of the next decade and prepare for them well in advance. I do not want you to be involved in a last minute panic, forced to dump your assets in a falling market at whatever price is offered.

I have tried to explain the economic background of the downwave to show you how to recognise that component of the downwave characterised by deep depression. The downwave will not move in a straight line. There will be many periods during the downwave where it appears that an economic recovery is about to take place. Such recoveries will be shallow and brief. Most of all, these recoveries will be treacherously deceptive. Businessmen will equate periods of mild economic improvement to the type of prosperity that followed during the upwave. They will think the world is getting back to the way it used to be. They will be wrong. Long term plans will be made which will be ruefully inappropriate.

The kind of business enterprises that prospered during the upwave will no longer be viable during the downwave. Property development and investment is probably the most notable example. I have focused on the type of business that should be resilient in the downwave and possibly be profitable during the coming decade. I have concentrated on investment that will help you protect your capital and hopefully enhance your capital during the dramatic changes in the economic, social and cultural environment which you will have to become accustomed to.

The downwave will produce many fortune-making opportunities. People who sell short, buy put options, buy bonds on margin, sell naked calls, and such will be able to amass and compound profits beyond their wildest dreams of avarice. Yet, I have purposely avoided any elaboration of these high risk strategies. The reason is that most people will not be able to handle the risks associated with these professional strategies. The majority who attempt these grandstand speculative plays will lose money when the most important objective during the downwave will be to preserve your savings above all, in both nominal and purchasing power terms. It would be very unwise to try to get rich quickly during the downwave. Adopt an attitude where you are content to nurture your savings. Try to get rich slowly . . . and there's a good chance that you will. The depression will run its course and then you will be presented with the most rewarding business opportunities of your lifetime. Needless to say, if you dissipate your capital before these opportunites present themselves you will not be in a position to take advantage of them.

The view of the future for most people is an exceptionally short-sighted one. The average businessman and investor becomes euphoric when the economy is booming, believing the boom will never end. He then becomes sombre, introspective and negative during a crisis, assuming crisis conditions are a permanent way of life. Successful planning is based on the premise that man will continue in the future to make the same mistakes that he made in the past. While circumstances change, the predictability of human behaviour is one of the most reliable constants in our economic environment. If people were to accept the inexorability of booms and depressions we would have neither. It is the lack of preparation for change, the anti-change mechanism which is part of the human psyche, that ensures booms and depressions will continue for as long as there are emotional development lags in our technological development.

There should be little doubt that man has a tendency to see the future as a continuation of the present moment while desirous of living in a state of permanent financial orgasm. People seem to forget, ignore or dismiss the inescapable truth that the whole cycle of growth and contraction must be perceived in order to gain a realistic view of the coming evolution. Like the panics and crashes that have punctuated history, the Great Depression of the 1930s; the 1973 to 1975 crisis and the depression which is now approaching, does not signify the end of economic growth in our industrialised society, as many people will soon think. We are merely coming to the terminal juncture of one particular economic period. Scientific discoveries, technical progress and the ensuing improvement in global living conditions has certainly not reached the pinnacle of man's achievement. A glorious twenty first century lies beyond the downwave. Humanity will continue its evolution undisturbed for the three decades to follow.

In the meantime, you must come to grips with the behaviour pattern implicit in the downwave. If what I have written has helped you to understand what has happened to the world over the past few decades; what is happening now; what is likely to happen in the future and why it's going to happen, then my research will have served its purpose. If you feel the possibilities that have been outlined are as inescapable as I do, then it is likely that you will be able to pick up the threads where I have left off, developing your own solutions to your own personal circumstances as the downwave unfolds.

If you are among the under sixties, you are about to experience financial, social and economic conditions unlike anything you have ever known. The world as you understand it is about to be turned upside down. You should now be able to profit from the downwave by using it.

Good Luck.

BIBLIOGRAPHY AND SOURCE MATERIAL

Alford, B.W.E.: "Depression and Recovery? British Economic Growth 1918–1939" Papermac, Macmillan & Co, London, 1972

Aliber, Robert Z.: "The International Money Game", Macmillan & Co., New York, 1973

Appel, Gerald: "99 Ways to Make Money in a Depression", Arlington House, Publishers, New Rochelle, New York, 1976

Aston, Peter: "Farm Business Management and Land Ownership", 1979

Bellini, James: "Rule Britannia: A Progress Report for Doomsday 1986", Jonathan Cape, London, 1981

Bladen, Ashby: "How To Cope With The Developing Financial Crisis", McGraw-Hill, New York, 1980

Branson, Noreen: "Britain in the Nineteen Twenties", Weidenfeld and Nicolson, London, 1975

Branson, Noreen, and Heineman, Margot: "Britain in the Nineteen Thirties", Panther Books Ltd., St. Albans, 1973

Burns, Arthur F.: "The Business Cycle in a Changing World", National Bureau of Economic Research, New York, 1969

Burton, Theodore E.: "Financial Crises and Periods of Industrial and Commercial Depression", Fraser Publishing Co., New York, 1966

Cardiff, Gray Emerson, and English, John Wesley: "The Coming Real Estate Crash", Arlington House, Publishers, New Rochelle, New York, 1979

Casey, Douglas R.: "Crisis Investing", Stratford Press/Harper & Row, New York, 1979

Cogan, L. Peter: "The Rhythmic Cycles of Optimism & Pessimism", The William-Frederick Press, New York, 1969

Delgado, Alan: "Have You Forgotten Yet? Between the Two World Wars", David & Charles, Newton Abbot, Devon, 1973

Dewey, Edward R. and Dakin, Edwin F.: "Cycles: The Science of Prediction", Henry Holt & Co., New York, 1947

Dewey, Edward R.: "Cycles: Selected Writings", Foundation for the Study of Cycles, Inc., Pittsburgh, Pennsylvania, 1970

Dewey, Edward R. with Mandino, Og: "Cycles: The Mysterious Forces That Trigger Events", Hawthorn Books, Inc., New York, 1971

Dines, James: "How the Average Investor Can Use Technical Analysis for Stock Profits", Dines Chart Corporation, New York, 1972

Eatwell, John, "Whatever Happened To Britain?", British Broadcasting Corporation/Gerald Duckworth & Co. Ltd., London, 1982

Galbraith, John Kenneth: "The Great Crash, 1929", The Riverside Press, Cambridge, Massachusetts, 1954

Gamble, Andrew: "Britain in Decline", Macmillan Press Ltd., London, 1981

Garrett, Garet, and Rothbard, Murray N.: "The Great Depression and New Deal Monetary Policy", Cato Institute, San Francisco, California, 1980

Gauquelin, Michel: "Cosmic Influences on Human Behaviour", Garnstone Press, London 1973

Gilbert, Bentley B.: "Britain Since 1918", Harper & Row, Publishers, New York, 1969

Glyn, Andrew, and Harrison, John: "The British Economic Disaster", Pluto Press Ltd., London, 1980

Grubel, Herbert G.: "The International Monetary System", Penguin Books Ltd., Harmondsworth, Middlesex, 1969

Guttman, William, and Meehan, Patricia: "The Great Inflation", Saxon House, Farnborough, Hampshire, 1975

Holt, Thomas J.: "How to Survive & Grow Richer in the Tough Times Ahead", Rawson, Wade Publishers, Inc., New York, 1981

Huff, Darrell: "Cycles in Your Life", W.W. Norton & Co. Inc., New York, 1964

Huntington, Ellsworth: "Mainsprings of Civilization", John Wiley & Sons, Inc., New York, 1945

Jennings, Sir Ivor: "Party Politics", Cambridge University Press, Cambridge, 1960

Katz, Howard S.: "The Warmongers", Books in Focus, Inc., New York, 1979

Kindleberger, Charles P.: "The World in Depression 1929–1939", Allen Lane, The Penguin Press, London, 1973

Kindleberger, Charles P.: "Manias, Panics, And Crashes", The Macmillan Press Ltd., London 1978

Lloyd, T.O.: "Empire to Welfare State: English History 1906–1967", Oxford University Press, Oxford, 1970.

MacKay, Charles, Ll.D.: "Extraordinary Popular Delusions and the Madness of Crowds", George Harrap & Co. Ltd., London, 1956

Madsen, Axel: "Private Power", Abacus, Sphere Books Ltd., London, 1981

Marriott, Oliver: "The Property Boom", Hamish Hamilton, London, 1967

McMaster, R.E., Jr.: "Cycles of War: The Next Six Years", Timberline Trust, U.S.A., 1981

McMillan, James: "The Way It Was 1914–1934", William Kimber & Co., London, 1979

Merritt, Giles: "World Out of Work", William Collins, Sons & Co. Ltd., London 1982

Milward, Alan S. and Saul, S.B.: "The Development of the Economies of Continental Europe 1850–1914", George Allen & Unwin Ltd., London, 1977

Myers, C.V.: "The Coming Deflation: Its Dangers and Opportunities", Arlington House, Publishers, New Rochelle, New York, 1977

Norton, Graham: "London Before the Blitz 1906–1940", Macdonald, London, 1970

Paris, Alexander P.: "The Coming Credit Collapse: An Update for the 1980s" Arlington House, Publishers, Westport, Connecticut, 1980

Phillips, Cabell: "From the Crash to the Blitz 1929–1939", Macmillan Company, New York, 1969

Pigou, A.C.: "Industrial Fluctuations", Macmillan & Co., London, 1927

Pigou, A.C.: "Aspects of British Economic History 1918–1925", Frank Cass & Co. Ltd., London, 1947

Reid, Margaret: "The Secondary Banking Crisis, 1973–75", The Macmillan Press Ltd., London, 1982

Rezneck, Samuel: "Business Depressions & Financial Panics", Greenwood Publishing Corp., New York, 1968

Rolfe, Sidney E. and Burtle, James L.: "The Great Wheel: the world monetary system", Quadrangle/The New York Times Book Co., New York, 1973

Rostow, W.W.: "The World Economy", The Macmillan Press Ltd., London, 1978

Rothbard, Murray, N.: "America's Great Depression", Sheed & Ward Inc., Kansas City, 1963

Ruff, Howard J.: "How to Prosper During the Coming Bad Years", Target Publishers, 1978

Sabine, B.E.V.: "British Budgets in Peace and War, 1932–1945", George Allen & Unwin, Ltd., London, 1970

Schultz, Harry D.: "Panics & Crashes and How You Can Make Money Out of Them", Arlington House, Publishers, New Rochelle, New York, 1972

Schumpeter, Joseph A.: "The Theory of Economic Development", Harvard University Press, Harvard, 1934

Schumpeter, Joseph A.: "Business Cycles", McGraw-Hill Books, Co., New York, 1939

Schumpeter, Joseph A.: "History of Economic Analysis", George Allen & Unwin Ltd., London, 1954

Shuman, James B. And Rosenau, David: "The Kondratieff Wave", World Publishing, New York, 1972

Smith, Adam: "Paper Money", Summit Books, New York, 1981

Spengler, Oswald: "The Decline of the West", George Allen & Unwin Ltd., London, 1926

Steiger, Brad: "The Roadmap of Time", Prentice-Hall, Inc., New Jersey, 1972

Stevenson, John, and Cook, Chris: "The Slump: Society and Politics During the Depression", Quartet Books Ltd., 1979

Stockbridge, Frank Parker: "Hedging Against Inflation", Barron's Publishing Co., New York, 1939

Stoken, Dick A.: "Cycles: What They Are, What They Mean, How to Profit By Them", McGraw-Hill, Inc., New York, 1978

Taylor, A.J.P.: "English History 1914–1945", Oxford University Press, Oxford, 1965

Terkel, Studs: "Hard Times: an Oral History of the Depression", Pantheon Books, Random House, New York, 1970.

Thomas, Gordon, and Morgan-Witts, Max: "The Day the Bubble Burst", Hamish Hamilton, London, 1979

Tinbergen, Jan, and Polak, J.J. "The Dynamics of Business Cycles", The University of Chicago Press, Chicago, 1950.

Toffler, Alvin: "The Eco-Spasm Report", Bantam Books, Inc., New York, 1975

Toffler, Alvin: "The Third Wave", William Collins, Sons & Co. Ltd., London, 1980

Wanniski, Jude: "The Way the World Works", Basic Books, Inc., New York, 1978

Warren, George F. Ph.D., and Pearson, Frank A. Ph.D.: "Prices", John Wiley & Sons, Inc., New York, 1933

Wilsher, Peter: "The Pound in Your Pocket 1870–1970", Cassell & Co, London, 1970

Winslow, Susan: "Brother, Can You Spare A Dime? America from the Wall Street Crash to Pearl Harbor", Paddington Press Ltd, New York, 1979

SELECTED PAPERS AND ARTICLES

Banks, Stephen J.: "The Great Inflation", The Financial Analysts Journal, May–June 1977, pages 43–55.

Bank Credit Analyst, The: "The Kondratieff Cycle", May 1973, pages 27–35

Bank Credit Analyst, The: "Kondratieff and the Super Cycle: Deflation or Run-Away Inflation", June 1978

Beckman, Robert C.: "Global Bankruptcy", The Crown Agents Quarterly Review, Spring 1979.

Beckman, Robert C.: "Bricks Without Straw: The Coming Property Crash", Penthouse Magazine, June 1982, pages 34–40 & 96–98

Cetron, Marvin, J. and Clayton, Audrey: "Turbulence & Tranquility: The Outlook for 26 Nations", The Futurist, December 1981, pages 50–55

Cetron, Marvin J. and O'Toole, Thomas: "Careers with a Future: Where the Jobs Will Be in the 1990s", The Futurist, June 1982, pages 11–19

City Bank Monthly Economic Letter: "Long Swings I – Kondratieff Invents History", January 1978

City Bank Monthly Economic Letter: "Long Swings II – Kuznets Explains History", February 1978

Cornish, Edward: "The Great Depression of the 1980s: How It Might Begin", The Futurist, June 1980, pages 29–34

Debenham Tewson & Chinnocks, Chartered Surveyors: "Money Into Property 1970–1980". August 1981

Forrester, Jay W.: "A New View of Business Cycle Dynamics", The Journal of Portfolio Management, Autumn 1976.

Forrester, Jay W.: "Changing Economic Patterns", Technology Review, August–September 1978, pages 47–53

Francoeur, Robert T.: "The Sexual Revolution: Will Hard Times Turn Back the Clock?", The Futurist, April 1980, pages 3–12

Garvy, George: "Kondratieff Theory of Long Cycles", Review of Economic Statistics, Volume 25, No. 4, November 1943

Hamil, Ralph: "Is the Wave of the Future a Kondratieff?", The Futurist, October 1979, pages 381–384

Kaiser, Ronald W. "The Kondratieff Cycle", The Financial Analysts Journal, May–June 1979, pages 57–66

Kitchin, Joseph: "Cycles and Trends in Economic Factors", The Review of Economic Statistics, Volume 7, No. 4. November 1925.

Kondratieff, N.D.: "Die langen Wellender Konjunktur", Archiv fur Sozialwissenschaft und Sozialpolitick, 1926.

Kondratieff, N.D.: "The Long Wave of Economic Life", The Review of Economic Statistics, Volume 17, No.6, November 1935

Land & Liberty: "Housing: A Crash in '84", November–December 1982, pages 110–111

Madron, Thomas William: "Political Parties in the 1980s", The Futurist, December 1979, pages 465–475

Michaels, Jane W., Baldwin, W. and Minard, Lawrence: "Echoes From a Siberian Prison Camp", Forbes, November 9 1981, pages 164–176

Peters, Ted: "The Future of Religion in a Post-Industrial Society", The Futurist, October 1980, pages 21–25

Speiler, Joseph: "The Possible Crash of 1980 and How to Make the Most of It", Quest, October 1979, pages 25–35

Stoken, Dick: "What the Long Term Cycle Tells Us About the 1980s: The Kondratieff Cycle and Its Effects on Social Psychology", The Futurist, February 1980, pages 14–19

Vallis, E.A., B. Litt. (Oxon), F.R.I.C.S.: "Urban Land & Building Prices 1892–1969", Parts 1–4, The Estates Gazette, May–June 1972

Vincent, Helen D. "The Correlation of Cultural Cycles with Business", the Society for the Investigation of Recurring Events, June 1980.

INDEX